Joan Lucas turned 85 years old in 2023 and following the loss of her husband, in the same year, decided that she wanted to share her life's journey, with the aim to inspire other women. Born into what would be a family of seven, in the dark wartime years, Joan had many challenges as a child but despite these and with help of other women, she became one of the first women to have a career in finance and live as an independent woman in the late 1950s. She went on to have further career success, fall in love with her soul mate, become a mother and travel the world. A story of a strong, resilient woman.

This book is dedicated to my husband, John Lucas, a life well lived.

Joan Lucas

## BRISTOW KID – UNDAUNTED

AUSTIN MACAULEY PUBLISHERS
LONDON * CAMBRIDGE * NEW YORK * SHARJAH

Copyright © Joan Lucas 2025

The right of Joan Lucas to be identified as author of this work has been asserted by the author in accordance with sections 77 and 78 of the Copyright, Designs and Patents Act 1988.

All rights reserved. No part of this publication may be reproduced, stored in a retrieval system, or transmitted in any form or by any means, electronic, mechanical, photocopying, recording, or otherwise, without the prior permission of the publishers.

Any person who commits any unauthorised act in relation to this publication may be liable to criminal prosecution and civil claims for damages.

The story, experiences, and words are the author's alone.

A CIP catalogue record for this title is available from the British Library.

ISBN 9781035893942 (Paperback)
ISBN 9781035893959 (Hardback)
ISBN 9781035893973 (ePub e-book)
ISBN 9781035893966 (Audiobook)

www.austinmacauley.com

First Published 2025
Austin Macauley Publishers Ltd®
1 Canada Square
Canary Wharf
London
E14 5AA

I would like to thank my family for their help and support in writing this book, my elder brother, Peter, who helped me with the early parts of my childhood and his wife. I thank my sisters, Wendy and Carol, for allowing themselves to be included in the book and I thank my daughter, Tracy, and her husband, Richard, for their encouragement to complete the book and Tracy's research into the family's ancestry.

# Table of Contents

| | |
|---|---:|
| **Preface** | **11** |
| **Chapter One: The Formative Years During the Second World War** | **13** |
| **Chapter Two: The Importance of Education in the Post-War Years** | **54** |
| **Chapter Three: Independence, Career Development Standing Alone** | **80** |
| **Chapter Four: A Wedding, A New House, A Mortgage**                                      Forging Ahead in a Male-Oriented World | **118** |
| **Chapter Five: The Adverse Years** | **159** |
| **Chapter Six: Finding Our Winter Home and**                                    **Dealing with Mental Illness** | **197** |
| **Chapter Seven: The Retirement Years, If You Want to Call It That** | **229** |
| **Chapter Eight: Our Final Times Together** | **261** |

# Preface

The inspiration for this book started with an email from a friend who sends me daily funny emails to enjoy; one email, though, led to some real thought. The 1% club; no, not the gameshow! I realised I was part of the last 1% in the world! This, in itself, is quite a mind-boggling concept and led me to realise that I was unique and needed to record my life experiences which formulated my life choices and drive to succeed.

Being a woman, belonging to this club, I feel it is also important that the struggles to depart from the traditional expectations of women at that time and the changes in the role and traditional views of women are recorded for future women, with the hope to inspire!

99% of those born between 1930 and 1946 (worldwide) are now dead. If you were born in this timespan, you are one of the rare surviving one-percenters of this special group. Their age range is between 77 and 93 years old, a 16-year age span. You are the smallest group of children born since the early 1900s. You are the last generation, climbing out of the depression, who can remember the winds of war and the impact of a world at war that rattled the structure of our daily lives for years.

You are the last to remember ration books for everything from gas to sugar to shoes to stoves. You saved tin foil and poured fried meat fat into tin cans. You can remember milk being delivered to your house early in the morning and placed in the *milk box* on the porch. You are the last generation who spent childhood without television; instead, you *imagined* what you heard on the radio. With no TV, you spent your childhood playing outside. We got black-and-white TV in the late 40s that had 3 stations and no remote.

Telephones were one to a house, often shared (party lines) and hung on the wall in the kitchen (no cares about privacy). Computers were called calculators; they were hand-cranked. Typewriters were driven by pounding fingers, throwing the carriage, and changing the ribbon. *Internet* and *Google* were words that did not exist. Newspapers and magazines were written for adults, and the news was broadcast on your radio in the evening (your dad would give you the comic pages when he read the news). You went downtown to shop. You walked to school. The radio network expanded from 3 stations to thousands.

You weren't neglected, but you weren't today's all-consuming family focus. They were glad you played by yourselves. They were busy discovering the post-war world. You entered a world of overflowing plenty and opportunity; a world where you were welcomed, and you enjoyed yourselves. You felt secure in your future, although the depression and poverty were deeply remembered. Polio was still a crippler.

Everyone knew someone who had it. You came of age in the 50s and 60s. You are the last generation to experience an interlude when there were no threats to our homeland. World War 2 was over, and the cold war, terrorism, global warming and perpetual economic insecurity had yet to haunt life. Only your generation can remember a time after WW2 when our world was secure and full of bright promise and plenty.

You grew up at the best possible time, a time when the world was getting better.

# Chapter One
# The Formative Years During the Second World War

Contemplating the idea of recording my life, I soon realised that I needed to go back further than I expected. To introduce the women who influenced my formative years and paint a picture of the times into which I was born.

By 1938, the Nazis had taken over Austria, the Anschluss, in March and there was a mass outbreak of violence against the Jews in Germany and Austria. Neville Chamberlain, as prime minister, was focused on forging a peaceful alliance with Germany and avoiding war, at all costs. My family, like most families, felt that war was a long way off and the only change to our daily lives was the arrival of *Big Bertha*, an anti-aircraft gun, which appeared at the end of the garden together with a few soldiers.

Gosport was and still is a military town, in the 20th century, a submarine base was established. In 1905, the local airbase was established, called the Grange, and by 1914 this was taken over by the Fleet Air Arm. In 1927, St Vincent training school was established for young sailors. A military town indeed.

My family lived in houses that were built in the 1920s to house the dock workers employed in nearby Portsmouth, as the rents in Gosport were cheaper, we lived in Elson Road.

In October 1938, a baby girl arrived, a note was sent to the doctor advising that a baby girl had been born, but the note was indistinct, and the poor man read it as a baby girl burned. He arrived somewhat the worse for wear, as he had needed a little Dutch courage to deal with such a horrific situation, to be met by this mother holding a newborn baby in her arms and smiling happily, poor man.

So, my life began, the third child and eldest girl in a family that was to become a family of seven children by 1950.

Figure One: Me aged 2 years and 11 months—1941

My father, prior to and during the war, was in the merchant navy. The merchant navy was a crucial part of the war, the fleet and the sailors transported troops overseas and kept them supplied, as well as civilians. It was a dangerous job, and, in the Second World War, 29,000 sailors were killed and 3,300 ships sunk. He also worked as an assistant chef on the big cruise liners that went from Southampton, travelling to New York in 1931 on the *Berengaria* and again in 1937 on the Aquitania, this was good money, which was needed to support a growing family.

The Bristow's, my mother's family, was large and lived close to each other, as was the norm at that time. My mother was the youngest of six siblings—Robert (born 1908), Elizabeth-Bess (born 1897), Flora (born 1899), Sybil (born 1902), Gladys born 1903) and Olive, my mother, born in 1912.

I was the one to benefit the most from the proximity of having a wider family living close by, as my mother's sisters, welcomed me with open arms, a little girl at last, these brave women influenced my entire life and are in my thoughts to this day.

I was not the first female grandchild born into the family, my mother's sister Gladys had two daughters, Mary and Marjorie, that branch of the family living in Bermuda at that time. They moved around the world as my uncle was a civil servant in the admiralty. Luckily for me, I was the one the aunts were able to spend time with.

Grandpa, William Bristow, had a tailoring business, where all the girls were expected to work. This work included cutting, stitching, pressing, whilst sitting cross-legged on the floor, working together and was seen as preparation for marriage and looking after the home, after all, women, even after the freedoms of World War I, were still being groomed for marriage.

My mother, Olive, was tasked with creating buttonholes from an early age, as the shop had a contract for navy uniforms, there were a lot of buttonholes. This was not paid work as we know it, but women were expected to participate until they married and began another form of unpaid labour, as a housewife and carer of the children. Women were not expected to work.

Figure 2: My mother Olive, on the left, with her niece Mary (eldest grandchild) and Grandma Amelia

There was no focus on education, although girls did attend school. The leaving age was 14 years, which was raised to 15 years in 1944, but it did not change to 16 years until 1972. Women in the 1930s still struggled with the focus on domesticity and running the home, although a third of all women did work outside the home, but mostly women had very traditional jobs in domestic service to the middle class and the rich, or they were teachers or nurses.

Well paid work was reserved for men and there was no chance of career advancement. Following the development of the sewing machine, many women worked from home, and the bicycle gave them the freedom to seek work further from home. The invention of the typewriter and phone opened new opportunities in offices and shops, but the roles were subservient and to serve the needs of the men who employed them, there was no equal pay, and they were segregated in the workplace from the men.

There was no paid maternity leave and women were expected to leave their work as soon as they married. Women in the 1930s did receive some form of education, could work, vote and get divorced on grounds of adultery and be given custody of their children but they still couldn't open a bank account in their name, pay tax in their name and have the same amount of national insurance as men, or own property in their name, abortion was still illegal until the 1960s and there was no access to contraceptives.

The world I was born into had changed a little for women, but there was still a very long way to go. I was lucky to be surrounded by strong female role models, some of whom had broken this traditional view of women.

Uncle Robert (Uncle Bill as he was known) was my mother's elder brother, whom I did not meet until I was 7 years old, he worked in Portsmouth's dockyard.

I recently learnt a little about his younger years from a letter, my mother wrote to my eldest brother Peter. Luckily for him and my Aunt Sybil, Grandma Millie, my maternal grandmother, received an inheritance around the year 1922, which enabled Uncle Bill to be privately educated and obtain his school certificate.

This was needed to obtain an apprenticeship in the dockyard. I was told he was situated in Singapore at the time of the Japanese invasion and was lucky to escape on the last ship leaving harbour. This inheritance also paid for Aunt Sybil's college fees, and according to the mother's letter, some much-needed new furniture.

Aunt Bess was a gentle woman who always had time for me, who spent winter evenings making dresses for my doll or making quilts for my doll's bed. The kindest, warmest person who loved unconditionally and who always had her arms open for a hug. The hugs I received were so important to me, as in my own home, hugs were not a common occurrence, more on that later.

Aunt Bess married in 1915, at the age of 18, which was very common at that time, to a Frederick Parkhouse aged 20, but he did not survive the First World War. She was one of the first recipients of the first state-funded, non-contributory pension that was granted to women whose husbands died in the First World War, this meant that they did not have to pay a contribution towards it. She died young at the age of 47 years.

Aunt Florence or Aunt Flo as we knew her, married Cecil Robinson in 1923, Flo was 24 and Cecil 26 years old, they had one child Robert Morley Robinson who was born with a disability which rendered him bedridden, this was common in those days, disability was managed in the home by family members, usually the women.

I spent a lot of my formative years next door as my mother and Aunt Flo were next-door neighbours on Elson Road, they were very close, and my mother helped with Bob. Cecil was a Drum Major, in the Royal Marines in Portsmouth, he joined in 1911 (14 years old) and served all through World War I. He accompanied the Prince of Wales on his tour to Australia during the 1920s. He died in 1956 at the age of 59.

Aunt Flo, this tough lady taught me how to sew, knit, tat, embroider and how to preserve food for the long cold winter months. So, my creative or maybe artistic ability was nurtured. Resilience was the key factor here, or to quote Aunt Flo, where there is a will, there is a way.

"You can do anything if you set your mind to it."

Whilst my kind uncle showed me that being kind, and considerate of others was important and that there is joy in everything, you just have to look for it. This positive viewpoint has stayed with me all my life. Uncle Cecil was young when he died and Aunt Flo looked after Bob alone until his death in his 40s, a very tough and resilient woman.

I spent many hours in Bob's (his family nickname) room curled up together in his bed keeping one another warm. During the day, Bob had a perambulator which was specially made for him because if he had not been stricken with the illness, he would have grown into a tall man. There was no access to wheelchairs and other equipment, families managed as best they could.

Aunt Sybil had a very big influence in my early years and is remembered to this day. She was a clear-minded lady who became a teacher, specialising in primary school education. She trained at St Mary's College of Education Cheltenham, formed in 1921, founded from the Cheltenham teacher training college established in 1874 and now the University of Gloucester. Achieving the job of headmistress at a local school. Unfortunately, becoming terminally ill and unable to continue with her life, she died at the age of 47 years.

This achievement of becoming a female headmistress at this time was rare and a huge achievement, considering she started off making buttonholes. Teaching was a growth area for women at this time, as primary education was made compulsory, for children aged 4-10 in 1880 and school fees abolished in 1891 and by 1902 literacy rates were 97% for boys and 96% for girls, which shows that parents knew it was important for their child to have the basics of literacy and numeracy.

Sybil's interest in me as a young child was fundamental to my life, she taught me to read and appreciate books and the knowledge that one can learn from history, Shakespeare and all the people who bothered to put pen to paper. She bought my first book for me, at a very tender age, a ladybird book from which I started the incredible journey of my life, reading and learning.

This wonderful woman came to my rescue time and again when the ramifications of family life became unbearable. She understood the loneliness of being too bright for one's parents to understand, after all, girls were meant to cook, clean and sew, not read books and have a thirst for knowledge and a drive to want more.

She was a single lady, who radically, for the time was a lesbian, and this she did not hide from me but showed me how to understand that just being myself was the most important thing in life. She gave me the strength to walk away from a life I did not want, and to understand that nobody has the right to control my life.

Mary and Marjorie's mother, Aunt Gladys, was the third of four sisters and worked in the family tailoring business. She was not such a positive influence in my life, looking down her nose at me as if I was orphan Annie, dressed in her daughter's hand-me-downs. She married Victor Prince in 1928, aged 25. Their daughters Mary and Marjorie were the eldest grandchildren who were brought up mostly abroad, Marjorie having been born in Bermuda.

Uncle Vic was in the admiralty working as a civil servant. The family spent a considerable time in Malta after the war. Mary was a musician playing piano and violin, Uncle Cecil coached her with the violin as it was necessary to have proficiency in two musical mediums to be able to attend the Royal College of Music, which she achieved. Marjorie trained as a nurse. Aunt Gladys and Uncle Victor retired to Stubbington.

Gladys concentrating on gardening and Victor with his group of friends. Maybe this was where I learnt that being disliked is not personal, just someone else's viewpoint. Look for the positive.

My mother, the youngest of the sisters. Married my father at the age of 19 years, after working in the tailoring business with her sisters, the same year she married, her father died, her mother dying 4 years later, leaving her with only the support of her sisters.

Bess, Flo and Sybil, three ladies who gave me so much in my formative years and who opened my eyes to what could be achieved, Sybil giving me the ability to learn, instilling in me the importance of education and joy of learning, Flo teaching me the skills of resilience and a can do attitude and Bess giving me confidence and the ability to like myself, these women gave me the strength and ability to live my life to the full, enabled me to go out into the world alone and stay true to myself. Modern women forging a path for the future. Amazing.

Figure 3–The Aunts and Mother with Grandad

Like most human beings, the formative years hold very little in the way of memories, just senses. The feeling of safety, warmth and comfort in a noisy household with two boisterous brothers. Aunts, Uncles and cousins living close by, to share our lives. This was not destined to last very long, as war was declared in 1939 and the evacuation of families living in areas deemed to be vulnerable in the case of an invasion. As the family lived on the other side of a naval port, Portsmouth, this meant us.

I do not remember this time being about 12 months old, but my elder brother Peter's tale is sad and amazing.

In September, Mother, Trevor (second brother) and I went by train from Gosport to Durley, South Downs. Peter went on another train with his school and was billeted with another boy in the countryside, he was only 5 years old. My mother, Trevor and I were billeted in a house near Durley. Peter must have been very lonely, no school, no brothers or sisters to tease or play with, just a boy he did not know.

He was strolling out on his own one day, probably bored, whacking the heads off the flowers along the lanes when he noticed his father's bicycle leaning on a cottage wall. He walked up and knocked on the door. Mother opened the door and screamed. He was filthy, clothes dirty and as ever hungry. As you have probably worked out, I was very small at this time so an account from me is not possible. Peter has written an account of his life during these years which is included in this book.

Needless to say, Mother brought the situation to an end, and we all returned to the family home, bombs be damned! The Gosport we returned to was a little different to the one we left, anti-aircraft guns manned by a group of soldiers were situated in the field at the back of Elson Road, together with an air raid warning claxon drone. Both the gun and soldiers left soon after we returned, leaving the area free for us kids to play in.

An Anderson shelter was built in our back garden, which was a hole dug down into the soil with a curved roof, topped with sandbags and turf. As the war dragged on, we spent a lot of time day and night in this creation. Tucked up in bed, warm and cosy, and the air raid warning claxon would sound, always just as we had gone to sleep and off to the shelter we would go, our record was 90 seconds from waking up to being in the air raid shelter. To this day, the smell of damp soil, stale air and toilet pots fills me with nausea.

I remember standing outside at the top of the steps leading down to the shelter with Dad's tin hat on my head watching the planes flying north and listening to the throb of the engines. Seeing the night sky light up as the bombs rained down on the harbour and towns.

Being pulled back down into the shelter by my brothers, as my mother was next door helping my aunt and uncle with Bob. Aunt Flo and Uncle Cecil also had an Anderson shelter to which Bob had to be carried, lowered in and tucked up. A very big job as Bob was not a small person. By now his head was abnormally bigger, which made transporting him difficult.

Stormy nights saw a respite in the waves of bomber planes flying overhead. No trips to the Anderson, instead lying in bed watching the lightning flashes through the windows, which were criss-crossed with tape in case they were blown in by bomb blast.

During the war, 11,000 houses were damaged in Gosport and nearly 500 destroyed. Furthermore, 111 civilians were killed and 289 wounded.

Schools weren't open, as most children were still evacuated, luckily Aunt Sybil made sure my brother's education wasn't disrupted too much. Otherwise, we were lucky, the boys and later me had the old gun emplacement and old recreation ground that we played on, we never went far, and mother only had to call us once to come in, which the other mothers were very jealous of. Mother felt lucky to have well-behaved children at this time.

Trevor would go off a little further and a neighbour once replayed a story to mother, that he had seen him sitting on a fence, seeing how far he could spit, using little balls of chewed up paper.

In 1939, we were all issued with gas masks in cardboard boxes and had to always have them around our necks, as I wasn't big enough for the box, I had a helmet-like contraption that you pumped air into by hand, mother felt very lucky that she never had to do this. The gas mask looked like a deep-sea diving helmet and covered the majority of the child except for its legs, which were for children up to the age of two.

In 1941, father was in the merchant navy at this time, and before he went to sea, he put a World War I tin hat on Peter's head, like an upside-down soup dish and told him he was the man of the house now. He took this very seriously and was marching around the garden and had to be dragged into the shelter when an air raid siren went off, he was only 8 years old.

Overall, the war years were characterised by a time of great community spirit, everybody was close knit, and everything was shared, we were lucky that the neighbours had two boys slightly older than Peter and Trevor, so their clothes were handed over in exchange for clothing rations vouchers. The mothers gathered regularly in the old recreation grounds, shared chats and laughter, which helped. Birthdays and Christmases were always celebrated. We made paper chains, painted Christmas cards and made Christmas calendars.

We even managed to bake cakes, made from rations of fat and sugar, with powdered egg and soya. My baby rations of concentrated orange juice were used to make jellies and David's (born 1941) baby rations must have been used for the same thing. Pastries were made with a cornflower filling. Sweets were too expensive for us and there simply was no chance of ever seeing or getting one's hands on chocolate. Washing day was on a Monday come rain or shine. There was a large tub in the corner of the scullery, water had to be heated by lighting a fire underneath it, this was seldom used.

Water was heated in the big kettle on the gas stove and used to wash clothes by hand. Whilst the whites were boiled in a larger vessel on another gas ring. Whites were vests and underpants together with pillowcases, which mother and I made from the less worn parts of old sheets, garments were taken out of the hot water and placed in the sink to be rinsed with cold water, from the tap, the only source of water in the house.

Beds were changed in a rota strictly adhered to, so no one had sheets on their beds for very long. Although there was a small mangle in the shed, the wringing out of the water was done by hand by mother. Out onto the clothesline to dry as much as possible. Rainy days meant clothes hanging up inside the scullery. Life for women was hard and long days of toil.

Mondays were bubble and squeak days. Sunday dinner leftovers were placed in a frying pan with lard and heated up until the edges became crisp. Who says frying cabbage is a 21st century idea.

Afternoon tea was homemade bread and homemade jam. Bread being homemade had no preservatives, which meant it became stale very quickly. All food scraps were used in some way, bread pudding was a wartime special. Aunt Flo would save her bread crusts and any stale bread for mother. All of this was torn into pieces and added to it was spice, egg, sugar and butter, dried fruit and hot milk, the resulting mixture packed into a large tin and baked. Eaten hot or cold, wonderful with a cup of cocoa on a cold winter's night.

Meat was rationed and mother had to stand in a queue at the butchers in the hope of buying something, sausages or as she called them bags of mystery, were cooked in a thick onion gravy which was really flour and milk with sliced onions and seasoning, in a large saucepan on the gas ring and served up with boiled potatoes. Cornflour and milk made what was called blancmange. What a luxury blancmange and blackcurrant jam.

Junket was not something I enjoyed, well, reading books and finding out how rennet was made did not help. This was added to milk, making the milk solids set. Which was served up with jam or on special occasions, Tate and Lyle golden syrup. This luxury was reserved for steamed puddings or spotty dick as we knew it. A mixture of flour, sugar and suet, and dried fruit placed in a basin and steamed. Cake was for birthdays and Christmas, and mother used to joke that her shortbread, laughing, she would say, "It is short of everything."

The sisters worked together to fend for us, and we were strong healthy children. Allocations of vitamin pills and cod-liver oil for children up to the age of 5 also helped, a teaspoon of cod-liver, how I loathed that taste.

The local primary school reopened early in the war and all children were allocated a third of a pint of milk every day, which in some way must account for my still having my own teeth here in the 21st Century. Well, something must have helped my teeth, as we didn't have toothpaste but instead used soot and salt. Can you imagine the young people of today with their *turkey teeth* coping without toothpaste. School dinners for us were free, all seated at tables in the hall. Must have been good although I cannot remember much about it. Tapioca pudding is not exciting, looked like frog's spawn.

Christmas dinner at school was good, roast chicken and Christmas pudding. Chicken a total luxury. Wartime Christmas was made exciting by the women in the family. Homemade presents, be it socks or a woolly hat. Our stockings holding an orange or a sugar mouse and something wrapped in homemade Christmas paper. Simple but most exciting and enjoyable. Big family Christmas dinner with all the aunts.

The Christmas tree grew in the garden and was dug up and brought inside each year. No need to worry about the needles falling off, the house was too cold. No central heating, just a fire in one room. Decorations were paper chains, strips of coloured paper cut out of old magazines and glued with flour and water paste. Pre-war decorations for the tree brought out each year.

As the war went on, some evacuees returned and the schools had reopened, so by 1944, life was quite like pre-war in Gosport, except for the air balloons, blimps, anchored in the fields and on street corners. We spent time playing and watching planes and 'doodle bugs' on their way to bomb London.

Figure 4 Top Left–Me, David and Wendy. Top right–Peter, Trevor, me and David–1942
Bottom Left–Playing in the rec Bottom right–Peter, Trevor, me and baby David–1941

Family life was always loud and chaotic with 4 children, and there were good times and bad times, but more challenging for an only girl. Aunt Flo and Uncle Cecil lived in the adjoining terrace house where the walls were so thin you could hear what was going on. We kids were racing up and down the stairs, Mother screaming when a nest of field mice were found in a drawer, one of my brothers having placed them there, looking after them well of course. Terror number two, Trevor.

When father was home, the rows with mother were loud and vicious, which had us three scattering out of it. The boys were out in the fields and allotments up to no good, and I was next door.

My refuge being with Aunt Flo and Bob, my cousin. Bob was severely handicapped having been born with hydrocephalus (Water on the brain) and completely bedridden. Bob and I together keeping warm and comfortable whilst

Uncle Cecil played the piano in the parlour or read us stories. Nights of old, Greek mythology and fairy stories for a little girl. Day time spent in the tiny kitchen preserving food, making jam. Topping and tailing gooseberries are things that little hands can cope with. Uncle Cecil had an enlarged pram made to accommodate Bob's disability as he grew to be very tall, this was in the dining room, and Bob could hear all we were doing and talking about.

So, my formative years were spent. The family home was a mixture of turmoil and anger, my mother coping with three little children and another on the way.

The water supply was a tap in the scullery, hot water was from the kettle heating on the gas stove or a pot on the iron bread oven in the family dining room. The toilet was outside in a shed in the garden. A big old cistern above the toilet, which flushed an enormous amount of water, this was wrapped up in old clothes during the winter to hopefully stop it freezing. No bathroom or running water in the house. A tin bath hung outside on the wall was brought in once a week and bathing commenced.

Half an inch of water per person was the allowance, like all things during the war, this was rationed. For most of these years, I was the smallest and had the first half inch and stood having a wash down, here was where my innocent childhood ended. My father was home and decided to bathe me alongside my mother, a little girl of 2 or 3 years, his hands exploring my genitals and the look in his eyes as I pulled away in shock, and my mother was laughing with him.

I remember Aunt Bess and her kindness at this time, the warm hugs and asking what the matter was, little one. Then the torment began, just old enough to go to the outside toilet on my own, and he came into the shed to watch me. Screaming long and loud, which brought my mother out to put a stop to it. The damage was done though, nowhere was safe, being too young to rationalise it, as I learnt to do in the years to come.

My terror was dismissed until my aunts became involved, Flo lived next door and heard what was going on, so I was packed off with Aunt Bess to stay with my mother's sister, Aunt Gladys and her family, living in Milford Haven in Wales at the time. I had cousins, Mary and Marjorie, to play with to look for eggs in the chicken run and to come to the bathroom with me and help me overcome the fear and enjoy my life again.

Father being in the merchant navy meant he was away for long periods, leaving the three of us to grow up together. Known locally as the Bristow kids.

Adventurous boys full of mischief, raiding the fruit cage on the allotments by climbing trees and dropping into the cage, filling pockets with fruit and then being pulled up onto the tree branch and back to the lane to eat the prize. Throwing apples over the top of the house into the front street, where they smashed and caused cars to skid. Oh, dear local bobby (policeman) calling again.

I, well, I admit to being a girl and not allowed to join in these boisterous games, fine as a look out and warning of danger, even better to bowl at them whilst they batted during our cricket games, the stumps were white lines chalked on an old tin. Mostly I was helping next door and learning the crafts of a woman's lot in life.

My third brother, David, arrived early in 1941, making my mother's life even harder, although reading her letter regarding these times, she seemed very happy.

As the war dragged on, we three, Peter, Trevor and I, became the three musketeers and had make-believe battles out in the lane and the recreation field. Playing cricket, laying down in the long grass and watching the clouds roll by, life was difficult during this time but we kids had freedom, never far from home and always near enough so that when mother called, we heard and ran home. Or the whistle when father was home, and meaning his putting me to bed, and all that entailed was once again part of my life.

Rationing was very strict, all and everything was rationed. Mother swapped our clothing coupons for second-hand clothes. These were remade into clothes for us kids, jumpers unpicked and reknitted. Aunt Flo would do most of the unpicking and washing the wool, which was hung out on the line to dry. Then the skeins would need to be rewound into balls.

Yes, there I sat in a chair in front of her holding the skeins between my hands with arms outstretched whilst she rewound them. Lucky for us, we all had big warm jumpers to ward off the winter weather. Knee socks, which had been knitted on four needles for all of us kids. Bare knees which were sore and chaffed, Wellington boots to wear outside, just socks indoors.

These were the years in which I experienced loss for the first time, my friend Shirley and her family lived with her aunt several houses along the road. They had relocated from Portsmouth; their home having been bombed. Shirley had a cousin much older than all of us who joined the Royal Air Force. He was such fun and always had time for a very small child like me. He would hoist me onto his shoulders and gallop up the street, taking me home.

Always smiling, always good fun. Then Shirley and her mother came to tell us that he had been shot down and killed during the Battle of Britain. A light gone out in my life. I can still see him to this day laughing and smiling.

Then in 1944 my sister was born, a sister for me in such a male-oriented household, unfortunately she was premature. No incubators or intensive care in those days, so instead I was called home from school to say goodbye to her as she lay in the cot dressed in a white romper suit.

Peter and I comforted one another as we walked back to school. I remember going to stay with Aunt Flo around this time, and it has transpired that mother accompanied father on the Queen Mary, a cruise ship converted to a troop carrier, travelling to New York and back. This was a time of great sadness in the family, my beloved Aunt Bess was very ill, Mother and I visited as often as we could.

Later that year, after being ill for some months, my beloved Aunt Bess died. The loss for my mother must have been huge, and for me, a time of deep sadness, still affecting me now 80 years later. I at last understood what she had told me at the time of my sister Christine's death, the only constant in life, little one, is yourself, learn to like yourself just as I like you.

The bombing stopped and it was just the doodle bugs overhead, which were still dropping on London.

Just down Elson Road was the Hardway slipway and in 1944, prior to D-Day, troops were gathered in the area ready to invade Europe and put an end to the war. We woke one morning to a deep rumbling sound, the road was crammed with army trucks full of soldiers, Canadians, Americans, men from all over the free world.

A manhole cover opposite Aunt Flo's front gate, popped out when one tank went over it and popped back in with the next, I can clearly hear that sound to this day and evokes that image of 1000s of soldiers on their way to save us and defeat the Nazis. The men were grim faced but kind to us kids, giving us pennies because they would be of no use in France, and more importantly, sweets and rations, which would be of no use for many. Peter recalls seeing me sitting on top of a Canadian Sherman Tank outside our home. Always a show off.

D-Day landing meant very little to me, as I spent time with Aunt Bess. Again, Peter and his friend knew a great deal more about the preparations for this enormous undertaking. The next section has been written by Peter to illustrate his memory of this time, which he titled, *Boy at War.*

The southwesterlies blew wet and cold along the English Channel on Christmas Eve 1938. The rolling, grey clouds splattered raindrops on the windowpanes of our house. The wind chopped the water into whitecaps in Portsmouth harbour.

Ours was an old house in a row of similar red-brick, slate-roofed houses. Its rooms had lath-and-plaster walls covered in faded wallpaper that had outlived Queen Victoria. Inside, in the living room warmed by a red-hot coal fire, aunts and uncles congregated and grew friendly over glasses of scotch whiskey and sherry. There was an aroma of cigars. And from the kitchen poured the smells of roast beef, baked vegetables and a heavy Christmas pudding laced with brandy.

As the temperature in the room rose and the windows steamed up with condensation, the red-faced, sweating men removed their suit coats and shirt collars and wandered away into the garden to cool off and guffaw over old jokes. As the daylight faded and nostalgia for Christmas past moistened her eyes, Mother switched off the electric lights and lit the hissing, gas lamps that hung from polished brass sconces throwing dancing shadows on the walls. Then we listened to Grandma Amelia say a prayer before eager hands reached out for bowls of food and platters of meat.

I was six years old. It was an unusually large family gathering that year. There was tension in the air. Something the children sensed. We ate and then, bored with grownup conversation and their loud laughter, sat beneath the loaded dinner table and played a giggly game of marbles with black olives and pickled onions.

Heavy grownup feet shuffled back and forth over our game leaving a smear of smashed olives and onions on the linoleum floor. Disembodied, hairy, calloused hands holding glasses appeared beneath the table and we took turns taking surreptitious swigs of dark beer. Delicate, white hands slipped us soft-centred chocolates until we became queasy with the rich mixture.

Dinner ended and the uncles and aunts left for home after watching us children eat a dessert of bananas and cream in a glass dish with maraschino cherries on top. Then we went up to our rooms to watch the winking lights of the town through the bedroom windows and searched in vain for a sign of Father Christmas's sleigh.

We lay awake as Mother clattered dirty dishes in the kitchen and Father clinked empty bottles. Then, when we could no longer giggle, wrestle and make guesses at the contents of the Christmas parcels stacked high on the living-room floor, we fell asleep one by one.

There were five of us. My father and mother, brother, baby sister and me. We lived in a garrison town on the west shore of Portsmouth harbour within sight of Horatio Nelson's wooden battleship *Victory* and the muffled sounds of the dockyard where the Royal Navy lay rusting and resting after the First World War.

Most of the families in the town were connected in some way to the sea. My father was in the Merchant Marine, an uncle was a Royal Marine and another a gunner in the Royal Artillery. Not surprising then, that as that Christmas Eve passed into night, the conversation downstairs had turned contentious at the prospect of war with Germany.

We woke as the sun rose on a cold Christmas morning. Downstairs someone with a raspy cough was raking out the fire ashes and snapping kindling sticks to relight it. After a hurried breakfast of toast and marmalade and dressed in our pyjamas and dressing gowns, we tumbled the presents onto the floor and in a frenzy of shouting and squealing, the bounty was revealed.

New, shiny pencils in boxes with hinged lids, hand-knitted sweaters, threepenny pieces, socks, gloves, *Windsor and Newton* painting boxes and oranges. And model cars. Mercedes Benz, Rolls Royce and Lagonda. Elegant cars that could be wound up with a metal key and raced across the linoleum floor. My brother's gift was a toy military truck full of lead soldiers. It was of little interest to him that it was labelled *Made in Germany*. The irony was not lost on Mother and Father.

The winter months passed and in the spring of 1939 the elm trees in the horse pasture behind our house broke out in a green mist of new leaves. It was a short distance from home to the little Flintstone church school next to the parade ground at Fort Brockhurst. At lunchtime we ran to the edge of the gravelled patch of ground where tall soldiers in peaked caps and shiny brown boots walked the snorting cavalry horses. They hoisted us up to feed them sugar lumps.

In the summer, the parade ground was deserted. The horses were gone. Then, overnight, soldiers arrived to set up conical, khaki tents and a field kitchen in the horse pasture. They hauled a howitzer, inevitably dubbed *Big Bertha*, onto the highest point and pointed the defiant, stumpy barrel towards the English Channel. The fat and sweating sergeant-cook entertained the local children with his dexterity with sharp kitchen knives and then fed them heavy desserts on tin plates.

During the next few weeks, the soldiers dug a complicated pattern of World War One-style trenches across the pasture in defence of the town. Then, as if they realised the futility of it all, they pulled down the tents, hitched up the howitzer to a truck and left. The abandoned trenches filled with slimy, green water in which the children played. Until a few fell in and had to be rescued by frantic parents. The trenches were finally placed out of bounds for fear of someone drowning in them or worse, catching some dread disease.

1939 passed from summer to autumn and the threat of war turned to a high probability. It was the time of the radio. The BBC news, read in those meticulous, melodic accents from London, brought news of far-off places. Finland, Danzig, Czechoslovakia, Poland and Latvia.

Exotic places that our teacher made us find on the pre-1918 oilskin map of Europe that hung on the wall behind her desk and then made us laboriously write the unfamiliar names on the blackboard.

On September 3rd, Mr Chamberlain got on the radio and told us what we were expecting. That we were at war with Germany. It had a chilling effect on the grownups, and they scarcely contained their anxiety for a few weeks as they remembered the First World War with the mud, the trenches, the bombardment of undefended cities by airplanes. And poison gas.

Gasmasks were distributed with strict instructions to carry them always. Bulky things in a cheap cardboard box on a string, which cut into your neck, but made a fine weapon with which to batter your friends in the schoolyard. They also had a wonderful ability to make flatulent noises when air was blown out of the tight rubber seal around your face.

20 children making dinosaur farts during a gas mask practice was more than a little fun. Babies got a red thing like a space helmet into which the whole child was inserted. It came with a hand pump and plastic window which fogged up when the baby breathed. The masks were never needed but we carried them for years.

On a cool, cloudy autumn morning, I dressed in warm clothes, a raincoat and a cap. My mother gave me a bag containing spare clothes and walked with me to the school yard. Unfamiliar, double-decker red buses with stairs winding steeply up to the upper deck (ours were green single-deckers) were lined up on the playground. We were marshalled into lines by patient teachers and whilst our parents watched mutely and submissively, we walked away in line and dutifully boarded the buses.

There were few tears and no confusion. All the children were to be *evacuated* to billets in safe areas inland among the country towns. Mothers and babies were to follow later with positive assurances that all families would be reunited at their new address.

My mother's final words were, "Be good, son. I'll see you soon."

How could a six-year-old know that across the English Channel, in Europe, similarly mute and submissive families were being herded away from home with promises of a better life in billets known as concentration camps?

There was a solemn procession of buses to the railway station where we transferred to a gently hissing Southern Railway steam train. I joined six other children and a teacher in a carriage without a corridor. We each had a large cardboard label attached by a string to the top button of our raincoats.

The label showed our name, address, destination and next-of-kin. I was destined for a place called Durley Village beyond the South Downs out of the way of the Luftwaffe's fury about to be unleashed on Portsmouth's dockyard.

We sat four to a side in the compartment and the teacher assigned to us began divesting each of us of our topcoat, hat, favourite toy and luggage. Then she stacked it all on the string-mesh overhead rack. All of which would have to be unstacked and returned to its rightful owner at the end of the journey.

The engine hooted and with a belch of white steam, pulled slowly away from the station. As we passed through the town the children chattered and wriggled but as the rows of houses and factories gave way to green fields and trees, they grew silent. Somewhere a child cried.

The slow, rhythmic clickety-clack of the wheels took us past HMS St Vincent, a naval barracks of imposing eighteenth century architecture. A tall, sailing ship's mast with a golden ball at the top was set in the middle of the parade ground where columns of blue-uniformed men seemed to be marching about aimlessly.

In the green playing-fields beside the railway track among the goal posts and pavilions, labourers were digging trenches and building gun emplacements. The children waved gaily as the train chugged past. The labourers waved back and leaned on their shovels.

Some openly cried and turned their backs in embarrassment when they realised, they were watching a trainload of children being taken away to God-knows-where.

"Why were the men crying?" we asked.

The teacher shook her head and held back her own tears.

By midday, the children on the train were hungry, rebellious and demanding toilet facilities. So, it was a great relief to us all when the train pulled into a tiny country station. The carriage doors burst open and frazzled teachers led us down the platform into the bathrooms. They tried valiantly to not lose a child and recovered most of those who had wandered off to seek friends in different groups. They sorted out piles of clothes and luggage.

Making sure each child still had his own label in plain view and then walked us to a nearby field and herded us into a large, khaki-coloured tent. We were fed sandwiches and glasses of milk. It was warm inside and with the food inside me and heavy clothes about me, I sat down and leaned against a tentpole. Then I slept among the noise.

When I woke, it was evening, and the teachers were gone. With hindsight, they were probably sitting glassy eyed with fatigue in the local pub with a drink in their shaking hand. Unfamiliar faces surrounded us in the darkening tent and homesickness welled up in the children.

Many cried for their mothers and fathers and were comforted by an earnest group of women volunteers dressed in Red Cross uniforms and Boy Scouts in shorts and safari hats who wandered among us distributing paper bags containing groceries and toilet items. They checked names and destinations on the ubiquitous labels, and we were split up into small groups. With our luggage tied on the roofs of taxicabs, we were driven to our final destinations.

In 1939, Durley Village was surrounded by rich, rolling farmland accessible by a narrow road cut deep into the earth and lined with ancient hedgerows. The taxi rolled to a stop at the gate of a tiny, wood-framed house where several large women dressed in wraparound pinafores and rubber boots were congregated in the evening light.

"Here they are!" called one woman. "My evacuees! Bring 'em inside. Poor dears must be tired out and hungry."

My roommate, Charlie, and I were scooped up in brawny arms, divested again of our parcels and raincoats and seated at a plain wooden kitchen table where we were fed again by the light of a guttering oil lamp. Then, bone-weary, we climbed the narrow stairs to our bedroom and slept together in the unaccustomed silence of the countryside.

It was early morning, to judge by the pale light outside, when Charlie woke me by shaking my shoulder. He was hopping from one foot to the other.

"Bathroom!" he demanded hoarsely. "Where's the bathroom?"

I shook my head. We padded the house in our bare feet, opened doors and climbed the stairs twice as Charlie's discomfort grew. Then our host, Mr Brown, appeared in his dressing gown and immediately perceived the problem. With a wavering flashlight, he led us to the privy at the bottom of the garden. Poor Charlie's embarrassment knew no bounds as he later lay listening to the muffled laughter of the Browns in the next room.

In the following days, we began to get used to the rigours of country life. School had not yet been convened, and Charlie and I explored the lanes and fields around the village. It was warm that autumn. Full of the smells of earth and contented cows. But where were my mother and father? Didn't she say, she'd see me soon? I had been a good boy, like she said.

It was one of those odd coincidences that when I was walking alone down the road one morning, idly severing the heads of wildflowers in the ditch with a stick, that I saw my father's Raleigh bicycle leaning against the brick gatepost of a house set in a large garden. I walked purposefully up to the open front door and loudly announced my arrival. My mother gasped in shock and grabbed the edge of a table for support before embracing me.

It seems that the omni-present bureaucratic bungling had placed me at the wrong address and Mother and Father had spent several days trying to locate me. My father had been bicycling the adjacent villages asking for me when I was, but a stone's throw away round a bend in the road.

So, we were reunited and spent the next three months together in the village. Until the reality of winter in rural Hampshire hit us in the form of mud, rain and unheated houses. In February we thanked our hosts and gladly made the trek back to our old home to face the war in familiar, if more dangerous, surroundings.

We spent Christmas Eve 1939 alone. There were presents stacked under the Christmas tree and there was no shortage of food. But there was no family gathering. My father and uncles were on active duty in the army or navy, leaving the women to put on a brave face for the sake of the children.

By now, the windows had been taped to prevent splintered glass from flying into the room. Frames had been made and covered with thick fabric. They could be fitted over the windows at night so that no light would escape and guide the Luftwaffe to our house. Air raid wardens wearing black steel helmets rode bicycles around the town checking that no house was guilty of showing a light. They reprimanded the guilty with cries of "Put that light out!" or, when the air raids began, "Put that bloody light out!"

By the spring of 1940, most of the evacuees had returned home and the local schools began to reopen. There were differences. Air raids had started. The classroom windows were taped. Morning assembly was held in a windowless corridor, and we were admonished to never, never be without our gas masks. During our absence in Durley Village, air raid shelters had been built in the school playground. Damp, smelly, rectangular brick boxes without windows and an almost airtight, felt-edged door-covering which supposedly kept out the poison gas.

Bare lightbulbs illuminated the dismal interior. We spent many hours in there as the noise and stink of war enveloped the town. We sat wrapped in army surplus blankets and learnt mathematics, English grammar and literature when the power was on. But when it was not our teachers read us stories by flashlight. And we could let their soporific voices lull us into a doze until the lights came back on and we were back to mathematics.

It was the airplanes that fascinated English children in 1940. Many a lifetime fascination was born during those days of the Battle of Britain. Boys made and compared balsawood models. They bragged how many different types they could identify. We played at being pilots high above the clouds. We ran the streets, arms outstretched, scanning the ground every inch of the way as if every crack in the pavement were a river, every stone wall a mountain and every other small boy a Heinkel or Messerschmitt to be chased and shot down.

The sight of squadrons of small boys, arms outstretched like wings, eyes lowered, making strange staccato noises and swooping from one side of the street to another in simulated aerial combat caused many an adult eyebrow to lift. And many a remark of concern for the parents of such demented creatures.

A parachutist landed on the seashore one afternoon and the leather-jacketed airman hurt his leg as he rolled behind the billowing silk. He sat smoking a cigarette as the solemn local children congregated at a safe and respectful distance. He had a round, square-jawed face, bright blue eyes and a strange way of talking.

"You a German?" asked an awestruck boy.

"No, No," said the airman laughing and shaking his head. "Polish."

They came for him in a drab khaki-coloured ambulance with a big red cross painted on the side and helped him onto a stretcher. As they drove away, he waved goodbye through the small window in the back door.

From then on we had heroes to go with our airplanes. No cornflakes package remained on the grocer's shelves long if it had a press-out model of an airplane on its back panel. More cornflakes were sold that way than by the life-size cardboard facsimiles of a smiling Shirley Temple that had appeared in the grocer's doorway that summer.

Our town was ringed with military sites. It was the Channel port for the British submarine fleet. So, when the Luftwaffe's attention moved away from the Royal Air Force airfields and onto the cities and towns, things got tense.

By the time the Battle of Britain was at its peak in the late summer of 1940, we had an Anderson shelter in the back yard. It was a hole in the ground lined with concrete and covered with a dome of corrugated steel and the dirt from the excavation. It had a tier of wooden bunks and a pallet on the floor.

At the first sound of the wailing air raid siren during the night, my mother woke us roughly and we ran sleepily down the garden path clutching pillows in one hand and holding up our pyjamas with the other. Then we dived in through the little doorway to the shelter and lay on our bunks until the 'all clear'. More often, we slept until morning.

Most of the time in late 1940, the German bombers passed over us on their way inland to attack London. The game of war was being played away from home. So, it was inevitable that we became careless about taking shelter. The communal shelters in the centre of town fell into disuse and soon, we took our time getting to the Anderson.

My most prized possession in those early war days was one of those odd-shaped steel helmets that French soldiers and firemen wore. At the time, the French fleet was impounded in British harbours and were being refitted with conventional, more austere, British equipment. French helmets and other things such as thick, green woollen blankets began to find their way into local homes.

During one of his infrequent leaves, my father had given me his helmet, the British type with a broad rim around the edge and informed me I was now the *man of the house* in his absence.

Instantly translated by me as the authority to sit on the roof of the air raid shelter and direct the war. Until a piece of shrapnel put a ding in the crown and reminded me that I was not immortal. My mother, being the *Lady of the House*, outranked me and henceforth, at the first wail of the siren I was to join her in the shelter with the other mortals.

Everything changed when the town became a target. Instead of sitting on the roof of the Anderson shelter arguing with my friend about which airplane was a Heinkel or a Dornier, a Spitfire or a Hurricane, I now sat in that hole in the ground wrapped in a blanket listening to the noise outside.

There were no airplane sounds now. The battered Luftwaffe was not as arrogant as before and flew higher in the sky. The black squadrons passed slowly overhead harassed by little dots of fighters streaming white vapour trails that made graceful, curving patterns in the blue sky.

First, the raids came by day but as the German losses mounted, they came by night. The darkness was filled with the flash and bark of anti-aircraft guns, the shriek and whine of falling bombs, the deafening explosions and the clang of emergency vehicles. Overall was the indelible stink of burning. The night sky turned orange, and, in the morning, anxious people walked through the rubble-strewn and smoking streets to find out if friends and relatives still had a home. Or if they still needed one.

With night bombing, the pattern of our lives took on a dull repetitiveness. We learnt to jump out of bed at the siren's first wail without prompting, put on warm clothes and head for the Anderson shelter. The shelter was dry and relatively warm with light provided by candles. Body heat was retained by layers of blankets and overcoats. Condensation formed on the cold steel roof and coursed down in little rivulets.

It became routine to spend the night in the shelter. Then, in the daylight, children emerged from the shelters to search the streets for shrapnel. Those lethal, jagged bits of anti-aircraft ammunition that rained down on us. The proceeds were kept as souvenirs or placed in buckets outside the air raid wardens' shelters to be recycled and hurled back at the enemy. Larger pieces were often too hot to hold.

Food supplies began to dwindle. Familiar things disappeared from the grocer's shelves. We were not to see a banana for four more long years. The British coalition government responded quickly to the situation and all children were given a ration of fresh milk, orange juice concentrate (which made a fine base for homemade wine) and the hated cod-liver oil.

But not all was doom and gloom. There was time for fun. Half-pint bottles of milk came in wire crates to be delivered to our school classrooms during morning break by the elderly, overweight janitor. He enlisted the help of some boys who made a cart of scrap wood and four mismatched wheels from old baby strollers. We loaded it with four crates of milk and raced along the corridors to the classrooms like a stagecoach being pursued by Red Indians in a *B* movie at the Criterion Theatre.

One boy sat on the front steering wheel with a loop of rope on the front wheels, two others pushing. The crates were heavy, the corridors long and smooth. And the cart had no brakes. There was an impatient waiting list of drivers and pushers.

It was in March 1941 that the war came too close. We had gone to bed early that evening because it was cold and there was a shortage of coal. My mother had placed hot-water bottles in our beds, my brother and sister, and I lay cosy between the sheets watching our breath condense in the frigid air in the bedroom. The air raid sirens wailed at about ten o'clock and with reluctance, we went through the routine of leaving our warm beds and going down to the shelter clutching hot-water bottles.

The bombs fell closer that night and with a greater frequency than usual. The ground shook. When the scream of a falling bomb grew louder, I threw myself from the top bunk and lay on the pallet with the others, my face pressed into a pillow. I covered my head with my hands, but still the thunder and crashing hurt my ears.

Showers of dust fell from the joints in the steel roof. Outside in the street, ambulances and fire engines added their clanging, high-pitched noise to the terrifying noise. And through it all came the sound of human voices.

When the raid was over, we lay together exhausted until the morning light filtered through the little rectangular door of our cell and Mother ventured out to make tea and toast for our breakfast.

The air was full of drifting smoke. Our house was relatively undamaged. Only a few broken windows and a small hole in the roof. The electricity was off, but the water was on. A policeman rapped on the door and asked if we were OK. In the street lay the debris from bombed houses and up the street, towards the harbour, one still burned white-hot in its brick shell with a column of sparks pouring high in the sky.

With a doggedness built on fear and determination, people began to appear in the street and hot, sweet tea laced with navy rum was being handed to smoke-stained survivors and rescuers. Across from our house, a family returned to find their house flooded. A bomb splinter had severed a water pipe in the attic. Mrs Witt's house had no windows. She feared the night air and had not opened the windows to mitigate the effect of a bomb blast.

The full extent of the damage was not apparent at first. As in any battle, a foot soldier sees only that piece of the action that immediately surrounds him and is necessarily ignorant of the larger picture. Half of the houses in the old town had been destroyed or damaged.

I went to school as usual that morning. Our house and those up the street towards the school had survived but as I turned the corner something was wrong. Funny place to find a school notebook. I picked it up. A few yards later, I picked up a small wooden box still filled with arithmetic cards from my own classroom. Debris covered the road and there was water everywhere. It wasn't raining.

Closer to the school building, there was chaos. The school had been hit, and across the street, a row of houses had burned. Roofs were gone. Walls had collapsed, exposing rooms full of furniture like a child's dollhouse with the side off. The elm trees lining the street were splintered and broken by the flying flint rocks that had been the school's walls. Furniture was stacked in front gardens and a woman dressed in a man's raincoat stood sobbing in the arms of a fireman. High up on a pile of rubble that had been a house, soldiers and firemen were digging frantically.

In one of the gardens, a woman dressed in a nightgown and galoshes stood screaming abuse up at the sky. She shook her fist at the departed Luftwaffe and with the other, pointed at her washing line where sheets and towels hung tattered and black-streaked. Behind her, her house still sizzled and smoked under the cascade of water from firehoses.

I stepped over the flaccid firehoses and paddled through pools of water and wondered if they would let me go to school. It was my turn to erase the chalkboard and set out the notebooks and pencils.

"No school today, son," said a dirty and tired policeman who took me by the hand and walked me away. "Better run off home now."

We got a new school later in the year. A larger building that had been almost completed before the war and now made habitable for the increasing number of pupils bombed out of their local schools. It had bomb shelters and the customary routine of confinement in them when the raids came. It came with a large, asphalted playground.

During one night raid, incendiary bombs were dropped on the school. The school roof suffered several holes, which were quickly patched over, but the holes in the playground were not. The incendiaries were the magnesium type. They burned a two-foot diameter hole through the asphalt before a fireman heaped dirt on them to extinguish them. They had quickly learnt to not pour water on them since that merely spread the flames. Soon, grass and thistles took root in the holes and the playground finally broke up into mounds of broken asphalt.

This organic growth achieved more destruction in a few months than Hitler's technology. In retrospect, the bombing of Germany with thistle seeds might have proved equally damaging to their war effort. Charlie, who was more inventive than most, secreted several of the 18-inch long, 2-inch diameter incendiaries in a cardboard box in his father's workshop. The filings from the magnesium carcass made excellent filling for homemade fireworks which were much prized in the victory celebrations later.

Local public transport during the war years consisted of a fleet of green, wheezing old diesel buses operated by the Town Council and one red, glossy, streamlined private bus. They moved slowly through the streets around piles of rubble and huge blocks of concrete that had been hurriedly poured in strategic locations under bridges and at bends in the road. Supposedly to slow down the advance of invading armies. In 1951, one was still in place under a railway bridge.

The private bus was owned by an ex-boxer who drove his route around town fortified by a case of Brown Ale beside his seat. He collected his penny fares as we boarded and drove at a sedate 25 miles per hour. But when the air raid siren started to howl, he was swiftly off out of town and safely parked behind Portsdown Hill.

It was bicycles that gave most people their ticket to freedom in the war years. Automobiles were rare. They were either confiscated for the military or suspended on wooden blocks in garages waiting for the day when petrol would flow again. When families could pick bluebells in the countryside or make daytrips to the seaside and eat sand sandwiches.

I got my first (used) bike during an air raid and rode it down the street on its maiden flight trying to steer with one hand whilst holding my tin hat on with the other. My gasmask didn't help much. It kept falling between my knees, collapsing both the bike and rider.

Bicycles are remarkable vehicles. Fast enough to outdistance the average angry dog or human on foot yet agile enough to be driven on trails only inches wide. Light enough to be carried over railway lines or hoisted up over barbed wire fences.

Being very young and having a bicycle was our passport to places denied to others. Charlie and I roamed far and wide around the town. We found anti-aircraft guns strategically placed in farmers' fields and camouflaged by immense tent-like arrays of nets intertwined with strips of green and brown. Underneath them, the guns pointed upwards, making peaks in the netting and soldiers and khaki vehicles hurried about.

On one bike journey into the woods behind Portsdown Hill where a little mist lingered among the pines in the morning air, Charlie stopped.

"See that?" he said, pointing.

"It's a plane!"

"Not a bomber."

"Nor a fighter."

We climbed over a five-bar gate and walked across the field. It was a shining aluminium biplane half-suspended in some trees with its nose on the ground and tail in the air. The broken fuselage was ribbed, and it had little curtains in the windows. Through the open doors, we saw seats. A casualty of war without explanation. Silence. Not a sound.

"Should we tell someone?" asked Charlie.

"Who?"

With the question unanswered, we solemnly got back on our bikes and rode away.

Memories of that plane lingered, and I later concluded that it was an Imperial Airways passenger plane. It had come to grief in the hands of the Royal Air Force and no news of its demise was reported in the newspapers.

The sight of crippled airplanes struggling to stay airborne or falling to earth was not uncommon. Salvage crews scoured the countryside looking for survivors and the rumour spread that the transparent cockpit canopies were made of a secret material ideally suited for making anything from rings to picture frames.

Charlie and I found the remains of a demolished fighter during one of our bike rides in swampland between a railway embankment and a patch of elm trees. The pilot had clearly sought out the patch of ground for an emergency landing and to judge by the lack of petrol fumes, was out of fuel. But the ground was soft, wet and muddy. The skid marks were very short and the airplane's tail was folded over the cockpit. The propeller was bent and thrust deep in the mud.

As the war dragged on, everything was in short supply. Food rationing meant long waits in line at the grocers and the portions were tiny. Many times, there just wasn't enough to go round and there were angry scenes at the counters. Music Hall comedians made light of the absence of bananas.

"—yes, we have no bananas,

We have no bananas today!—"

We ate a lot of potatoes and onions. Fried fish and chips, that gastronomic disaster, featured more and more in the national diet. When fish was available, a 'Frying Tonight' sign would appear about once a week at our local shop.

Being fleet of foot and armed with a half-crown coin, I was assigned the task of lining up at the shop and asking, "Four pieces and a shilling's worth of chips, please," of the tall, thin man who sweated over his deep-fat fryer trying to diplomatically enforce his own form of rationing.

Then, stuffing the newspaper-wrapped parcel under my aromatic sweater to conserve the heat, I ran home. But not without exacting my fee of a few gratuitous chips winkled out through a small hole in the paper.

Rubble from bombed houses was piled high on the town parks. There was a desperate call for scrap metal to feed the armaments industry. Without a *by-your-leave* metal garden fences were cut down with acetylene torches. Church gates, the iron decorations from Victorian graves, toys, the railings around the park were swept away to make bombs and tanks.

Repair kits for fixing holes in the bottom of worn-out cooking pots were sold because replacement pots were unavailable. They consisted of cork rings sandwiched between metal washers and tightened with screws through the hole. They lasted for a few days or weeks. Less if one puts them on back-to-front with the cork on the outside in contact with the gas flame.

"How many cooking pots did they need to make a Lancaster bomber?" I asked my teacher.

She shook her head and laughed.

Wartime food shortages and consequent rationing had a variety of effects. Children whose diet had been inadequate in the years before the war were getting better nutrition through cheap milk and orange juice and well-cooked, if starchy, school lunches. The absence of sugary candies no doubt contributed to the remarkable improvement in dental health in a generation of children.

But our parents often deprived themselves to give the children more. Years later, the deprivation had its effects on their health as did cigarette smoking which had multiplied among women.

After the battles of El Alamein, Stalingrad, Kursk and the death of German U-Boats and their crews in the Atlantic, the air raids began to diminish. The mood in town and the rest of the country became more hopeful. The Germans would be beaten.

Then, in late 1942 and in 1943, unfamiliar uniforms began to appear in town. Different languages and accents were heard in the pubs and streets. Frenchmen in pill-box hats, Poles in red berets. Bright, eager young men in British battledress with shoulder flashes reading *Norway*, *Denmark*, *Canada* strolled about. And Americans wearing round helmets and spats on their boots joined the others.

Rows of wooden barracks sprouted among the trees in the forests and private estates around the town. Barriers appeared everywhere and soldiers in wooden sentry boxes guarded the entrances to the camps. Some of those young men had Wrigley's gum, cigarettes and chocolate bars to share. And overhead, squadrons of Lancaster bombers and B-17s escorted by flocks of fighters headed south towards Europe. The tide had turned, and we cheered.

One evening in early 1944, I got my first sight of a V-2. A small, unpiloted airplane launched against Britain from concealed sites across the English Channel. It had a crude ram-jet engine which glowed red in the dark and puttered like a lawnmower. When the engine stopped, the plane became a bomb. A new engine of war. An indiscriminate weapon designed to intimidate. Which it did until the Royal Air Force found fighters fast enough to shoot them down by their hundreds. The population took another deep breath.

There was more to come. There was no warning of the approach of a V-2, and we were rarely in the shelter when one fell. The V-2 was a supersonic ballistic missile with a 1-ton Amatol warhead that rocketed into the stratosphere and fell to earth with a devastating explosion.

Fortunately, their guidance systems were inaccurate, and few fell near our town. So, we went about our business knowing that chance played a major part in where the V-2s fell. There was no fighter fast enough to shoot the V-2 down. No defence at all.

In the spring of 1944, Charlie's and my bicycle expeditions were suddenly restricted. An invasion army was assembling in Southern England. The country lanes and fields began to fill with a multitude of men, women and the massive material of modern war.

We became captives in our own town, hemmed in by tent cities and thousands of tanks and trucks with a big white star on their sides. Huge mounds of boxes and oil drums were stacked in fields and covered with tarps. Then, in the weeks before June 1944, the country roads and streets began to fill with an army on the move. It had to filter down from the countryside to the loading docks in some prearranged order.

There was not enough room on the narrow roads. Two lanes of traffic had to become three at the expense of front gardens. Sherman tanks, trucks, DUKWs and a plethora of strange contraptions rumbled across flower beds and lawns. Roads became miles of churned-up asphalt. Manhole covers flipped like so many tossed coins.

Soldiers bivouacked in the street and temporary field kitchens sprouted on bombed sites. All the time, women and children brewed the inevitable tea from scant rations and handed up cups to the patient, bored men in their vehicles.

Those piles of rubble in the town parks had been put to good use in 1944. Landing craft (LSTs) needed ramps for the tanks and trucks to run down, enter their gaping bow doors and be swallowed in their cavernous interiors.

The town children had sat on the sidewalk and watched as the promenade beside the harbour was destroyed. In past summers we had strolled along it and climbed down to the water's edge to collect cockles and mussels from the stony beach.

Now, it was cleared of its poplar trees and viewpoints and rubble had been dumped over the edge to fill the space between the sea and the upper road. Hundreds of labourers with bulldozers worked to pack and smooth a shallow ramp that ran down into the water at low tide. Then they laid huge paving blocks that would support the weight of loaded trucks and tanks. A rickety-looking pier was built of scaffolding material.

Closer to the date of embarkation for the Normandy invasion, a company of British soldiers arrived during the night and set out 2-gallon-sized containers at fifty-foot intervals along the street. Mother turned out the lights so that we could open the blackout curtain and watch them at work.

Days later, we found out what was going on. With the town full of troops and machines and the water of Portsmouth harbour covered with ships of every description, we were about to be hidden from the enemy. Those canisters set out so secretly were full of naphtha and when ignited, poured forth a thick layer of pungent smoke which covered the town in a noxious blanket. An old-fashioned smokescreen. It lingered for days until the winds, happily, blew it away leaving more ugly black streaks on the buildings to add to those from the bomb fires. The crates the cannisters came in made excellent kindling wood.

In early June 1944, there was not a vacant space on any road in the town. We woke at first light to find three lines of vehicles stalled in the street below our bedroom window. Over everything was the stink of gasoline and diesel engines. From the harbour came the rumble and throb of a thousand boat engines. Then, very slowly, the lines of tanks and trucks began to move.

They moved all day and all night and still they came. The excitement grew and Mother became tense. Next morning, I could stand it no more and slipped out into the traffic to follow it down to the loading ramp.

I found a vantage point on the very edge of the ramp by wading with other boys through the water at low tide. Soldiers lining the ramp shouted and waved at us to move back and one fired a burst in the air. But there was no going back. The tide was coming in. So, we sat and watched as history was made.

The harbour was filled with every variety of vessel from battleships to torpedo boats. In front of us, two landing craft at the ramp were swallowing up columns of tanks and trucks. Others waited out in the navigation channel. Blue smoke belched from engines. Loadmasters waved their flags, cursed and shouted. It looked like total chaos to me. But around the bend of the harbour to my right, a stream of landing craft was moving out into the English Channel towards France.

Days later, the landing craft returned. They moved gently up to the ramp and lowered their hinged bows like a castle drawbridge. Showers of French sand dropped onto English concrete. Columns of medics carried khaki stretchers down to the waiting army ambulances. The long lines of ambulances moved slowly along the shattered streets towards the temporary hospitals set up on the outskirts of town. No tea for those soldiers.

Only quiet, awed sympathy from those of us who had sent them on their way so recently with cheers and flag-waving. Close to the ramp, a morgue was set up in the garden of a house for those who did not make it home. It was concealed from view by billowing tarpaulins hung from trees.

With the insatiable curiosity of small boys, we inspected a wired-off section of the loading ramp. To find it filled with the boots, helmets, torn uniforms and piles of discarded, blood-soaked stretchers. We left the scene quietly with the reality of war indelibly impressed in our memory.

At the end of the European war, a great bonfire of wood from destroyed houses was built on the ramp. A tower of sparks rose high into the night air and illuminated wild scenes of drinking and dancing. Out on the harbour, sailors emptied the ships' lockers and fired flare pistols and distress rockets into the air until the scene looked like the blitz at full throttle. Finally, in the early hours of the morning, the fires died down and the fire brigade moved in to douse the embers.

Christmas 1945 was a time of thanksgiving and stark austerity. Food rationing was strict and was to be in force for several years. I have a ration book issued to me in 1954. Oranges appeared briefly in the shops and were quickly snatched up, split into sections and shared between the children.

Over the holidays, we visited an aunt in Southampton. The city was smoke-stained and desolate. Rows of houses were reduced to rubble. The streets were cleared and eerily deserted. Only the clanking trolley buses moved about.

With each New Year, the living memories of World War Two diminish. Today, the bomb damage is long gone. The loading ramp is the slipway for a yacht club. More names have been added to the weathered granite war memorials in the churchyards of towns and villages. Faded red poppies lie on the trimmed grass beside the old inscription that chides us—"Lest we forget."

News began to filter in that the Germans were on the run. Gradually the terrible stories of death camps and concentration camps became known.

1945 and the war was over. Rationing was still in place, and remade clothes continued. I had a sister at last, Wendy, who the boys nicknamed Wendy Whiffles, born in 1945. Dick Barton, a TV show, became the high light of children's days, the streets emptied with shouts of Dick Barton's on. Father came home from the war and became a milkman, as there was not much work around for his skills. This meant he was able to obtain a box of ice-cream, something we had only ever heard of.

I was doing one of my chores, scrubbing the draining board, they shared the whole box between them, and I can still see the malice in his face when he said, "Oh, dear none for Joan."

Here I am, 7 years old, and this person was exercising his power over me. I had learnt not to get upset, just walk away. Aunt Flo had heard. Sybil arrived with a small bowl of ice-cream which she had made just for me. These brave, caring women.

My formative years were about to change with the arrival of my Uncle Bill, returning from the far east after the war. Someone I had never met, a tall man with dark hair greying at the temples. He walked into the room where a fire was lit and we were all gathered round talking, reading and playing board games. The snakes and ladders board was bent and battered from many years before. As he left, I remember him saying to my mother, I am going to get myself some of this.

Some months later, Uncle Bill brought a lady to meet us all. She was so glamorous, wearing the new look in red with a little hat on her glossy curls. Lipstick and mascara are so attractive, mesmerising. My new Aunt Joyce, known as Joy. My parents were horrified as if this person was some sort of jezebel, and to crown it all, she was Uncle Bill's fiancée.

The wedding was to be set for April 1946, and they announced that I would be a bridesmaid, I was beyond excited. Well, who would not be. I was totally in awe of the way she looked and her confidence whilst dealing with my parents. Given confidence by Joy, I boldly asked if I could have my hair curled. Joy backed me up and I had my way, my eyes were well and truly opened.

So, a bridesmaid with curls I became.

The wedding caused uproar in the Bristow family, Uncle Bill had inherited the family home in Gosport, being the only male. It was a semi-detached house near the town centre. Whilst he was away during the war, Aunt Sybil had lived there, and I had visited on numerous occasions. Sybil and her female partner did not cover up their relationship, nothing was hidden from me. I knew they shared the same bed. To me, it was quite normal.

This was one of the places I was safe and was full of books, always one left out for me to read, and my opinion sought at the end over the content of the story. The morals they taught as well as the delights of a story were fundamental to my core beliefs, even today. Sad that society meant they had to have a secret relationship and were not free to express themselves beyond the confines of their house. Homosexuality was not legalised until 1967 in the UK.

Now, Uncle Bill needed the house for his bride. So, Sybil had to move out. Uproar, poor Joy got the blame.

The war had damaged so many lives and hopes of the future for many, fiancés, husbands and boyfriends did not return, leaving grieving women. No hope for a future with the men they loved no family to care for and nurture. The women they worked with left their jobs, as the men who had survived the war, prisoner of war camps, and injuries slowly returned, and the women were expected to step aside and return to the role of housewife only.

Joy had been a fitter in the dockyard during the war, dressed in dungarees and hair covered in a scarf. Uncle Bill singled her out, he told me that she was intriguing. A future for both of them, having both been affected by the war, two people who came together to find some happiness, and make the most of their lives. Joy's fiancée had been killed in the war, and therefore, all her hope of a family. Uncle Bill provided her with that hope and security, even though when they married Uncle Robert was 42 years old and Joy was 22 years old. They went on to have a daughter, Cheryl, in 1948 and two sons, Paul, in 1951 and Timothy in 1970.

My mother's dislike of her was palpable, but I was allowed to visit them in Inverness Road. All the uproar started again when Uncle Bill moved to Alverstoke to run part of the dockyard, and they moved to a house nearer to his work with Inverness Road being rented out. Joy was to have the rent as her own money to do with what she wished.

Their new house was nearer to our home and my visits became more frequent. This lovely woman introduced me to a side of life I did not know existed, hair rollers, pan stick, rouge, lipstick and French knickers made of black lace, not knee-length bloomers. Sitting together at her dressing table, Joy in her lingerie, putting on her make-up, brushing out her hair, perfume spray, the smell intoxicating.

Perfume goes here, sweetie, on the main pulses, dabbing it on my wrists and neck pulse. Then on with her shoes followed by her dress. Another amazing woman entered my life bringing me a new depth of self-respect and confidence. A realisation that being a woman could be great fun!

My elder brothers were a fundamental part of my formative years, Peter was the eldest, born into a family unit which included our grandmother Millie. Mother's sisters welcomed him with great joy, as did grandma.

Gladys had two daughters living abroad at that time and Flo a son born with a disability which precluded them all from cuddles and doting care for a little boy.

Peter's character shone through from an early age, a big-hearted boy, looking after the younger ones as they came along, he was 5 when I was born and 3 when Trevor was born. Old enough to remember being evacuated in 1939 to Eastleigh, having been separated from Trevor and me. A strong independent boy of five, finding his way around the area until he found the rest of us.

With the help of Aunt Sybil, he completed his lessons each day, the schools being closed at that time. Missing primary school didn't affect him and being a clever young man, he passed his 11 plus and went to grammar school in Gosport and then moving with the family to Cheshunt, from where he struck out on his own at the age of 16.

Trevor, or the holy terror which was the name my aunts used for him. Full of mischief, a happy-go-lucky child, or so it seemed, we were close kids, Peter, Trevor and I, fending for ourselves to a large degree. Growing up during the Second World War, we formed a strong bond which lasted all our lives. Trevor was a kind, vulnerable child who sought attention by any means. It is only in recent years that I heard of the damage our days and nights in the Anderson shelter caused him.

Claustrophobia being down under the earth with the doors shut tight. I remember the darkness and being huddled up together. For me, the trauma caused something similar but not such a life-changing situation. For me, it was and is the smell of dank cellars and surprising the smell of a wine cellar in South Africa. The nasty smell of rotting leaves. Small fry against Trevor.

Trevor and I had fun, though away from the house, playing cops and robbers in the trees out in the back lane. He could run a lot faster than me. Yep, always it. Although he did go and get my mother when I fell out of a tree, getting caught on a branch and dangling from my dress hem. Eventually, he took his time as he thought it was funny.

Come the cold winter of 1947, I think, we ran about during the day coming back mid-morning for hot cocoa. Sweet and warming.

The ponds down by the creek were frozen, Trevor came to fetch me, come and see. Of course, Trevor was a holy terror, but he was never boring. Out onto the ponds we went, laid flat on the ice to look at the plants deep down, frozen in place. Eerie and beautiful. Home, we went wet through and grinning. He got a rollicking for that, and the clothes brush came out whack. He walked past me, rubbing his hand on his pants and whispered, "Worth it, wasn't it?"

Oh yes, brother of mine, it was.

He had his own circle of friends, one lived on the opposite side of the street, who was given a chemistry set. The boys were banished to the Anderson shelter in his parents' garden. They were missing for days until they became too adventurous and caused an explosion, Trevor with singed hair and eyebrows, but his friend was seriously burnt. Chemistry lessons were taken at school thereafter. David and Wendy were born during the war, and their formative years were spent in a new world.

David, the younger brother born in 1940, a stoic, quiet boy within the family home, was off out with the other two boys as soon as he was able to walk. Peter and Trevor were at school, and I was still very small. I have little recollection of him during these early years, but one incident comes to mind. The three of them were down the creek messing about in the mud as boys do and David sliced his foot open on some broken glass.

He was probably around three years old. Mother was not happy, the two elder brothers had to line up in the family room and she whacked them both on the hand with the back of a wooden clothes brush. This David and I had to witness, left me a bit afraid of that clothes brush.

Luckily for David, he was cleaned up and iodine applied to the foot, that stuff stings something awful. Foot bound up and no walking on it. I have no recollection of a doctor being involved, no NHS in those days. Doctor appointments cost money, and most of them had come out of retirement, and treatment was old-fashioned.

Antibiotics had not been discovered, no penicillin.

David as ever a tough little boy came through this ordeal and never complained at being pushed around in the old pram.

David and Trevor were playing Roman soldiers, the old pram being the chariot, up and down the garden path. Oh, dear, Pram and David ended up in a bush. Mother out of the scullery like a shot, another rollicking and a whack with the clothes brush for Trevor, David, and me watching on. Trevor, as usual, just rubbed his hand on his trousers and walked away.

Peter and Trevor were considerably older, and this stoic little boy became the butt of fathers nasty belittling ways, he learnt to stay in the background staying out of the family rows and bullying ways of father. The quiet observer who walked away as soon as he was able.

The only one in years to come, offering comfort at a particularly difficult time in my life. Not much passed David by.

Like all of Mother's children, Wendy was born at home, her rainbow baby after the sad time of Christine's birth. It was late October, weather cold and dreary. We were ushered in to greet our new baby sister, so precious, so tiny, a sister for me at last.

The boys, true to form called her Wendy Whiffles, as mother had rinsed out her nappies and hung them to dry on the fire guard. Nothing quite like my brothers.

We four were all attending school now and had our own groups of friends, World War II was over. Wendy was very precious to mother, and we had very little to do with her whilst she grew from babyhood to starting school.

No Aunt Sybil to help with reading and writing no encouragement for Wendy. This is not something mother undertook with any of us.

Wendy went off to school in Cheshunt where we moved to in 1950 to be taught by a new method of learning. I remember reading about the new method of teaching children, the play method, which sounds good in theory, but lacked the grounding us four oldest benefited from.

Like David, I remember her being a very quiet, happy girl with the loveliest smile. Craft work is the area in which she excelled, and in later years, an incredible wife, and mother. Coming to my aid in later years when my apartment was to be inspected by my future mother-in-law. An hour is all it took her to turn it into a coordinated, pleasant and shiny main room. Window cleaned; furniture polished; you name it. An exceptional home maker.

Recently I discovered, from Wendy herself, that she had a very successful career as a pharmacy manager, managing a large team of staff, having worked her way up into this role from being the cleaner and then a shop assistant, something she is and should be very proud of. Seems to run in the family !

So, as the war drew to a close and I was heading for 7 years old, I had been lucky to be able to read and write and developed a thirst for learning that remains with me today, I had faced adversity in terms of the war and had and would continue to suffer abuse, that would make me the woman I am today, and I was beginning to realise that I was much brighter than my parents.

# Chapter Two
# The Importance of Education in the Post-War Years

The war was finally over and it was a time for celebration for us all, it was very exciting times for us children born in and brought up in time of war, as war was all we knew. On VE day, in May 1945, tables were set out in the street, with food on the tables, including jellies, sandwiches, and cakes, we children had never seen so much food and were allowed to eat as much as we liked, we were amazed. Bunting was hung outside every home. Our Mothers were all smiling laughing and happy, singing and dancing to the radio.

It was also a confusing time, for us children, who had never known a time before the war, with no longer spending nights in the Anderson shelter, no more planes flying overhead. Families began to return from evacuation, there were many more children in school, meaning new friends to make, which was great fun. As the men returned from fighting, they took up their old jobs, and for the first time we were taught by men, who were much stricter than our gentle female nurturers, which meant it was time to learn more important things, with focus on needing to pass your 11 plus, lessons became much more serious. Singing in the assembly hall became more patriotic.

Geography became a new subject, learning about the world and the British Empire. Playtime or break time was more relaxed. Skipping ropes so long that three of us could skip side by side. Bouncing tennis balls against the wall to a rhythmic song. One a penny, two a penny, three a penny. And so on. Playing tig, screaming your it when you managed to catch someone.

A visit from John Betjeman had the staff very excited and we practiced our singing longer than usual. After our performance, a little pep talk about the winning of the war and the freedom, we now had due to the sacrifices of so many.

"You girls and boys have to build this great country again."

Confusion reigned, the need to succeed a new concept in my life. School was a refuge away from the family rows.

Learning by reading was a form of osmosis really. The main constant in my life was books, information. Imaginary journeys. The world and all it holds, all there in books. Images and stories firing my imagination, building blocks for the rest of my amazing life. History books, which were pre-war, of course, medieval Britain or the dark ages. How cruel the human being can be.

We were hearing and reading all the time of the atrocities carried out in Europe and Russia. Let alone the stories coming across the world about the war against the Japanese. Of terrible POW camps, men reduced to skin and bone, and again even more atrocities. The atomic bombs which were dropped on Japan brought this conflict to a close.

Working and stretching my mind, getting ready for my 11 plus exam, only to be told not this year, she is too young, the woe of being born in October. My school life had started at 4, a year earlier than most, as thanks to my Aunt Sybil I had been able to read for some time. Numbers no problem, really enjoying the neatness and rhythm they represented.

Life was not all work and playing with my brothers. They had grown away and formed new friendships as indeed had I. Several girls moved into the houses nearby, a little group of us joining the brownies to learn how to tie knots, which was new for me. Oddly enough, this was something I did not use in my adult life. This is where I learnt about teamwork.

The ability to work with others to achieve a common goal. They were happy days holding rummage sales and raising funds to send to Africa as little children were starving and needed our help. Odd, I thought, after all we had fresh pea soup for dinner with homemade bread, they would be welcome to it. Had to be hungry to eat that soup.

Sunday school for me, the boys refusing to go. It was something that irritated me as I questioned everything now, beginning to form my own opinion, what was the point of keeping quiet, so quiet that you can hear a pin drop. Reading the psalms, which preached forgiveness when we had all endured such hardship inflicted upon us.

I began to see how unfair life really was, no party dress for me when invited to a birthday party for a friend at school. Still wearing hand-me-downs and remakes, which had never bothered me until I saw other girls in dresses made of parachute silk with ribbons in their hair. Proper shoes with a bar which buttoned across the foot. Not my brother's old plimsoles which mother had lovingly whitened for me. Hair cut so it fell in soft waves, not chopped off with mother's sewing scissors and scrapped into bunches.

Unfortunately, two of my beloved aunts died during these post-war years, leaving me sadly alone without them. How I missed them, just how much they did for me. Brushing my hair, "have to brush your hair every night, little one, one hundred times to keep it smooth and shiny." The hugs and caring all gone. Time to grow up.

My father had finally returned from the war and took the only job available for a man with his skills and started redelivering milk each morning on his milk float. He was worse than ever and as I was no longer small enough to be put to bed, he became more devious. Telling my mother, he could hear me crying and came to comfort me. Those creepy hands had escalated to kissing and licking.

Things were not good for me as I began to have nightmares and screaming at night. Aunt Flo heard and gave my mother what for to the extent that these two sisters stopped talking to one another and the adjoining garden gate was locked. Father was home, life was grey again.

In hindsight, I blamed myself for losing my refuge. I should not have gone running around there whenever I could to get away. Well, it was probably nothing to do with me, just my father throwing his weight around as usual.

Everyone at that time had enormous adjustments to make. Men returning home to their pre-war employment, finding this had been done by women. These incredible women had kept the factories working, made the ammunition, felled the trees, farmed the land and brought up the children. Suddenly, they were back being housewives again.

However, the world had moved on, the Americans had arrived during the later years of the war and women witnessed a different way of life. Nylon stocking, amazing. English women had thick Lyle stockings, or if they could afford it, silk stockings.

Mother had to toe the line of a dutiful wife ordered around by father. His life had also changed, no vacancies for men with his skills, a milkman being the only employment available. Working on cruise ships was not an option, most of the ships have been adapted for war service. No more adventures, no more trips to foreign countries, this sedentary life soon lost its appeal.

Watching my mother struggle at this time brought enlightenment to a young girl, visiting my friends in their homes where they laughed and sang along to modern songs on the radio. Glad to have the men home. Out dancing, bopping to the big band sounds.

Shirley's uncle took us girls to a Pantomime in Portsmouth, all sitting together in a box next to the stage, amazing the dame coming in to our box and pretending to jump down on the stage. Whispering to Shirley, "That's a man."

Understanding that, Mother was fighting for survival, and she was fighting for her children. The situation could not continue, something had to change.

Peter and Trevor had passed the 11 plus exam and attended the local grammar school. Homework in the evenings for those two boys and sewing for me. Reading to David and Wendy, who were still very young, and early to bed. Solace and peace for a while, lull before the storm.

Change came quickly and suddenly, Father had been home for about 18 months, and we were now in 1947. Still rationing, still not much food, and the milkman's pay with five kids did not stretch very far. I had learnt to suppress my nightmare screams but the visits were still occurring.

Mother began to tune the radio to the news in the evenings and sit with me as I sewed shirts and underpants, all the necessary things of life, which were still in short supply. Father began to join us and we three discussed what was going on in the world. These times seemed to be of help to them, no shouting or arguing when Joan was about. My mother found a way to survive this turbulent time.

Aunt Sybil had attained her ambition to become a headmistress, and the news of her illness was a shock. The sisters rallied round, and Aunt Sybil came to live next door for her final days. I was taken to say goodbye to her, that lovely smile just for me, tears in her eyes, and she turned away groaning in pain.

I learnt many years later that she had provided for me in her will, leaving me a legacy and her gold watch, at the time, my mother was very angry as the bulk of her estate was left to a charity. I wonder where that watch is now.

London was now thriving and bustling again. Lyons tea shop became even more fashionable, during one of the evening discussions the decision was made for Father to contact some of his mates from his time on the ships to see if they knew of any opportunities in catering. One of the pursers came back with information about a new restaurant which would be opened by the Cooperative Society in Enfield, there was a vacancy for a manager.

Great excitement as Father left for the interview and was appointed, what an upheaval for us all, the boys were delighted as the only future mapped out for them was working in the dockyard or into the armed forces. These were three highly intelligent young men who saw the opportunity and welcomed it with open arms.

Father was gone and into lodgings with his old seafaring friend. Mother was left to clear the house and wait for father to secure somewhere for us all to live. No mean feat at that time. The elder children had to reduce their belongings to one box each, not terribly difficult as we had very little. My dolls had been passed down to my sister long ago.

So, books, my friends, went into my box, all three of them and of course my sewing kit. Then came the shock, I was going to be left behind to live with Aunt Flo and help with my cousin Bob. I was not very old in years, but thanks to the aunts I had a brain which could look at the situation laterally. Why, after the telephone calls I had had to make with my mother, when he had not sent funds, telling him that we could not eat or pay the rent.

Only thing I could reason was Aunt Flo protecting me. What would this mean for me? First and foremost, separation from the three musketeers who had become four and my young sister. Left to become a maid to an aging couple with a tough life looking after Bob and eventually marrying a sailor. I may have lost two of my beloved aunts in the past few years, but they had influenced my life, and I felt them there with me as I stood in front of my parents and said, "No, I am not staying here. I am going to London."

The worm had turned into a force to be reckoned with, who had ambitions and aspirations, the quiet one. This was my life, and I would survive the coming years. Despite what this meant I would have to endure; this was an opportunity not to be missed. Like the boys, we saw the world as it was, ready to make our way in this world. Father with his bullying and controlling ways be damned we would be together.

Eventually, after many bonfires to dispose of all unwanted possessions, we moved to London. My adventures had begun. We all now understood just what our mother was having to do and put up with. It was for her children, for the boys in particular, but I was the one she had to sacrifice to this man in order for all of us to survive.

I was 10 years old.

Moving day arrived, Mother, my sister and I took the bus to the ferry and crossed the hardway to Portsmouth railway station. Emotional time for my mother, I could feel her anxiety, such a change for her, away from her sisters and into the unknown. She was very curt and ordering me to hold on to your sister and look after her.

Onto the train we went, Wendy jumping up and down with excitement. I was more tuned into my mother's stress. Stepping into a different world, with the hope of improving the family's life and following her husband's choices, as he was the breadwinner. The place of women at that time had changed, but not for my mother, with no skills to offer employers and small children to raise, there was no choice for her. Always a risk where father was concerned, but he needed to be more than a milkman, also a growing family needed to eat. She had little or no choice. When we arrived in London, we were met at the train station by father's friend's wife who took us to her home in Enfield where father had been lodging. Wendy and I stayed there overnight, I continued to look after my little sister, whilst the parents went to our new home to meet the furniture van and to help unload our belongings.

The three boys had helped to load the van in Gosport and travelled to London with the driver and his mate in the van, something which would not happen in the 21st century. Health and safety rules just did not exist, but there was no other way, as there was no way we could afford three more train tickets.

The next day we two girls were taken by Mrs Manson to our new home, we were both excited and apprehensive, but it would be good to see the boys.

The property was in Cheshunt, a borough in Hertfordshire, to the north of Enfield, along a parade of shops, we were located over the top of the local co-operative. The flat consisted of three bedrooms, one family room, a small kitchen and an indoor bathroom, oh the luxury. The bus stop was outside the family room window and people in double-decker buses could look right in. We kids loved it, everything was so different and lively.

First night was a bit traumatic, we all managed to squeeze into the family room. Peter, who was now very tall and athletic, tried to move closer to the only source of heat, a small open fire and managed to break a window. It was a very small room. The three boys slept in the room on the ground floor, which was at street level. Wendy and I shared a bed in the small bedroom, which held a bed and that was it, the parents had the other room.

Freedom from the night-time visits at last, whilst sharing with Wendy, but affected by the feeling of being so very unimportant, after all, the parents wanted to leave me behind. Why I thought, why, so many thoughts going through my head.

The role of women at that time was still to be subservient, after all, they only got married and had children. Household duties were their lot in life. Carers, nurturers, bring up the children. This was how they were viewed and had been for many generations. Men were the ones to work and provide the family income.

This sounds like an ideal situation, but as with all things in life, nothing is simple. Some men were good at supporting their families and many more were not.

The two eldest boys, Peter and Trevor, went to Cheshunt Grammar school whilst David and I went to the local primary school, which was in walking distance. More 11 plus preparation for me, but best of all the school had a library. Sewing came into its own again as we girls stitched clothes for small children to sell at the school sports day.

I was asked by the teacher what stitches I was making in a tiny hem; the teacher had never seen it before. Run and fell seam tailoring stitch which is almost invisible. The aunts to the rescue again. I knew more than the teacher. Life was good.

September found me being fitted out with a school uniform, two blouses one gymslip and a blazer. Best of all a pair of shoes. I had passed my 11 plus with flying colours and joined my brothers at the grammar school. First ever pair of new shoes!

The grammar school was very formal and traditional, with assembly to start the day, with classical music playing on a speaker system, followed by an explanation of who wrote it, the meaning of the music, and the period in which it was written. Lessons were varied and interesting, I was learning on every level. Sciences, geography, English language and literature, art classes, cooking and needlework.

Once again, the aunt's teaching had the needlework teacher staring at me as I could roll a tiny hem and stitch it as I went along, not tacking first, she was amazed. Talking of tacking, we all girls had one length of thread about two feet long to tack with, using it time and time again, the aim being to save thread and costs, as rationing was still in progress in all areas. My mind just soaked everything up at this school.

Sports lessons were as ever for females limited to netball in the summer and hockey in the winter. Sports day, we girls gave a PE display whilst the boys did athletics. Our parents did not attend ever, so once again the three musketeers supported one another at each event.

The school was in walking distance, and I soon made a group of friends, older girls who chatted as we walked home together. School uniform meant that there was no nastiness because you all wore obvious hand-me-downs or remakes. All equal. Talk covered many areas, but was typical of girls, for example, having your hair cut by a stylist and how to make your hair shine.

The only product available was Amami setting lotion, a sticky solution used to control one's hair and the best curling method. Thanks to Aunt Joy I could participate in these conversations. How to apply mascara so it was not a cloggy mess. How to dust one's face with powder. Cold cream to soften one's skin. Not that I was allowed to use such things. According to mother, powder and paint make a nice girl, what she really ain't. All the school gossip. Great fun.

Home life was easier as the home being compact left mother with more time to relax. She had time to write letters to my aunts, her sisters, and even asked if I would like to add something to the bottom.

That was the way we all kept in contact in those days, the only option. This is called snail mail in the 21st century, with all the technology available that makes communicating so easy, but an important part of life during this time and something that was important to mother.

Having a bathroom with an inside toilet was my mother's pride and joy, after a life of outside toilets and the old tin bath. It was cleaned every day, not just a quick wipe over and a promise to do better next time. Thoroughly cleaned every day so it was shiny and bright. So much pride. Makes me feel humble today as I take for granted the house in which I live in currently which has four bathrooms.

Figure 5—Top pictures are me, and me as a bridesmaid at Uncle Bill and Aunt Joy's wedding 1947, the image underneath is Shirley.

That summer the two eldest boys worked in the local greenhouses picking tomatoes, Peter earning enough to buy himself a bicycle. Which he duly rode south to Gosport. Very tall now and athletic, winning the long jump at the school sports day. That was an enormous jump. Talk of the school for some time.

Mother was carrying another child, not so easy for her this time, I helped in the house, preparing the evening meals and running errands, taking Wendy and

David with me. A hot summer, walking to the park opposite the grammar school. Playing with the younger ones in the yard at the back of the shop. Passing the days until I could return to school.

So, my life continued the feelings of unimportance gone. The aunts had taught me well. Believe in yourself sweetie. That the one constant in life is you, learn to like yourself, and that is all that you need.

Come December of 1950, my younger sister was born. As with all of us children she was born at home in the room next to the family room. Getting the meal for the family and making tea for the midwife was down to me. Everyone else carrying on as if nothing untoward was going on. Father sat in front of the fire, a large bag of nuts beside him, throughout this time of waiting, he cracked open and ate every single nut.

I knew my mother was having a more difficult labour than normal. Although she made no complaints, just the soft murmur of the two women talking. At last, the cry of a newborn baby, joining in with carol singing on the radio. Father was allowed into the room and then we all welcomed our new sister. Perfect little girl with perfect tiny fingernails, amazing.

I was at home the next day as school was closed for the Christmas break. Mother and baby were resting. The rubber sheet used to protect the bed during mothers' labour was dumped in a bucket in the middle of the bathroom. It was in the same state when removed from the bed to make mother more comfortable. He had not dealt with it, I just looked at him and said, "Perhaps you should see to that."

Next thing I knew, he had gone to pick the bucket up and had a pain in his chest. Could not move. Called the ambulance and off he went. Leaving a 12-year-old girl to look after her mother and the family. Yep, cleaned the rubber sheet in the bath and put it out on the line to drip. Poor mother in bed with a newborn relying on her eldest daughter to hold things together. He was brought home on Christmas Eve as they could find nothing wrong.

Christmas was different but the new baby made up for that mother sitting in front of the fire holding her. As she joined in with the carols on the radio when she was born, there was only one name for her—Carol.

In the New Year, Mother's health improved, although she seemed to have lost some of her softness. During our time preparing the evening meal, she asked me what had happened to the bag of nuts at Christmas time.

"Oh dear, well, I was not going to cover for him. What all of them," she exclaimed. No wonder he had a pain. She was not a happy lady.

Back to school, no matter the weather, it was great. My daughter, a teacher, told me recently of parents complaining about their children being told to line up before going into the school building and how horrified they were in the cold weather, how times have changed.

1951, here I am, really enjoying my life, art lessons where you could express yourself, mix the colours instead of reading about how to do it. Amazing, the art teacher allowing for free thought and opinion, debating the different art forms down the generations to modern-day art. How these teachers helped me to believe in myself again. I could feel the aunts smiling. Latin, I was learning Latin, and a tiny hope began to grow. Maybe just maybe I could have a career.

The family was growing up and beginning to take new directions, Peter had passed his leaving certificate, GCSEs as they are now called. These results were so good he was able to obtain an apprenticeship with a company called Sangamo Weston.

This company was an American company which designed and manufactured a wide range of electrical measuring and control equipment for the aviation industry. He began what was called a sandwich course, working part-time and studying part-time, attending courses at Enfield Technical College. Later in life, Peter moved to work and live in America for the aviation company Boeing, so this apprenticeship really set him on his way to great opportunities.

Undertaking this apprenticeship meant Peter leaving home and going into lodgings. Like all apprenticeships at that time pay was minimal, hardly enough to pay for board and lodgings. How he managed I do not know; father was supposed to contribute. The unreliable money troubles that plagued mother whilst waiting in Gosport for father to find accommodation returned.

We all missed Peter so very much, my mother most of all, being her eldest son and first born. This parting was a mixture of sadness and gladness, he deserved this. From my viewpoint, this was not loss, just Peter leading the way, showing us, the Bristow kids, that it can be done and have the confidence to strike out on your own.

In the autumn of 1952, Mother told me I had to take a day off school to look after my baby sister Carol, as she and my father had to go to Gosport, coming back later that day. Still the same mindset from my parents, girls' education was not important. Off they went, Peter saw them travelling on the A10, heading south in an old pewter coloured car, as he cycled to work. Neither of us had a clue where the car came from, father most likely borrowed it.

Gosport, I found out later, was not the destination, when they returned during the afternoon. I was right in thinking, how could they get to Gosport and back in that time, now came the bombshell. Father had secured a much better job managing two restaurants, a ballroom and a hotel, which was great for him and potentially for us but meant another move, this time to Oxford.

So, in the New Year of 1952, we were all packed up and ready for the off, minus Peter though as he stayed in Enfield. No bonfires this time, nobody had much to pack.

Mother, Wendy, Carol and I arrived at our new home during the afternoon, travelling by bus and train. The rooms were above a shop once more. Having two sitting rooms, a kitchen and bathroom with a separate toilet on the first floor, three bedrooms and a box room on the top floor. Situated over a shop, once more, my mother was horrified.

The first time I had seen her in tears.

"It is so big and bare, our furniture will look lost, the windows are huge, and we have no curtains," she was so very tired, all too much for her.

Carol was still a toddler, and her birth had left my mother drained. I thought the opposite, it may have been huge against our previous homes, but the winter light coming into the room was amazing, and Oxford itself was a beautiful city.

I had lost my great school, my friends and hope to a certain extent.

"Would we always be moving because of Father?" I questioned.

Would there be such a good school as the grammar school and the opportunities but mother seemed to have lost something much bigger, she seemed increasingly out of her depth, out of tune with the modern world, afraid of a rapidly changing world, whereas for myself the changes hinted to more opportunities for women and a chance to do more than running a home and not being reliant on a man.

Time for positive thought.

I said to mother, "Come on, Mum. Let's check to see if there is anything to make a fire with, look there is a gas stove, the kitchen sink is by the window and there is a big market where we can go and buy fabric to make curtains, it will be alright."

First thing was schooling to be sorted out, Trevor went to Oxford Boys school to finish his leaving certificate, Wendy to the local primary school and

David to a secondary school called Cheney school in Headington. I went to the all-girls' grammar school, Milham Ford School.

Strangely, this is the moment Mother began to smile again, as having written to her sister Gladys, now living in Malta, telling her of our latest exploits, she received a reply which pleased her, Milham Ford was a very famous school, and I was going there.

Gladys' daughters, Mary and Marjorie, had travelled the world with their parents, but little woebegone me, receiver of hand-me-downs all her life, was going to Milham. The poor woman never got over it. Such one-upmanship and jealousy between sisters. But as I said, this small opportunity for one-upmanship made my mother briefly smile again, which was a good thing.

I started at Milham Ford School, the Monday after we arrived in Oxford, an all-girls grammar school which had a very high-grade image, although I did not know this at the time.

On my first day at my new school, as was expected, Father accompanied me to school for the introduction to the headmistress, pleasant words of welcome to me, but Father left in the background. This was a girl's school, and the meeting was an introduction for me, so what did he expect?

Unfortunately, he got the huff and gave the order, "I do not want her learning any dead language," and promptly then left. Any hope of me becoming a doctor went out of the window in 5 seconds. After father's bombshell regarding Latin, I was a bit shell shocked. Never shown the least interest in my schoolwork, surprised he even knew I was studying Latin.

The school system took over, Head Girl was called in and we were introduced. Given a tour of the school, explaining the front staircase and the quad were out of bounds. Introduced to my mentor and shown to my allocated class.

Cheshunt Grammar had been focused on producing a well-rounded student versed in as many subjects as possible. Whereas, at Milham Ford, the focus was on the academic subjects. The artistic subjects, for example, music, art, cooking and needlework, were part of the curriculum but not the most important.

The school, as there were just girls was very different, it felt far more civilised and I was surprised how easily I was accepted, also there were no paper pellets flying about the room and sticking in one's hair, which was a bonus. Coming from Cheshunt Grammar seemed to be acceptable, I knew it was a good school, but it seemed so did everybody else.

After all this is Oxford and most of the students were daughters of Oxford academics working in the education system.

Lessons were just as interesting and varied so I soon became engrossed, art lessons were exactly that no debates or discussions but also no boys to keep occupied. Physical exercise was undertaken in many more forms, Physical Education with ribbons and hula hoops, gym jumping over equipment as well as outdoor pursuits. Tennis and cricket in the summer and hockey and netball in the winter.

After school activities were numerous, I joined the choir and returned to singing, which I always enjoyed.

Eventually, I was given a bicycle to get myself to school each day, instead of costly bus journeys. As always second-hand but a bike for all that. This enabled me to join the cycling club, a route was planned to cover as many historic places as possible, and I grew to know the villages outside the city centre.

One of these trips took us to Dorchester-on-Thames to walk around abbey, visit the iron age fort and dykes, of particular interest to the teacher was a thatched wall. This was an important place in Roman times.

I made friends with several girls in my own peer group and because we had lunch in mixed age groups, a lot of the older girls as well. My closest friends were Yvonne, who I met when joining the school in 1952, and Susan, who moved from London and joined the school in 1953. These friendships would last a very long time, one for the rest of my life.

The role of women in the 1950s was changing and the school reflected this. Students were being prepared to go out into the world and make a difference. Women teaching the women who were destined for a different life to those of our ancestors.

In this environment, I thrived as the school ethos was carrying on the job my aunts had started so long ago, and I was driven by a desire to live like some of my aunts had done by achieving my full potential, experiencing life to the full and being independent.

During this time of change in my life, periods had started. There was no kindness or understanding from Mother, a sanitary pad and the funds to buy myself a sanitary belt and pack of sanitary towels. When I asked what I should do with my soiled towel, she simply said, "Give it to me, I will deal with it."

This she duly did when the two boys and father were sitting around the fire that evening, she took it through and burnt it on the fire. Humiliating maybe, but it served the purpose. A warning.

A sanitary belt is something most women born from 1970 onwards would not know about, my daughter was certainly amused when she discovered what they were. A sanitary belt, together with thick pads, was used before self-adhesive pads and before tampons were available.

Basically, when your time of the month rolled around, you attached a non-adhesive pad to the sanitary belt, and you dealt with the discomfort of these and awkward undergarment lines, that came your way. Nowadays, we are a little spoilt for sanitary products. The first challenge was figuring out how to wear the belt, and the second was attaching the pad to the belt, which was nothing like the pads available today, basically changing your pad and using the belt was hard work.

My reaching womanhood enabled me to concentrate on my education and friends, most of the girls at school were good company, how different we all were. Some excelling in English and a joy to listen to in class as we read Shakespeare plays out loud. Trying to take on the character of the part we were reading. Miss Overend, the English teacher, so big-hearted and expressive. She did a good job indeed, as going to the theatre became a favourite pastime of mine, not at this time but later in life. Others excelled in science, mathematics and geography.

To this day, I can draw the rail network in Australia. Some girls were sport-oriented, and this was catered for as well. Exercise in school, at that time, followed the pattern of the 1920s/30s, bending and stretching to music, using ribbons and hoops, which was great fun.

PE lessons for us girls were the normal, Hockey in the winter, tennis, cricket and netball in the spring and summer terms. Domestic science was still taught, we may have been getting an exceptional education, but the basics had not changed to any great degree, women were still expected to do the housework, shopping and child rearing.

In 1955, I passed my O-level exams, and it was suggested that I stay on into the sixth form with a view to taking A levels in general science and mathematics. Mother was very proud and immediately wrote to Aunt Gladys, such rivalry. Father though was not very impressed, he couldn't see the point of me staying in school, I was a woman and it's not as if it would lead anywhere, and it meant I wasn't getting a job and adding to the household coffers, nothing new there.

I had started a Saturday job around Easter time of 1954, just before finishing school, because one of the cashiers in father's restaurant had been sacked. Wearing a uniform with a cap on my head, taking the money. This turned into a summer job, after my exams, as a locum cashier in the co-operative butcher shops. Mother sat me down at that time to have a little chat.

There was a tiny room at the top of the stairs which would make a cosy little bedroom. I thought she was talking about Carol going into this room, wrong. I was to go in there and use the money I had earned to buy the furniture. My two sisters would be in one room, together. Not a lot I could do about it, I was still at school and had started studying for my A levels, which neither of my elder brothers had been able to do. Or in Trevor's case, wanted to do.

Trevor passed his O-level exams with flying colours, immediately found a job through his father in the co-operative offices where he remained until the age of 18, when he joined the Royal Air Force for three years. Simply by joining for three years instead of doing national service, he received higher pay. Go with the flow my brother.

Trevor had a wide circle of friends and was not really a part of the family now, he became proficient at billiards and games of that ilk. A great fan of jazz music of all genres. Dressing in the fashion of the time, a teddy boy. Black jacket, string tie, and tight pegged trousers which made his feet look enormous.

Most of all was the haircut, sleeked back over his head with Brylcreem and combed into a DA (Ducks rear end) at the back. How the local girls loved him and his mates. Jiving on a Saturday night at The Holyoak Hall in Headington, Oxford. Sunday morning, coming down for breakfast, found Wendy and me stepping over bodies sleeping on the hall floor, these lads had a good time. This is Susan, my schoolfriend's lasting memory of meeting him for the first time, a teddy boy.

I cleaned my new room myself and painted the walls, not as well as I had never done anything like it in my life, and my parents certainly had not. The furniture arrived and consisted of one single bed, one kidney-shaped dressing table and a single wardrobe.

Nobody had thought to measure this stuff. Father had been instrumental in its purchase, but it all squashed in just. It's not as if I had a lot of clothes so no problem. Being on my own again could be a problem though.

Homework had increased in volume and intensity, this meant I needed space for my books, this was not possible in my little room. I ended up working in the spare room next to the family room, which had a desk and loads of black furniture. The old chaise lounge from grandma's house was under the window, and it was cleared for my books.

Susan, my friend from the days we both started at Milham Ford, had also stayed on into the sixth form. True friends, no one-upmanship, enjoying one another's company, and this is something we still do today. So those were happy days. My Saturday job bringing in a little cash so I could buy my female necessities or wool to knit myself warm jumpers. But I should have known this would not last, it never did somehow father always got his way.

It is now 1956, David was 16 and leaving school, an apprenticeship was obtained for him with the co-operative, of course, which meant very little in the way of pay. One of the little chats with mother ensued, and it had been decided that I would have to leave school because father and mother could not afford to keep me at school whilst supporting David, apparently Father had found a job for me in the co-operative offices, what a surprise. I cannot describe the emotions I felt, it just wasn't fair and so small-minded, would David complete the apprenticeship? What about my future?

I went to school and told Susan; this is the first time I cried. We were both very upset by the unfairness, mixed feelings of anger and frustration, her immediate reaction, well, if you are not staying, then nor am I, what a friend!

My father notified the school, and to my surprise, I was summoned to a meeting with the headmistress, which was amazing. She expressed her sense of sadness and total exasperation with the decision made by my parents, anger, but controlled.

She said to me, very clearly, "You, young lady, can do anything, you have talents you have not found yet. Cooperative office girl, let me think about it."

Oh! The joy to hear she believed in me, and I remembered this my whole life. Just like the words from my aunts.

I left the all-embracing safety of school and went to work in the co-operative offices, well I had always been pretty good at making tea.

Uncle Cecil died in February 1956 when I was 17 and had been working at the Co-op offices for a couple of weeks. Sad day, my parents went to his funeral, leaving Wendy in charge of the household. Another family member gone. Aunt Bess, who had passed away several years before, told me at the time of my sister's death, the only constant in your life, little one, is yourself, learn to like yourself as much as I like you. Those kind words came back on that dark day.

The dark clouds began to lift when I received a letter from a bank, it seemed the headmistress, at Milham Ford School, had intervened. I travelled up to London on my own, paying my own fare, which the bank reimbursed. This piece of information was not shared with my parents. Across to Threadneedle Street on the underground to Bank Station, for my first ever interview. Scared all the time but determined. This was an opportunity not to be missed and time to do something for myself.

My career, it seems, was to be in the world of finance.

I started work at Westminster Bank in the spring, at the Oxford branch. It was still a very male-oriented world, banking, but my experience of growing up with my father and brothers helped. What a great surprise, my friend, Yvonne, who had left Milham Ford School in the previous summer, was also starting work at the bank on the same day.

She told me that the headmistress of Milham Ford had been contacted by the bank about two vacancies and she had recommended us two. That kind woman had set us both on a path to the future knowing we were close friends. A far-reaching influence on both our futures.

In life, you occasionally meet people who think of you and give you a helping hand, this was especially important at the time, when women were almost non-existent in the banking world.

Susan's parents were very supportive of her desire to leave the sixth form at the same time and encouraged her and paid for her to go to secretarial college, in Oxford, attending secretarial college was what a lot of middle class young women did, at that time, being a secretary, in an office, full of men, gave these women the opportunity to meet and marry a well to do young man, so was an aspiration for a lot of parents. She attended the Oxford and County Secretarial college, which, at the time, was a prestigious secretarial school for young women.

Interestingly, in 1999, it became the Oxford Business school and the concept of a secretarial college disappeared as the roles of women and equal rights law changed but it is telling of the times that even in the late 1950s and early 1960s the so-called age of liberation for women, young women were still encouraged towards *female* roles and families lacked aspiration for them due to their role to marry and have children, past their 18$^{th}$ birthday.

Susan's parents enrolling her in a Secretarial Training College left me feeling sad. How lucky she was to have parents to help and guide her. Looking back now, I wonder if this was another form of female oppression, as the prospects of building a career from this training were not great, and it seemed very much a time filler until marriage and babies, very much the old view of women's status.

David dropped his bomb shell that summer, which was a nice big slap in the face for father but bittersweet for me. He had cancelled his apprenticeship with the co-operative and joined the Royal Navy. Good for him. No hard feelings from me. He did not order me to leave school. Now, two of my brothers had gone their own ways and I wondered how Trevor would cope without them. Trevor was the brother most like Father, in looks as well as some personality traits, and he was influenced by Father.

That summer Trevor was twenty years old, he enlisted with the Royal Air Force, for three years. Eventually, Peter and David forgave him for joining the boys in blue rather than the Royal Navy.

At the bank, the work itself was paper bound. My first job was to visit Lloyds Bank on the corner of High Street and Cornmarket Street to exchange local clearing. All the other banks sent clerks for the same purpose. Cheques which were drawn on branches of banks in Oxford City were cleared through the banking system every day. Cheques drawn on branches in other areas were sorted into banks, totalled up and despatched to the clearing house in London where they were exchanged.

This sounds complicated but in fact was a well-run system which depended upon accurate sorting and totalling. So much so that the girls in the office carrying out this work would have to stay at the office until the daily work was balanced to the last penny. Interesting, at that time, that this work was very much women's work, with the men holding the higher-level positions.

The sorting of cheques and cash receipts and credit slips, carried on during the bank's opening hours, was called collecting the waste. Which was also part of my introduction to banking. This is the area which was to play a very important part in my career, meeting the customers.

I found the work, although at times repetitive, was interesting and stimulating, and I was very glad I had made the change from the co-operative.

One problem remained, clothes. I had only my school uniform and one dress and that was it. Most of the girls in the office were good company, talking about boyfriends, going out on dates, clothes, and make-up. Such fun to listen to.

Always ready for a laugh, usually at one of the male bankers' expense, which was fun. As in life, there is always one person who acted in a superior manner to us all, and for some reason, especially me. I arrive one Monday morning in my one dress, sponged pressed and with a fresh white collar, to a tirade of haven't you got anything else to wear, from this person.

Sponge pressing is when you use a damp sponge and wipe your clothes, especially the lining and then press, making clothes look smart. Did not see that statement about what I was wearing coming, and I was blindsided, my skills of self-control and not reacting, a lesson learnt well, came into play that day. I just got on with my work, with words of sympathy from others, but it was not needed, I just had to up my game and show her a thing or two.

We girls were late home that evening because the accounts did not balance, what a shame, she was late for her date, nothing to do with me. One of the older girls gave me a wink, oh dear, someone had reversed the numbers when transferring to a new column. The senior clerk was called in, she tried to blame me, so he gently but firmly informed her it was her job to check, then pointed out that I was working on a different section. Enemy for life.

After a quick sandwich for dinner and a look in my wardrobe, which did not take long. Ah my school uniform. So out with my sewing box, which I had not used since O-level time. I had made a two-piece suit, a pencil skirt and fitted jacket for my O-level needlework practical exam. Mother bought the fabric, a nasty grey cheap stuff which frayed when cut and stitched so all the seams had to have bias binding.

So, we have a skirt, not the jacket over the top for my present status at the bank. Two white school blouses. That's a good start. Flat shoes cannot do much about them at that precise moment, but I did have the London fare reimbursement money. So, I wore the same old dress the next day. It seems a certain person had calmed down, not that it mattered. I was greeted by the rest of the girls with a grin, and how are you feeling today?

What a group, such fun. At lunch time, I went off to Selfridges for a pair of black shoes with heels. They had to be comfortable, as they would have to stand me in good stead for a while. Walking in heels was a new experience, and I liked it, only in the last few years have I stopped wearing heels. Then the next day, I went down to the market and the second-hand clothes stall, I was looking for some coloured silk, no success, I would have to wait until payday.

On Saturday afternoon after work, I slipped into Selfridges fabric department and found half a yard (just under half a metre) of blue patterned silk which was perfect. I was later home than usual, but nothing was said, everyone assumed I had to stay to balance the books, which suited me. I curled up on my bed and set to work stitching a square scarf, with the aunt's trusty run and fell seams. Even today I have a great selection of scarves, well, why not, you can't beat the feel of silk against your skin.

On Monday morning, I dressed in my skirt and blouse tying the scarf at the back of my neck, father looked a bit shocked and my sisters wide-eyed. I wore my new high heels and found I towered over both of my parents.

The girls in the office were great. "I want one of those," they cried, and it matches your eyes came from the girl who had winked at me. I received compliments from the male members of staff and a thumbs up from the senior clerk. This was accepted in that day but nowadays would be seen as inappropriate of male staff and as sexist remarks.

One person not happy and sour-faced, oh well. This became my style of dressing for the years to come, nowadays it is called a business suit, and it was not long before the pleated skirts and twin sets, normally worn by the female staff, changed to high heels, pencil skirts, shirts and blouses.

Life was not all work; the weekends saw Yvonne and I going to a dance academy known as Brett's over Bakers department store, now known as Boswells, on the Corner of Broad Street and Cornmarket Street. This was a dance school and concentrated on traditional ballroom dancing.

No alcohol allowed on the premises, but many friendships blossomed and floundered at this academy. Susan, who lived several miles outside the city, was still attending secretarial college and forming her own group of friends under the watchful eye of her parents.

Yvonne, Susan and I also went to the cinema and theatre together, this was cheap entertainment, as we all had to help with our families' incomes having younger siblings. All three of us went to the cinema to watch Bill Hayley and the Comets. Amazing rock and roll, so lively such fun, all three stunned by the screaming of young female members of the audience.

After six months, Yvonne and I had a raise in salary as our probation period was over, and we had to open a bank account to receive our salaries. This is 1956, very unusual for women to have bank accounts in their own name at this time.

Normally, in 1956, women wishing to have a bank account in their own name had to have permission and a signature from their father or husband, but as we worked for the bank, we were allowed, even as single women. This remained in force until 1975, 19 years later.

When you think about this fully, this inability to have your own bank account meant women were not free and any money they earned went into the husband's name and in many cases the women or wives were given housekeeping money only. I would see the impact of this on the lives of women, in the future, when I meet my mother-in-law.

Women would be very restricted when needing to leave a relationship for any reason, and also protection in old age, this led to a lot of women being very fearful of the 'workhouse', for example, and heavily reliant on their eldest son. The Sex Discrimination Act 1975 changed this situation.

Banking rules were strict, you could not have an account with another financial institution, everything had to be upfront, this suited me as now my parents did not know what I was earning. Friday was pay mother day, which was fine by me, and we all handed our contributions over.

However, this was not fine a few years later when witnessing Trevor's contribution handed back to him on the Saturday morning. What on earth was going on? I kept out of it; some skulduggery I expected, in cahoots with Father.

1957 came in with little inkling of the changes about to happen in my life.

One day, I was called into the manager's office, holy of holies, I was asked to sit down as he wished to talk to me. This was an ex-army major, so I sat thinking, what have I done? Nothing that I could think of, but that still did not stop me wracking my brains. The only worry I had was I just seemed to upset Madam by being in the same room. The answer was simple, no need for all that worry, he was so impressed by the way I talked to customers, whilst collecting the waste, that he wanted me to become a cashier, good grief.

A female cashier, just how many do you think there were in this male-oriented business, absolutely none. This change in role reflected several changes for women in the workplace in banks, following the importance of women in the Second World War in banks, in relation to the simple fact that they kept the banks running in the war and undertook all the jobs of the men.

In 1946, there was a special committee report, which marginally improved the scope of opportunity for women. It recommended that the field of women's work be extended, from typing and filing and that jobs done by men in all departments from time to time be given to women.

This achievement was to lay the foundations for the 1955 special committee on women's work, its conclusion was that a gradual integration of male and female staff of the bank was practicable and desirable and that women should have the opportunity to graduate from women's work to the work done by men and be promoted in competition with the men, after an initial period of five years of service, and I was one of the first women in the banking world to benefit from this change and also the pioneering work of the women during the war. But it wasn't until the 1975 Sex Discrimination Act that any further change of any note occurred in the banking world.

I went back into the office with the girls, a bit stunned, but quietly got on with my work, the senior clerk then came in to congratulate me, followed by the chief cashier, amazing.

Most of the group were happy for me, some giving it rather you than me and some saying get it right kiddo so we can follow. The person who had taken such a dislike of me, most unhappy, beside herself with anger. What was her problem?

Oh, I got a raise as well but didn't share that with the family!

I was not sure if the family were happy for me as they never said a word, but it was not a surprise, as the family had no understanding of what work I did. Life for them seemed to carry on as usual, but for me life was changing and so was I.

Aunt Gladys wrote to my mother telling her that my cousin Marjorie was getting married in April, and Marjorie would like my youngest sister, Carol, to be her bridesmaid, and would I make her dress. Why not ask me herself, I thought, but that was the way things were communicated in those days. Simple really, Carol was told first, so she was fit to burst with excitement when I came in from work, she was going to be a bridesmaid, every little girl's dream, so there was no way I could say no, and a dress was made.

The dress was perfect though as I didn't want Aunty Gladys looking down on us and especially Carol. Getting time off work to go to the wedding was a very different matter. The chief clerk gave me a categoric no. The other cashiers, all men, were not unpleasant, generally they were good fun and understood that dirty jokes were not something I could or would tolerate but as I had worked a few extra Saturday mornings to enable them to shop with their wives or helped with their paperwork so they could leave early and go to school meetings, I hoped, at least one of them, would be willing to repay the favours.

So once again, I went in to see the manager, different now.

"Sit down, my dear. I hear you would like to go to your cousin's wedding and the chief cashier tells me that members of his staff had volunteered to cover this time for you? So yes, you can go but be back here on Monday morning, ready for work. No bleary-eyed cashiers allowed."

The wedding was back in Gosport. The parents, Wendy, Carol, and I travelled down in Father's Morris Minor. David arrived the next day. Trevor was in the RAF by now and could not make it, that's even if he had wanted to. Peter was living in Enfield and unable to join us.

The girls and I slept in one room that night, which was an evening of giggles and excitement. The parents went off to Aunt Flo's. The bridesmaid's dress was duly scrutinised and approved of, well, it was a bit late to remake it. What had I done to this woman?

The wedding was fun, Marjorie's new husband was a bundle of laughter, good company, although her sister, Mary, was not certain of the reason Marjorie married him, she expressed scathing remarks about his money and not being able to manage on her nurse's pay, but that's sisters for you. There was a reception in the garden which was lovely under the apple trees in full bloom. A simple family wedding, a real time of celebration and nice for everybody to see each other.

The happy couple left on their honeymoon, and the rest of us cleared up whilst the two sisters, mother and Gladys had a cup of tea and a natter. Mother and the girls were staying overnight with Aunt Flo, taking Carol in her bridesmaid dress and Marjorie's flowers.

So just a little bit of the day for Aunt Flo as she was still looking after Bob. I had to be back at work on Monday, as in fact did my father, he would call back for me, and we would travel back to Oxford together. Mother's parting words were, "Look after your father."

Oh, dear god, could she have been any more blatant? Angry does not cover how I felt. Cold fury did because this was over, never again would that man touch me. I sat in the garden for a long time thinking about this situation. I had read enough books to know that most bullies are weak, and he felt he had power over me. I had to take this power away from him. Aunt Bess, remember little one, believe in yourself.

David came out to the garden with a cup of tea for me, saying I wish I could help Jo. That kindness was enough. I let him know that there was no need to worry, I was going to deal with this once and for all.

The journey was uneventful, I was still thinking and completely ignoring him. I went into the house, saying I have to go to work tomorrow, so I am going straight to bed. I did, but I did not undress, just waited for the door to open.

When the inevitable opening of the door happened, I sat up and told him to get the hell out of my room and if he ever laid hands on me again, I would talk to the chief constable who I knew by name, his boss who I knew by name and my boss who had more influence in the city than all three put together, all were Free Masons, a group he aspired to join.

He went puce in the face and stormed off. Not a lot of sleep that night but also no further interruptions. Mother and the girls returned next day, and, apparently, there was an almighty row. Oh, dear, upset the applecart again, most certainly was not going to worry about that.

Susan had finished her course and obtained a secretarial job working in the Oxford High Street Branch of Barclays Bank. We enjoyed one another's company again. Often going shopping after work in Oxford City, having coffee and cake in the Cadena. The dancing at Brett's academy had lost its appeal, as it was very small and same old group all the time and the other option Carfax Assembly Rooms was a no-no, as it had a very bad reputation and Susan's parents refused to allow her to go there, I did not want to set foot in the place father ran it.

We three girls Susan, Yvonne, and I went to the forum along the High Street, where they held a dance every Saturday night, no problem for me as I could walk home. Susan had a group of friends who already frequented the dance hall and offered her a lift home. Susan and I would meet at Iffley Road, having fun getting ready for the evening.

Early in 1957 Peter had come to Oxford for a visit prior to reporting to HMS Collingwood in Gosport, for his national service. As normal Susan walks into the house and to use her own words 67 years later, "there he was," her future husband.

Life for us three girls continued, working each day. Meeting at weekends, occasional dates, but nothing serious for Susan and me. Yvonne now had a regular boyfriend and spent less time with us.

My wardrobe had expanded and included a couple of decent dresses again, reflecting my new image. One Saturday night, it was just Susan and I; Yvonne had a date with her steady boyfriend, I decided to wear a navy-blue cap sleeved dress with a large turn back collar which dipped in the front, with a straight fitted skirt and an artificial gardenia stitched in the front, a dress that made me feel happy.

Susan had been going to meet her friend Brian, at 9.30 pm in the forum, but of course he had not turned up as it was too early. Susan, being of a nothing ventured nothing gained sort of person, stormed over to the Eastgate Hotel and into the bar area, to see what he was doing. Up to the bar she goes and orders two gin and orange, well, no gin, just orange juice, but who was to know that. Brian her date comes over to her profusely with apologies, sorry, sorry, he says and pays for the drinks. I loved it, she had me in stitches, so bold for a woman to order her own drinks! Up until 1982, it was perfectly legal to refuse to serve women in bars and pubs, very much seen as male environments.

Susan exclaimed to me that there is a chap called Luke over there, explaining that he is always so touchy about his hair. She walked over holding her glass of orange juice above his head. He shot out of his chair.

Oh my, but she still is quite a girl.

Brian went white and said, "OK, Susan, we will be over shortly and back to the dance we went."

Both having a good time whilst waiting around for these young men to pluck up courage to come to a dance.

Luke, this young man who I had never spoken to in my life comes over and asks me for a dance, he said as we danced, "What is a nice girl like you doing with that person?"

Meaning Susan. *How rude,* I thought, so I replied indignantly, "We have been friends a very long time."

And I walked off the floor, not realising just how important that meeting was to be for the rest of my life. I had just met the love of my life.

A lot had changed from the age of 10, a lot of challenges had been faced head-on and were no longer being endured. I had managed, with help, to break into the male-dominated banking world and was pushing forward, undaunted, with my life, and unlike many other women I had my own bank account.

In the 1950s, the focus for women was on equal pay and in 1951 equal pay for teachers was granted, 1954 equal pay for people who worked in the civil service, but very little else had changed for women, 75% of women were married and still engaged in domestic activities, the 1950s was a bleak time, rationing still in place. Focus following the war was on family and the establishment of the welfare state and the NHS.

# Chapter Three
# Independence, Career Development
# Standing Alone

National service was a standardised form of peacetime subscription. In 1947, it was announced that all able-bodied men between the ages of 18 and 30 were to be called upon. The conscripts initially served for 18 months. It was ended in 1960. The young men, who were impacted, had to time their national service around college courses, families and careers.

Late in the year of 1957, Peter joined the Royal Navy to carry out his national service training, he was then aged 24. We were lucky that he was able to take a break with the family in Oxford prior to enlisting and Mother was very happy to see him, as indeed were all of us. It was a memorable time as the house was full of laughter and fun again. He was such a charismatic young man.

During the time of his visit, Susan and I were due to go dancing at the forum, in Oxford, on the Saturday night, with both of us getting ready at my house before we set off. Peter was sitting in the family room chatting, and in Susan waltzed, it did not take much to persuade him to join us. We had a great evening together and my brother had met his future wife.

At the same dance, Luke came over and asked me to dance, which was surprising following how our last meeting ended, both chatting away as we danced, we were so at ease with one another and got on well. It was very exciting to see him again and I did find him very intriguing and attractive.

Peter left for his training with the Fleet Air Arm. They had an interesting custom, if you did maintenance work on an airplane, you could have the chance to fly in it afterwards! Especially national service petty officers, which Peter was. He flew in a Fairy Gannet, a 3-seater submarine chaser on a sortie over the western approaches, sitting in the rear, very exciting and exhilarating, scary but not very comfortable due to having to sit on his parachute. Such a memorable event that Peter can recall it as if it was yesterday, at the age of 90.

Life soon returned to normal. Susan, Yvonne and I went out on dates, with all three of us meeting interesting young men, but none of us ready to settle down or it seems meet someone special. I had met one young man when visiting Susan and her friends, he was so kind, and I admit to being flattered, at the time, and I hoped that, maybe just maybe, he would understand me and all that had gone before, just maybe.

Saturday nights out dancing, working five and half days a week, occasional visits to the cinema or theatre, life was busy and exciting, a good time to be young and with our lives ahead of us.

The young man I had met at Susan's parents also had national service to do and in 1957 he also went off to undertake this period of service. Whilst away this kind and caring man sent me drawings and letters, I had little to write back about other than work and my friends, but it was lovely to receive his letters.

One Saturday night late in 1957, I had just turned 19 years old, I was a bit late leaving the forum and had to be home by 11.45pm before father returned home himself. As walking would take too long, off came my shoes, and I ran all the way home.

Halfway there and a voice called out, "Goodnight, Joan, see you next week."

It was Luke, it transpired he was walking home with his friend Keith, both lived very close to my home on Iffley Road.

The following Saturday, we three girls were having fun and dancing to a live band, towards the end of the evening, Luke came over, no would you like to dance, simply, "let's dance."

We walked home together that evening. I knew very little about him, he played cricket every weekend in the season and was busy most evenings. Transport was a push bike (bicycle). We talked about what I did with my life, and he appeared to be a very quiet, private man.

He walked me to my garden gate and said to me, "I might be free Tuesday night but then I might not."

I thought, *enough of shilly-shallying about*. I replied, "I will meet you over there by the lamppost on Tuesday at 7 pm, be there or don't bother, up to you. Goodnight."

On Tuesday evening, I was pleased to see there he was under the lamp post at 7 o'clock, with a big grin on his face. These Tuesday walks became a weekly event. We were simply two people enjoying one another's company, talking of our ambitions and what we were hoping for in life. Arguing at times because we did not agree about everything.

The busy evenings he talked of, were spent either at night school or preparing for his next course at the technical college. This was on top of a full day's work, in the drawing office of a company called Pressed Steel Fisher. How he managed to find a couple of hours a week to go walking with me, I do not know. The two of us just walking in the air, getting to know one another.

The weekly dancing on Saturdays with my friends continued and I was often asked to dance by more members of the cricket team Luke played with, getting to know them all. I was told by Luke's close friend, Keith, that Luke was his nickname, and his real name was John Lucas.

Walking home after the dance together, I asked him why he had not told me his name when turning up every Tuesday to go walking with me and dance with me each Saturday?

His reply was, "When I am with you, I am just myself, not the Oxfordshire County Cricket Team player, not the local low handicap golfer, I did not gush over him thinking he was handsome or swoon over him, you liked my company, just me."

I was left speechless.

Gradually, on our walks, he talked of his ambitions, the reason for his time spent studying but very little about his home life or childhood. Just a little about himself and of course he still had to do his national service. This came quicker than I expected, and January of 1958 saw him signing on with the Royal Air Force.

With John gone, as well as the other young man I liked, I found myself writing to two men in the forces, I thought, *what am I doing? I needed to think all of this through and decide what I wanted, as it wasn't fair on them.*

One man so kind and thoughtful, whilst the other annoyed me, irritated me and intrigued me. So simple it was staring me in the face, John Lucas made me feel alive.

I did the one thing a girl at that time should never do, I sent a *Dear John* letter to that kind and gentle man telling him I had met someone else.

I then had another conversation with myself, *what was I doing wasting my time listening to Radio Caroline in my room during the evenings or making my sister's clothes, if people like John can work hard to attain their ambitions in life, why wasn't I? Time to make lists. What do I want?*

Marriage and enduring the life so many women had, still largely subservient maids, no, not that kind of marriage or life, not for me, I wanted more for myself and a relationship that was equal. So, I decided what I wanted was, firstly, to progress in the career I already had at the bank, to enable me to leave home and have my own place to live. Secondly, to be an independent woman standing on her own two feet, whether that was in a marriage or not.

Life took on a new slant as I began studying for my banking exams, whilst still a cashier. Men held all the posts above me, how will I fit in with this, a difficult one, and I could not see a way forward at that time. I just got on with day-to-day tasks, getting to know many of the customers calling into the branch by name. I also was no longer the only female cashier as my friends began to join me.

At times, staff in the administration department would be on holiday and required to cover to ensure the daily balance continued, after all, we are dealing with the customer's money. Working back in the administration department, amongst this friendly group of women was fun, but I couldn't see a way to progress, in either the administration department or as a cashier.

Figure 6—Top picture is *Luke* or known as John, and the second image is John on a cricket tour.

Oxford University had a large intake of students each autumn, students from all walks of life, all needing bank accounts. Who would have thought that something so simple would change so much for me. The banking hall, the area for customers to approach the tills, was nowhere near big enough, which meant the bank was losing potential customers as there was not enough staff to open accounts, let alone space in which to do so.

The premises were to be renovated, the existing cashiering desk to be removed entirely and the cashiering section pushed back against the wall and windows, leaving a wide-open space for customers. The administration department was relocated to a new floor built above the chief clerk's desk. Interview rooms were to be included in the newly acquired space together with additional space not yet allocated or designated.

The chief clerk approached me one morning, advising that the manager would like a word. Entering the manager's office, I was invited to take a seat. A group of three men were all there, the manager, office manager and chief cashier. I felt very daunted and intimidated, especially with no warning.

First question, "How would I envisage the post of receptionist?"

Luckily for me, I had noted the spare desk in the new layout and had tried to work out what it might be for. Right in front of the main door could only be one thing really.

I replied after taking a few seconds to calm down, "Perfect position to welcome customers, especially those who presently had to queue to speak to a cashier, before being referred to an appropriate member of staff. This could be carried out quickly and more efficiently. The manager's diary could be duplicated and handed to the receptionist so they could greet the customers by name and then be taken into the manager's office and introduced."

I went on to explain it would be a very good opportunity to amalgamate the daily task of customers' requests to make certain transfers, university club fees, purchase of bonds under one control.

That was the end of the meeting, and I resumed my normal work for the day. Three other people were also asked into the meeting room after me, two men and, believe it or not, the person who had shown such dislike from the beginning of my employment.

Nothing came of these meetings, business as usual with the branch renovations being carried out around us. A few mice scuttling across the floor, poor little things, well, the field mice in the drawer all those years ago and my mother's disposal of them had left me sympathetic to the mice.

Towards the end of the summer, the renovations were almost complete, the cashier's desks readied and the reception desk in place. I was then notified that I had been successful. Branch Receptionist I became, a job I achieved above two males. I was very happy and a great step forward for women. So, progress I was beginning to make and my strive for a home of my own, one step closer.

Oxford University Michaelmas term commenced, the city filled with young men and some women all needing bank accounts. The new banking hall was very modern, with neat, clean lines instead of the heavy carved furniture that used to grace it, beautiful but not right for the new generation, appealing to these young men and women. The new set up of reception and introduction to a member of staff who opened an account for the customers worked very well and I thoroughly enjoyed the role.

Meanwhile, John transferred to Weston Super Mare from his induction course in the north, and I sent him a packet of cigarettes, having been told by all my brothers that pay was bad for those doing national service and they could always use a packet of these.

One Saturday a few weeks later, he was on leave and turned up at the forum dance hall with the rest of his sport mad friends. John came over and said thank you, nobody else had written to him, let alone sent cigarettes. We all walked home together that evening, Keith, John, a few more of his friends and I. I had known this man for a matter of months and already my circle of acquaintances had grown beyond recognition.

John was on leave before being posted to Christmas Island. The British and American tested nuclear weapons on Christmas Island, Operation Grapple, which had profound and lasting cultural consequences for both atomic veterans and the island nation. Preparation for the posting to Christmas Island included having inoculations for tropical diseases, even yellow fever.

Not one at a time, all together. John told me he shivered so much the bed vibrated against the wall, perspiration soaking him and his bedclothes. As it transpired, all for nothing, he was called back to barracks, due to his studies, he was to be posted to Abingdon, a town very near Oxford. He was very lucky. Arrangements would be made to enable him to continue his studies, he had officer potential. To Abingdon he went, getting to the technical college was another matter.

During our walks we talked of our first jobs, mine as a cashier in my father's restaurant and John's a paper round from the age of 12. Like me his earnings were expected to be part of the family income, he was no idiot, being male he was able to open a savings account with the Trustee Savings Bank, each week he put part of his earnings into this account, continuing to do so as he progressed at work, to the drawing office. Enabling him to buy himself a scooter, a Lambretta.

July 1958, Peter had completed his national service and returned to civilian life, taking an apartment in Bracknell. Bracknell was one of eight London new towns. All designated before 1950, most designated to hold 50,000 people. The apartment was part of a new block with wide windows filling the rooms with light. I remember Susan and I visited him and his friend, the only thing to eat was canned salmon, bread, butter and pickled onions. We diced the onions finely and added them to the salmon, mixed and made sandwiches, happy days. We saw more of Peter now, and it was no surprise when he announced his betrothal to Susan with the wedding in June 1959.

John was stationed at RAF Abingdon for the latter part of his service, so we were able to meet during this time. Still walking in the evenings, because pay for the men in the forces was very low, going to the cinema was out of the question, I could afford to pay for both of us, but this was a proud man, so we continued to enjoy our walks.

One spring evening in 1959, we were strolling along in the local area, not far as we both had work next day, unknown to us, his father passed us riding his bicycle on his way to the Liberal Club. Apparently, they were surprised he was with a woman, and when was he going to bring her to meet them.

We were good friends but the time for anything more serious had not arisen until now. I was invited to Sunday tea when he was next on leave. John came to collected me from my house, we walked to his home, the house was a terraced property in a cul-de-sac, with a tunnel gap between two adjacent properties giving access to the rear entrances and gardens.

I was ushered into the kitchen at the rear where his mother was working at the sink. John motioned for me to sit down whilst he put the water on for a cup of tea.

She remarked to him as she went into the tiny scullery, "Well, she is no oil painting" was what I heard. I had been nervous at the idea of meeting his family, but had not expected such a welcome, part of me fumed in anger, there she stood with a woodbine cigarette tucked into the corner of her mouth, speaking to him as if I was not in the room and being obviously offensive and judgemental.

I admit to wanting to be rude right back but knew this was no way to deal with this situation. I must be a threat, and this is the treatment she would mete out to any female John brought home. Rational thinking again, I am not going anywhere, this man is my friend, there is no way I would walk away from him over this. He deserved better, a friend in need is a friend indeed. John simply said, "This is Joan."

His father came home shortly after having been to the Liberal Club, another woodbine smoker and asked me what I did with my life.

"I work in a bank."

This seemed to shock him, a man locked in the traditions of the past, not the answer he expected. Somewhat bewildered by my reception, I wondered why I had been invited. I knew very little about these two people, John had chosen not to discuss them or his family with me, he had chosen not to introduce me to them during the past few years. We were friends, good friends, this situation had nothing to do with me. Maybe one day I will find out. Time would tell.

Peter and Susan's wedding was approaching fast; I was to be her bridesmaid. The wedding was to be held in her local church with the reception at a hotel on the Oxford to Witney Road. Susan's mother was the happiest I had ever seen her.

The task of making Susan's wedding dress, something she relished, would I please make my own bridesmaid dress. No problem I thought. Later, all three of us travelled to London to purchase fabric, we had a great time, coming back with our arms full of parcels. The wedding and bridesmaid dresses were to be white, a very modern wedding indeed.

The wedding morning dawned, a beautiful day, soft air and flowers in the garden. Susan and I were chatting together whilst Susan had a bath, true friends.

When I was in the car with Susan's cousin, the other bridesmaid and Susan's mother on the way to the church, catastrophe, the blue bow on the back of my dress came lose, panic set in and a safety pin was quickly fetched, tension released, all three of us laughing and smiling.

The church was beautifully dressed in summer flowers, guests all talking softly, my two brothers standing at the altar, Peter and his best man Trevor. Susan's Uncle George and David were acting as ushers. David, in his naval uniform, standing near us, two bridesmaids keeping us company until the wedding march was played.

Once the ceremony was over, we went back into the sunshine, photographs were to be taken.

Figure 7—Peter (second from the right), Trevor and David (far left), not sure who is on the far left—on his wedding day—below is an image of the bride and groom—Peter and Susan

The wedding reception was to be enjoyed, a very happy time and such a glorious day. One of the best days of my life, let alone Peter and Susan's wedding day, as this is the day my family met John, as he called over late in the day to collect me. No longer in white tulle but a slim flowered dress cinched in at the waist, but the dress had to be hitched up to enable me to get on the back of the Lambretta. I didn't think this through and broke the rules of modesty for ladies.

Seeing me on the back of the Lambretta gave my parents a bit of a shock and set the tone for John's meeting with them. I wish I could say the meeting went well, but of course not, father the worse for wear, trying to sneer at this young man almost a foot taller than him, mother a bag of nerves. My sisters enjoyed the Lambretta though, and seeing me on it, they were laughing and smiling, this was nearly the 1960s after all and the world was changing quickly.

At that time, there was always a price to pay for independence. After work the following Saturday, mother confronted me, something along the lines of letting the family down, not being a nice girl, slap, a big hand landed on my cheek.

I turned to her and said, "People who think like that must have lived like that, would you like to slap the other cheek as well?"

My brother Trevor then came into the room with one of his friends and I fled to my room. How father must have goaded her for her to do this, a young man in my life, taller than him and able to put him down with ease. Worse still, seeing me riding on the back of a Lambretta. Well, I was no longer ready to accept this treatment, no longer willing to follow their old-fashioned guidelines, with two young sisters coming along in my wake, I needed to break loose but needed to make a plan.

John was demobbed from his national service in July of 1959, returning to work, he found that the engineering union had the men on strike for a longer paid holiday entitlement, what a choice he had to make, having just come out of the forces he had very little money. Whilst in the forces he had been unable to pay his union dues, so no strike pay for him. It was either go hungry or cross the picket line.

Approaching the picket line, he explained his dilemma. To be met with an amazing response, because he had been in the armed forces, his dues had been waived. Strike pay was there for him. What a summer that was, cricket each weekend, golf during the week with his friends and cricket net practice two evenings a week. We were walking during the other evenings, still broke but having fun.

On the August bank holiday afternoon, we planned to go to Bablock Hythe on the river, riding on the pillion again, fine by me as I had been on the back of the Lambretta a few times already but definitely needed to wear trousers for comfort. This was 1959, and I had bought myself black jeans, a yellow tee-shirt and flat yellow shoes. Trevor was in the main room with Mother and Father, the girls probably in their room. The reception was one of shock, I was wearing trousers.

"Nice one, sis," from Trevor, grinning hugely. A lot of shouting by the parents, I simply picked up my jumper and left.

During September John dropped a note through the door to say he was unable to meet me as arranged, he was taking his mother to the cinema for her birthday and hoped I would understand. I already knew John was a kind and thoughtful man, taking his mother to the cinema was fine but why John and not his father.

In October 1959, it was my 21st birthday, this being the age when I could legally strike out on my own, as a woman. I had begun to collect my belongings together in my room over the preceding months and by the end of the summer it was completed, and I was ready.

Work was good, life was enjoyable, home life was not, tyranny ruled. I was instructed to be home one evening, we had visitors. That was surprising, not something that happened often, other than my mother's sister Gladys coming to stay. Father motioned me to sit in his chair, unheard-of, Mother and sisters sat on the settee. A neat family group, everything neat and tidy. Two men were ushered into the room and asked to sit in two of the dining room chairs facing this happy scene.

Father perched himself on the arm of his chair where I was sitting, so I was only partially visible and put his arm round me. I had my knitting on my knee. A little small talk and questions, where did the girls go to school, who did the grocery shopping, did mother work outside the home, turning to me, did I work outside the home, as I went to answer, father gripped my right breast and squeezed a warning. I answered that I was the receptionist at the bank. A bit more chit chat and they left. Why the warning, why was I kept quiet? Everyone sighed in relief. What on earth was going on?

My birthday arrived and my parents arranged a party for me, to be held at home, a large number of friends from work, Trevor and his mates, together with Peter and Susan, arrived.

John was unable to come as he was representing the Company at the Earls Court Motor Show in London.

Father and Mother had bought me a gold cocktail watch.

John, charms for my silver bracelet, these I have to this day.

Trevor an expensive lipstick, and Peter and Susan pictures drawn in a Japanese medium. A happy day before the storm broke.

Back in 1958 I had talked to mother about purchasing a radio for my room, this was difficult, there being no electric socket in my tiny room. Father to the rescue, he had found a radio for me powered by batteries, which I could pay for on a weekly basis, giving the money to mother. Great, now I could listen to Radio Caroline, I duly paid for it and carried on thinking nothing of it.

Which is why in 1959, I was surprised to be told father had taken the radio back for a while as he needed it. The reason for me being kept quiet during the visit when the family were asked questions was that they were the investigators from Father's work.

Like so many things in my father's life, he had taken these things without paying for them. If I had not been wearing my watch that day, it would have gone back as well. This was just the tip of the iceberg. Trevor knew far more than I did about what he had been up to.

Following the visit from the investigators, mother announced that we are all moving to Plymouth, no regard for my two sisters' education, absolutely no regard for my employment, an airy "oh you can get a transfer." Trevor, well, who asked him?

The evening paper was on the dining table, and I took it to my room. Trevor knocked on my door, asking what I was looking for, sis.

"A bedsit or lodgings," I replied.

With his usual big grin, "Good for you."

He was quicker on the draw than me, having already sorted out accommodation for himself with his friend Don, he also looked after me and told me of a young couple with two small children who had a house with an extra bedroom which was empty, and they needed the extra income. I was welcome to come lodge with them, but I would need to furnish the room.

Money was very tight for them with two young boys, a mortgage and only one salary. I would be welcome, especially if I would babysit so they could go out with their friends. This would be on a Saturday evening, meaning my evenings at the forum would be curtailed. A small price to pay. One problem remained, how would I get my furniture boxes and myself from Iffley Road to Headington?

My parents were in uproar, we were all expected to toe the line and obey father, well, the reality was Trevor and my contributions to the family budget would end, Father's new job was a big step down, so money would be tight for them again.

I had a problem to overcome whilst helping mother to pack, she was obviously hoping I would change my mind, no way, I just assisted her as best I could. She was uprooted again, having to follow the drum like army wives in Napoleonic times, how difficult life was for her generation and so many generations before, unable to work with two young daughters, no real chance of employment or choice but to follow father.

I had benefited from the influence of my forward thinking, brave aunts, what did I benefit from my mother, I thought at that time, I did not know the answer to this, gradually I grew to understand in later life.

I was friendly with two ladies who lived in the house next to ours, they had both been army girls during the Second World War, and always kind to me, earning their living by delivering milk each morning and always interested in what I was up to. They loved hearing about us three girls out dancing and dating.

They had heard of the move and asked me how it was progressing.

I explained that I did not want to go, I had a large circle of friends and a job I really enjoyed.

"Sorry, dearie, we have no room, how kind."

That's not the problem, I explained and told of my transportation difficulties, no problem, we will take you Sunday afternoon, we will use the milk float, they replied. This is a small electric delivery van with open sides and a roof, ideal. Sunday came and the three of us moved the furniture out of the house onto the float with my boxes, Wendy and Carol were visibly upset and Mother tired but resigned. My father and brothers were all missing.

If I expected a pleasant parting from my parents, I would have been disappointed, so the actual departing was true to form. Mother, I will let you borrow the bedding for now, but I want it back. Father, you will not last five minutes, you will come crawling back. My sisters a smile from Wendy and tears from Carol. Thank you, Aunts, for the strength to smile and wave goodbye, without retorting what I really thought, you will have your bedding back, mother, and to him, not a hope in hell.

Life had a new dimension now, was I lonely, no, did I miss my home life, no, did I worry about my sisters, yes, could I do anything about it, not really.

The city library supplied me with plenty to read, any subject I chose. Work was busy and my friends rallied round, making sure I was OK.

John was still doing endorsements to his engineering degree, and I still had studying to do. Instead of meeting outside of my parents' home, he now called for me at my lodgings and we still went walking in the evenings, as we were now both strapped for cash. A new dimension indeed, in our relationship and we became closer, calling for me one evening going to the rugby club, we began to be viewed as a couple.

1960, life was far simpler now, Susan and Peter were living in Bracknell and Trevor still in Oxford. Yvonne was with her steady boyfriend. Dancing at the forum a few times, but mainly work, walking with John and babysitting. My landlady was a hairdresser. Friday night saw her friends coming round, hair styling, discussing make-up, men and boyfriends; they then went out each Saturday night all out on the town, John and I babysitting, talking, discussing our week.

My landlady had a book on the top of the bureau, the book related to modern medicine, modern well, 1920s. Whilst babysitting one evening I started reading it whilst John read the local paper. I had studied general science at A-level during my short time in the sixth form at school and fully understood the workings of the female body and just how easy becoming pregnant could be.

John and I had discussed many topics, but sex was one we had so far managed to avoid, probably because sex outside marriage was not socially acceptable, even though it was 1960, but we had a highly charged sexual attraction to one another.

Not lovers but very close. John finished reading the paper and asked what are you reading there, no use lying, I replied, the rhythm method of birth control. His reaction, what the hell is that, let me read it. As ever, we had an analytical discussion, culminating in no wonder his grandmother had so many children. To the library, books on the rhythm method to find out as much as possible.

Neither of us was very enamoured with the idea of marriage, having witnessed our parents' relationships, both of us were very wary. The social norm was to marry young, and before you had sex, if you were over 21, you were on the shelf, potentially an old maid or marrying because you had a baby on the way, men being forced into marriage having been trapped into a compromising position.

Neither of us wanted any of these scenarios, we didn't want to marry or have children now, maybe later, but definitely not now, we had careers to progress.

Abortions were not legal until 1967, and the pill was only made available via the NHS in 1961, but for married women only; this changed in 1967, so we had to think about how we could be lovers but not marry and how we could not get pregnant.

Christmas 1960, John invited me to Christmas Day lunch with his parents. The house had no Christmas decorations at all, except a few Christmas cards, but no festive feeling whatsoever, it was horrible. The afternoon was spent listening to the Queen's speech whilst his parents snoozed. John took me back home and stayed awhile with the young family. There were toys everywhere and two very tired little boys, Christmas as it should be, something John had obviously never experienced, which was sad but would definitely change in later years.

My parents seemed to be settled in Plymouth, although I did not hear from them very often. Originally, they had lived at Mutley Plain in Plymouth and then moved to the Crown Hill area. One day, I received a letter from my mother, unusual in itself, requesting I visit them, as this was not something I wanted to do, I wrote back saying I could not afford it. Another letter enclosing funds for the train journey arrived, much to my surprise. I guess it was time to return the bedding, sheets, and pillowcases, seeing my sisters again would be good. John was off to Denmark on a cricket tour, so I thought I might as well take some of my holiday entitlement and go visit them all.

Seeing my sisters again was a joy, Wendy now a very attractive young woman, Carol a slim young girl.

Wendy and I talked about her clothes and how to put outfits together, using a base colour and adding different coloured tops, scarves, bracelets to make a small wardrobe become a large one. Great fun. My time of the month, or period, happened whilst I was staying with the family, and I left my packet of tampons by the side of my bed. Wendy saw them, and we discussed what mother had supplied her with.

Once again, sanitary belts and sanitary pads, Wendy's description, "they felt like huge duvets, so uncomfortable." I left the packet behind. Life had not changed for my sisters, nobody did anything, no visits to the cinema, no strolls along the beach, no walking along the promenade, living a kind of limbo.

Off to the department store we three went, purchasing fabric to make ourselves dresses, a simple shift dress for me, I also found a pair of shoes, pretty deep blue high heeled sling backed sandals, with a lacy insert over the toes. My but I loved those shoes. Time to return to Oxford, I was happy to go, sad to leave my sisters, but glad to leave the boredom behind.

Changing trains at Reading to catch the connection to Oxford, not in the least difficult. Buying a case to carry my belongings had been out of the question, I had made a bag, very much like a sailor's gunny sack. Basically, a tube with a circle sewn in at one end and a drawstring on the other. Easy to pick up and carry. Well needs must.

Stepping off the train having reached my destination and preparing to walk to the bus station for the final leg of my journey, there was John. How did he know which train I would be on, he did not, he simply met each train that afternoon.

In January 1961, Katherine was born, Peter and Susan's first daughter. She was a gorgeous little girl with eyes that looked right at you. I was sitting on the settee in the living room of their new house in Bracknell, baby by my side, the family dog, a corgi, watching intently, leaning over to stroke the baby's soft cheek, the corgi growled and gripped my hand before I got anywhere near her. Not a mark on my hand, not a scratch, just a warning hands off.

Peter and Susan rushed in to see what was going on.

"Do not blame the dog, he is doing his job protecting his family," I said.

Later that night, I lay awake wondering what my life would be like if I had a dog to cherish me in this way.

Katharine's christening day arrived, I was to be godmother, together with Susan's aunt. Off to the church we went, I felt so honoured. When we got there, Susan's mother took me aside, Mavis will be her real godmother, of course, as she has no children of her own, so you need to take a step back. Life had not been an easy road for me, it had made me tough, upsetting me took some doing, this cut me to the quick. Even to this day, this still hurts.

Life continued, the pattern much as before, both of us working, me to enable complete independence in the future. John his ambition to be a fully qualified mechanical engineer.

The car factory where John's father worked, closed for two weeks in July, his parents went to Brighton for a few days, and John asked if I would please come and cook him a meal on Saturday, he would pay for the food. Me being me asked if this was to see if I could cook, laughing, the reply came just cheaper than taking you out for a meal.

I went shopping that afternoon, then travelled on to his parents' house. Both of us working in the kitchen, John preparing the vegetables, boasting this is something he was good at following his time in the forces, chatting away and me being teased as usual.

John, standing behind me with his arms around my shoulders, asked, "will you stay with me tonight?"

The time had come, the time I had dreaded, as this could be the time when my life, without this amazing man, would start. I asked him to sit down, stood in front of him and told him of my childhood and the abuse, instead of being repulsed he stood up and pulled me into his arms, "oh scamp." He held me in his arms for what felt like ages and stated to me, "Cry it out, just cry it out."

John and I became lovers that night and successfully managed to not have children for another decade, thanks to that book and the library!

Later in the year, problems arose at my lodgings. Firstly, the young couple needed to borrow some money, they had a mortgage payment outstanding. Well, I could help, but warned I would need the funds repaid. This was the last time I lent money to anyone. Something else was amiss, they were rowing and arguing, late at night, it seemed she was not fulfilling her wifely duties in the bedroom. Abstinence, the only guaranteed form of birth control.

One Saturday afternoon, my landlady had taken the boys to visit her parents, and I was in the kitchen having a cup of tea when her husband started to get amorous. No way this might be the sixties, but as the expression goes, I did not give out, except to one person! But it meant I needed to move lodgings quickly and let them sort it out, which was a bit annoying, especially as I had done nothing wrong.

My mother had been befriended by one of the co-operative managers' wives whilst living in Oxford, helping her pick out evening dresses to wear to masonic lodge balls, something my mother had really enjoyed. Her name was Sally, and we bumped into one another quite often going to and from work. I met her a few days after the incident at my lodgings, on the bus coming home from work.

An astute Yorkshire woman who called a spade a spade saw something was worrying me. After I told her my sad and sorry tale, she simply said, "We have a spare room you can use, until you can sort this out."

I jumped at the opportunity and had moved to the outskirts of Headington within days. My furniture I put into store, thanks to one of the cricketers, John knew who managed a removal firm. Life was never simple for single women in the late 1950s/early 60s.

My original landlady's father dropped into the bank on a Saturday morning, telling me he would pick me up after work and drop me at my new lodgings, he needed to talk to me. He handed me the money, which was owed, which was great. Then the burning question, why are you moving out, he thought it was because they had not repaid me the money owed, but I stated to him, there was more to this move than money.

"Tell me," he said.

So I did, and explained the rows at night, what I considered to be the cause (lack of marital duty as she didn't want another baby yet), and the husband being amorous towards me. Having spent time at the library finding out as much as I could about how to not get pregnant and still have sexual relations, I suggested he gave them a couple of books, available on the NHS, to read, obviously this didn't go down well but something had to happen, or this marriage would be on the rocks.

I was being given more locum work in the out-of-town branches around this time, the embezzlement and corruption at the co-operative being the talk going around the office. My father had never acknowledged my work; therefore, luckily customers did not connect me to him. Getting me away was probably a good move of the banks, no gossip sticking on them, a close call for me though, and the potential impact on my independence, if this had happened and connections had been made.

In September, John and I went on a package holiday to the Costa Brava on the Mediterranean coast of Spain. Travelling by train to London, a ferry across the English Channel, yet another train to Paris, then on an overnight train journey south to Barcelona. The journey was exciting, travelling south through France, through the Pyrenees, waking at dawn to see the sun rise over the peaks, a sight never to be forgotten. We were the only two travellers to continue south from Barcelona, until this point, we had been looked after by a tour guide.

From this point to our destination, we were on our own. We were given verbal instructions on how to get to our destination, an adventure indeed. For this last part of the journey, we travelled on a local Spanish train which had wooden seats and was full of local people, goats, chickens and baskets of provisions. The whole train smelled strongly of garlic and cigarette smoke, mingling with the heat of the day, it was incredible and so different to the UK. We had been told to get off three stops down the track by the travel agent, so off we get, luckily it was the right stop, and we could see our hotel sign standing out amongst the houses, Hotel Canada situated in Calafel. Calafel is in the tourist region called Costa Dorada now and is a jungle of concrete and hotels.

We stayed in a lovely Spanish family hotel, which served wonderful food, and you could step out into the courtyard, which was sheltered from the sun, cool and aromatic with herbs growing in pots. This was such a romantic setting for us, and we had an amazing time as two young lovers, who weren't married, which was still very much frowned upon in those days, especially by the older generation, but it was a time when we had total freedom to just be ourselves.

We got up at dawn each day to see the sun rise over the water, romantic happy days spent swimming, sunbathing, and strolling around the local area. In the evenings, for dinner, it was just the two of us, delicious, home cooked food and a glass of local wine for John, water for me, as over the years I had discovered that alcohol and I did not get on and this still applies, it simply sends me to sleep.

The village was always humming with life, music playing from the little bars, shops open late into the evening and people calling and chatting to one another across the street. We walked into a local village in the hills where there were tapestries hanging from the balconies and little rivers of water running down the sides of the streets, almost medieval, poking our heads into little shops.

We often went down to the water's edge during the evening to watch the fishing boats which were not far from the shore, lights hanging over the sides of the vessels to attract shrimps to the surface, which they scooped out with nets. I can still remember the aroma of herbs cooling in the evening air, the sound of music, the boats' lights twinkling out on the sea, reflected in the moonlight.

We stayed there for two weeks, the days taking a similar pattern of walking to the beach each day or into the local village, John swimming and me wading in as deep as I could (I had developed a great fear of putting my head under water), sunbathing, having dinner each evening and watching the people coming and going. Two weeks when time stood still for a while, just the two of us, it was magical.

Later in the year, my landlady, Sally and her husband let me know that there was a problem with the building, and we would all have to move out for a couple of weeks. *Wonderful,* I thought, *where on earth was I to go.*

Luckily, John came to the rescue and offered for me to come and stay with him at his parents' house. This was a good temporary solution, I thought, but I was proved wrong. I thought I would not be a great burden, as I ate my main meal at lunch time, so all that was needed was breakfast, which I purchased on my way to work anyway. His mother made us cups of tea, as it was her kitchen, she insisted, it was obvious she found it very hard having me there, another woman and potentially the woman who could take her son away, I often asked if I could help and received a curt no in reply. I tried to be understanding and can look back now and see that she was afraid of losing her son, there was no need to be so rude though, but this continued to be the theme of my relationship with my to-be mother-in-law.

One Sunday, John was off playing golf, leaving me with his parents which was never pleasant, as they obviously had issues with me and the way I was living my life as a woman at the time and out it came, the question they had been desperate to ask, "I hear you are getting married?"

My reply, "Well, that is news to me."

It turned out that they had heard some gossip from the inner grapevine of Oxford, Sally, my landlady, had talked to her friends about this young couple she knew, so right together and would obviously marry, a few Chinese whispers later and the future father-in-law was told that John and I were getting married.

I left it at that and left them to talk to John, but it highlighted that it was time for me to take the leap and to find a place to live on my own, this was a challenge, as I was a single woman, and many landlords wouldn't rent to single woman, but I got lucky.

At work in one of the local branches the next week, I was chatting to one of the young men in the office about the problems young women had whilst in lodgings and how I would like to rent my own place.

The thoughtful man said, "Have a word with James, he runs a letting agency down the road, and he is due in the bank today to pay in the rent money."

When James arrived, he called me over and I explained my situation. He said, "There was the possibility of a flat becoming vacant when the couple living there had confirmation of a job move, would I like to view it?"

At that lunch time, I saw my new home, a sitting room, a bedroom, a bathroom and a kitchenette on the fourth floor of an old Victorian house, the lower floor being the letting agency. The young couple were there at the time, and as the rent was due for payment the following week, they wanted to vacate before that and would move in with his parents, I could afford the rental deposit and the monthly rent, so all was set, I would move in the following Monday.

I was beyond excited, my own home, my own space, all that I had worked for over the last few years and above all, total independence. Sometimes in life, you speak to the right people, who know the right people and it all fits together.

I bounced back to John's parents' house, ready to share my good news but was met with two men just standing around waiting to be fed, informing me that his mother had taken to her bed, very unwell. Someone or something had upset her, and this was common behaviour when this happened, a behaviour I would see repeated many times in the years ahead. They didn't have a refrigerator, so food had to be bought daily from the local shop. *It was like being back in the 1930s,* I thought.

Fish and chips not an option as these shops didn't open on a Monday. The only option was that I had better look to see what they had, bread, eggs, and milk, so they had a dinner of omelettes and toast that night, and the future mother-in-law stayed in her bedroom all evening. What a come down from my exciting day, typical. John and I went out walking, of course, as usual, leaving his parents to get on with it. Apparently, there was nothing I could do.

I asked John what on earth had happened, it seemed his mother could not let well alone and confronted him regarding our chat the previous day about marriage. This had incensed him, and he exploded, asking them why they had not talked to him first, what had I done to them, how badly they had treated me since the first time I had been introduced to them. When John was incensed, there was no holds barred.

I simply told him it did not matter, put it to one side, then gave him my news about my new apartment, which was much more important. John, always worried about money, said, "Are you sure you can afford it, Scamp. Are you sure?"

I said, "Yes, but that my finances would be tighter, and he might have to pick up the theatre tickets costs from now on."

It was now 1962 and I was independent at last. That first night I slept on an eiderdown on the floor, but it didn't matter, it was just so amazing to be in my own space, not sharing with anybody else, like I had been for all of my life, able to have a cup of tea in my pyjamas if I wished, oh the freedom. My belongings were with Sally and all I had was some clean underwear.

One of my friends had taken my washing home and her mother had washed it for me, one never forgets true kindness. I was excited to get started and get what I needed, as I didn't have much and there wasn't anybody to help me, not that I minded as whatever I bought would be mine, so during lunch time the next day I found myself in a local hardware store. I bought two cups, two saucers, two plates, two knives, two forks and one saucepan. There was a local grocery shop along the parade of shops, so I had everything I needed nearby.

This was an area that catered for university students, which was just right for me at the time. That weekend saw me in the Oxford Covered Market buying myself a sheet, towels and a pillow, it was basic, but it was a start, I was just so happy to be independent, the rest didn't matter.

In 1962, Peter and Susan had their second daughter, Elizabeth, this made then very happy, and the baby was lovely, as was little Katherine.

John called round, when he was not busy with studying or sport, no longer walking but talking in the comfort of my little living room. In this relaxed and cosy environment, he really opened up to me further and at last, he began to talk of his childhood, and the problems that made his home life so unhappy.

His father was a very sociable man, who enjoyed being the centre of attention, he attempted to behave like one of the toffs, a member of the rich upper classes. A wood turner and cabinet maker by trade, even though he was seen as a skilled worker, he was not a toff. His mother had been a book binder at the Oxford University Press before she married and was the youngest of thirteen children. When she was born, her eldest sibling was 22 years old, three of these siblings died in the Great War, and her father died a year after the war.

John went on to explain, having decided to marry, the question of finding accommodation arose, and they purchased a house on the outskirts of Oxford, which was seen as well to do.

At that time, women were unable to continue with their employment once married, so his mother gave up her job. They married when they were 25 and 23 years old, which for the time was reasonably late. Running a home was hard work, at the time, as there were no modern conveniences, and everything was done by hand. The house was simple, as was usual with a toilet outside, with a small bathroom off the kitchen but over the years some modernisation took place, and it became his mother's pride and joy.

In the 1930s before John was born in 1934, came the great slump as it was called, following the great depression that started in USA in 1929 but his mother and father were very well-to-do, due to his skilled job and didn't suffer from a time of great unemployment, they enjoyed their lives fully for four years, not burdened with childcare they were out in the evenings to the pub and dance halls, dancing the Charleston, even entering a dancing competition in London, his mother able to spend money on dresses and make-up.

John's birth brought great change to the relationship, as his father, aged 30, just carried on his life of going to the pub and dance halls, taking no part in parenting or interest but his wife, then aged 28 and perceived as very old to have a child in society, was left behind and became bitter and depressed, reliant on her husband for money and nothing to do all day apart from housework and childcare, which she obviously did not relish, she wanted to be out with her husband dancing and receiving attention, she was a very attractive woman at that time.

To quote his father, "You ruined my marriage."

The decision was made, and they had no more children. John, when he was a toddler, spent his early years in the family room, prevented from leaving the room by a chair blocking the doorway, all alone, whilst his mother continued with her weekly routine. Family life was bitter and acrimonious, his father out with his friends at least three nights a week playing billiards, weekends at the Liberal Club betting on horseracing.

Money was short, due to his father's gambling, and tempers raged. Like me, John had cut down clothes and second-hand shoes, football boots which were not a pair just a right and left foot, no underwear, and was therefore often chaffed and sore. My pyjamas might have been my cousin Bob's hand-me-downs, but at least they were warm, John had an old shirt from the market. Is it any wonder that he was off out and about as soon as he was able. An independent little boy, watching his mother suffer but unable to help.

In 1939, he was five years old and went off to school. At his school there were children of all ages in one class as the Second World War had started and there was a lack of teachers, so his education start wasn't the best. Every morning his mother gave him a farthing, into the baker's shop for a bread roll he went, as this was his breakfast, he was five.

Sunday morning all the local lads gathered to form football teams in the local park. Jackets down on the grass, used as goal posts. John was a very skilled football player. In the summer it was cricket. John's father played cricket for a local team, together with John's Uncle Cyril and a friend named Den (short for Dennis).

As John grew older and began to show proficiency at cricket, they practiced bowling to him, aiming at his feet. When John told me of this, I questioned it. I could see what they gained, but what for him? His reply, "I am good at blocking balls and can see the ball coming through the air at me, very useful with fast bowlers." So funny.

War time for his family was not the horrors I grew up with, no Anderson shelters and no bombs. But they did have an evacuee living with them, a young boy from London, which was great as it was company for John.

John's father did not join the forces but was employed in manufacturing in Swindon. John and his new friend, the evacuee and his mother worked in the garden growing vegetables and strawberries. One autumn day, he went with his mother to the cattle market and purchased three fruit trees, apple, pear, and plum. Travelling to town on the bus and walking back, carrying fruit trees, that was a long walk.

Schooling was of no importance to his parents, lessons being in a large room with all age groups, nobody interested in this young boy. His young life revolved around sport with his friends, learning to swim, running and exploring the River Thames, with Keith his lifelong friend, who lived in Iffley Village close to the lock, his father working for the university, this is the life John enjoyed at that time.

When it came time to prepare for the 11 plus, it was not to be for John, as he had been off school a great deal during the year with sickness and stomach pains. Eventually, he was taken to the doctor and was rushed to have an appendix operation at the Radcliffe Infirmary within days.

His parents fetched him from the hospital, no transport had been arranged by them, and he had to travel home on the bus. Can you imagine the discomfort of stepping up into a bus, let alone walking from the bus stop to the house. This was a major operation, no National Health Service to facilitate this.

The only person who could have paid for this was his grandfather, the one who stood up to his father at this time, telling him how he neglected his son and should treat his wife better, one day John would become a man, a force to be reckoned with. He was right.

When John's health improved, he went to the local secondary modern school, unable to go grammar school as he hadn't sat his 11 plus, but at that time it didn't matter as sport was still foremost in his life. When he was selected to play football for Oxford City Boys, he had a glimpse into another world. He played with other confident young men who were attending grammar school or privately educated at Magdalen school. The importance of education was staring him in the face.

At twelve years old, he had a paper round, delivering the papers in the streets near home. His earnings had to go into the family purse, as was expected for children that worked, this was the life envisaged for him, a steady but boring job and little other aspirations, what did John do, he took on a longer delivery route, opened a savings account with the TSB and put a large part of his earnings into it, what the eye does not see the heart will not grieve over.

School work had a new urgency, and he began to study for his leaving certificate, although he had a lot of gaps educationally.

On 1 January 1947, his family were down the pub celebrating the new year, having left John with his grandfather, who was already very ill. The two of them lay in the bed talking, his grandfather told John he believed in him and told him to work hard for his leaving certificate, demand an extra year at school and believe in himself. The family returned to find John sound asleep, his grandfather next to him having died in his sleep.

Work hard he did and demanded an extra year at school to accomplish his grandfather's request, as this incurred a cost, this was a big ask. On leaving school, the only employment on offer was to become a gardener with Oxford City Council, he had little or no help from his parents, who just needed him to work and pay his way.

Luckily, his Uncle Cyril intervened and helped him gain an apprenticeship at Pressed Steel Fisher, a British car body manufacturing business founded where John was brought up. Uncle Cyril was married to his father's sister, Addie, as she was called, they had two daughters, Susan and Lynda.

As John had purchased a bicycle some while before, transport was no problem. He attended evening classes at the local college to gain the qualifications he had missed and needed to further his career; his life was certainly very full. Cricket and football still filling his weekends.

John, being a very adventurous young man, also learnt to ride horses at the equestrian centre in Littlemore. He continued to play for the Oxford Boys Club and when they played against Balliol College boys in 1951, the team became the champions winning the Amos George Cup. Cricket became the main sport he played, and he started playing for an Oxford City Club, called Cowley St John's.

John had been invited to play for the Oxfordshire County Team at a very young age. Having, by now, moved to the drawing office at Pressed Steel Fisher, he had to get permission from his supervisor for time off to play for the county side, this request was received with a categorical no.

However, the Oxfordshire County Cricket Club chairman, telephoned the Company Director and the situation swiftly changed, he was to have the time off required, it was prestigious for the company and reflected well on them.

At this time, he was also given day release to study, so no more night school, which meant he could also go to net practice at the university parks with the team. Sport had triumphed. Mixing with a wider sphere of people made John realise what opportunities there were, and when we went on to have children, he was determined that they had access to the best education, which they did.

I learnt a great deal about John in the quiet evenings of early 1962, but very little of his mother. I knew of his father's attitude towards them both and could clearly see he was a product of his times, a man in a man's world, with women in a subservient role, there to provide for him.

Before I questioned John, I had to get my mind cleared of any preconceived ideas and take a long hard look at his home life and that of his mother.

I learnt from conversations with John over the years that what was now the little scullery housing the gas stove was once the pantry. John and Keith had installed a modern sink unit for her with cupboard space, underneath the window. The only other furniture was a table and three chairs, the fourth being in the sitting room, next to a fold leaf table.

Nothing else, not a modern appliance to be seen. Washing was boiled on a gas ring, everything, sheets, shirts, night shirts and towels, she then carried this washing into the kitchen area to be rinsed, then out the back to be put through a mangle to remove as much water as possible, finally onto the line to dry or hung over the little bath on wet days.

Very hard manual work. Ironing was done on the kitchen table with an old-fashioned iron made of wrought iron and heated on the gas ring. Monday was always washing day. The meal was always the same each week. Left over Sunday joint with mashed potatoes on a Monday for example.

A regimented daily and weekly routine. She didn't even have an electric kettle to make her life easier for herself, and it seemed she never asked her husband to buy her anything, and he had no inclination to make her life easier, if it meant spending money that he spent for his amusement. A life she seemed to tolerate or think herself worthy of nothing more, living in a time warp, fearful of change and progress.

She wore slippers most of the time, with a pleated skirt, hand-knitted button-up cardigan over a white blouse buttoned up to the neck with a little collar, one brooch and puffing on a woodbine cigarette. Suddenly, instead of thinking, I was the problem; I realised there was much more to this.

So instead of trying to find out why his mother disliked me so much, I asked why no electric kettle to make tea, he grinned at me, wondered when you would ask. It transpired that his father kept her short of money, simple as that. We talked then of her younger years, coming from a family of 13, losing 3 brothers in the First World War her father almost immediately after this, her mother running a laundry, euphemism for taking in laundry which the young girls helped with, this was a university city and most of the domestic work was outsourced.

Living in the Walton Street area of Oxford, at the time. How she would have been drawn to Walter, a sociable young man, the centre of things. A toff as she thought. Subservient and browbeaten, his own father having to warn him about neglecting his son and ill-treating his wife. Sometimes, it pays to look beneath the surface, what security did his mother have, no money, no prospects of change in her situation. Take away John's contribution to the family budget, who would suffer, not his father.

John's paternal grandmother died in 1959, she had been living in a home at Longworth, Oxfordshire, the family house standing empty for several years. Unable to sell the property prior to her death, John's father proceeded to clear it out and put it on the market. Probate and selling the house took time, and, in 1962, Walter and his sister inherited a sum of money. Invest for the future, put in central heating, of course not.

Altering the house by reducing the size of the sitting room to make room for a narrow hallway was the reality. Buying a television set, a new gas fire for the greatly reduced room, new furniture, two single beds for themselves, purchasing a refrigerator. Then the cruncher booked a package holiday to Sitges on the Costa Brava, travelling by train.

What did John have nothing until he pointed out that it was time he had a new mattress as his had a hole in it. New dresses for John's mother, new shoes, a bit of a problem as she had large bunions on her feet, from her dancing days. The new dresses a throwback to the 1930s, a sleeveless straight top with a pleated skirt, nothing modern. Almost flapper style. Happier than I had ever seen her, she was busy decorating the inside of the house, new curtains, cushions, the works, I realised the house was her domain and this made her happy, after all, it was all she had. Many women at that time struggled with the new age and modernisation, they were fearful and could not understand modern women, who wanted more and to be independent. All she had were her other sisters who were born of the same era.

This was the year my younger brother David advised my mother that he was getting married, the wedding was in April and was to be in Manchester. Carol was to be a bridesmaid again. John and I received an invitation, we were both happy to go as David was a firm favourite.

A few weeks later, a letter from mother arrived, Carol my sister hated the bridesmaids dress, as it was like a puff ball, would I please make her a white suit to wear for after the ceremony. I thought it must be bad and duly set to work.

I had been making clothes for my friends at work for some time, making a little extra money to keep myself afloat, so this was not a big problem, especially as one of the girls from the office had a sewing machine I could use.

Off to Manchester we went travelling in John's first motor, a grey van, map in hand, we arrived at the bride's home and were introduced to my future sister-in-law, who handed me a buttonhole which was a nice surprise, double flower like all the married women, she coyly smiled and saying, "I know all about you."

I thought, *no, you do not, I am not living in sin.* Of little importance on this special day. On the way back, I wondered just what the family had to say regarding John and me. Nothing good that was for sure. Carol was right that the dress was awful.

September came around, and it was vacation time. We decided on a different holiday this year following a letter from my Uncle Bill, which had arrived in the new year, advising me of a small inheritance. This was a complete surprise to me, it came to light that Aunt Sybil had left me funds which I was to receive at the age of 25, or when Uncle Bill thought it appropriate.

Apparently, he and Aunt Joy were delighted with the progress I had made in life and considered now was the appropriate time. Amazing, I no longer had any worry regarding money, life-changing indeed. We carried on saving for a summer holiday, but it meant that John and I were able to afford something new and adventurous.

We flew to Palma airport in Majorca and took an onward flight to Ibiza. Such an adventure, as there were no package holidays in those days and mass tourism.

This was 1962, one dressed smartly to fly, no trainers or jogging bottoms. John dressed in slacks, a shirt, tie and blazer. My outfit was a silver-grey Prince of Wales check box jacket and pencil skirt with heels, handbag and sunglasses. This was the way one travelled, celebrity style today. The journey to Majorca seemed to take a long time, up above the clouds, a sight to behold. The world is a beautiful place.

Landing at Palma airport we were whisked away just the two of us. Driven to a different part of the terminal to be confronted by a Lysander aircraft. We were the only two English people on board. It was a brilliant flight over to the island and landing directly onto the beach.

This island was untouched, no high-rise buildings, just a warm, sunny landscape, the smells of wild thyme in the air. We were entranced, an adventure indeed. Our hotel was in San Antonio and the only hotel in sight, a beautiful new Spanish style building, floors polished like glass, a courtyard and flowers surrounded by the hotel rooms.

The dining room overlooked the tiny harbour. Exploring was a major part of this vacation. A local fisherman was offering trips to the next cove, just a small boat taking maybe 6 passengers. The Mediterranean Sea, colours of blue through to turquoise at one's fingertips, fish clearly visible, the water was so translucent. Stepping onto a tiny jetty and surveying the amazing little cove.

People swimming and splashing in the warm water, resting under the shade of trees at the top of the beach. Perfect place to spend the day, all you needed was a little lunch and water, both supplied by the hotel. A wooden shack also stood under the tree line, nothing going on there, so basically ignored it.

Late morning, a rowboat appeared around the headland, one Englishman with a barrel of wine. The shack was a beach bar, red wine out of the barrel. John soon made himself known and they sat chatting for ages over a couple of glasses. Transpired the bar keeper was a retired civil servant who spent his days on the beach, selling a few glasses of red to keep himself in wine.

Living in St Antonio for him, it was the perfect retirement. Late afternoon, we walked back to the hotel through farmyards and olive groves past water tanks full of frogs, nasturtiums rambling around the gardens. Walking and exploring the area every day, lunch and water provided, resting on the beaches in the heat of the day, back to the hotel in the evenings to shower and dress for dinner. Wonderful romantic holiday.

As always in life there is a downside. John and I were some of the first English people to visit this island and here we are among a large contingency of German people of our own age able to afford holidays. Back in the UK, rationing had only recently finished, scars of war were deep. One young lady came across to our table and tried to chat John up, he replied with his clear Oxford accent. We are British, where do you come from? Gotta love this man!

Spring of 1963, and I was back at the main bank office full-time returning to the reception desk, to be greeted with a good to see you welcome back from the assistant manager. I soon found out why, it took several weeks to sort out the mess.

No matter, it was good to be with my friends again and cries of joy, "Are you able to make me a new dress?" and one shy request for a white coat. A registry office wedding. Life was on an even keel again. My school friend, Yvonne, was not herself, unusually quiet and withdrawn.

One lunchtime, she asked me to accompany her to a second-hand shop to buy a trunk. As we walked along, she told me of the difficulties which had arisen in her life. The long-term boyfriend had been seeing someone else; it was called two-timing in those days. She had applied for a new job, which she had been successful in and would be leaving at the end of the month. The job was in Toronto, Canada, the reason for the travelling trunk revealed. The first of our trio to emigrate to pastures new.

John was still studying, the last endorsement. Once this one was achieved, it left him with one exam outstanding. This had been a long hard road for him, an enormous achievement, considering his educational start. Just the last steps to be taken, and as with all things, finishing the course is difficult. I saw less of him during those weeks as he knuckled down, sitting in his bedroom studying.

Summer saw both of us getting on with our lives, dress making for me. John being promoted to the sales department. Still playing sport at every opportunity, whilst waiting for the result of his endorsement. All the technical and mathematical work completed. Successful, just an O-level exam to go. David and his wife Carole had their first child in 1963, a son called Mark, followed shortly after by Jane, I didn't see much of them, as they lived so far away.

Holiday time again, one with a difference this year. We had a driving holiday and drove in a mini through France, travelling through the Pyrenees to Spain, once more. A few days, one would have thought, not John. We drove to Hythe on the south coast, stayed overnight in a bed and breakfast and flew over the

Channel in a Lysander airplane, mini strapped in behind us. Travelling along French roads which were still two lines of cobble stones with grass growing between them, still old carriage tracks. Down through French Towns and cities. Stopping for fuel when and where we could and picking up food in the local villages.

The afternoon saw us well down into the south of France when fields of sunflowers began to appear. I had never seen anything like it. Round the Mediterranean edge of the mountains and into Spain we went, but the journey was getting arduous now. My map reading is not the best, as I have no great sense of direction. Driving through Barcelona, I could not make head or tail of the map, still we were on the right road. John had followed the river, I had the map upside down, hopeless.

That evening, we arrived at our destination, twenty-four hours after we had left the UK, Calafel, the place we had enjoyed so much before and would remember for the rest of our lives. Still, the same atmosphere, so romantic. Happy days.

Having transport on vacation opened a new way of taking holidays. Travelling further south around narrow mountain roads to Salou, and further south. Inland to see the olive groves in the hot September sun, orange and lemon trees on hillsides. Peach and nectarine trees dotted in between.

A stark contrast to our lush green fields and orchards back in the UK. Turning back from a journey to Valencia because of a heavy storm, hail stones rattling on the car roof.

The journey back at the end of our vacation, we broke our journey, staying overnight at an inn. The inn was an amazing place, very old roadside inn, a bowl and jug of water outside the door in the morning. Toilet facility communal in a small closet along the hall, one did not spend long in there.

Off to Calais we went the next morning, we were catching the regular ferry for Dover, the car kept overheating, and we had to stop in the shade. Nerves getting frayed now as we could not afford to miss the ferry, we arrived at the ferry terminal, which was in total chaos. Having a small car paid off, as we were directed to the shortest queue, little cars take up less space, so they can squeeze more cars on.

That experience was outstanding, and this style of holiday a recurring theme throughout our lives, a holiday with a bit of adventure.

The winter of 1963 was bitterly cold, the bank office was large and keeping it warm was difficult. Steaming hot tea and coffee made for everyone was brought up from the basement and delivered to your desk, in the administration department, this was around the big main desk and a great time for gossip. Talk of boyfriends and weddings. The wind was icy, so cold one needed a hat and to cover one's face as much as possible. Freezing rain, covering cars with a sheet of ice, making it impossible to open car doors as they were frozen solid.

Luckily, my apartment was small, and I kept warm by bringing my eiderdown into the sitting room and reading. Also having purchased winceyette pyjamas, I was warm and comfortable curled up under the eiderdown in bed.

Christmas morning dawned, with heavy snowfalls overnight, the roads had not been gritted, which would make driving difficult. So, I decided to walk to John's parents' house around two miles away. Wellington boots and a warm coat, which I had made myself a few years before, and I set off, arriving around midday.

John was outside digging his car out, endeavouring to come and fetch me. Calling out, "I should have known scamp I should have known." Laughing and throwing snow at me. Well, I did not need to think, let the battle commence. Inside we go laughing, wishing his parents "Happy Christmas." Oh dear. Unseemly, I guess, the restrictions of behaviour in the 1930s still prevalent.

After lunch we dug the car out together, leaving his parents to sleep through the Queen's speech, yet again. John and I walked back to my place, and he returned home whilst it was still light. The best Christmas together, happy together.

New Year's Eve arrived, and it was still bitterly cold, but the roads were passable. We celebrated the New Year with our friends at the rugby club and had a great time welcoming the new year, but awkward questions began to come, drink loosens people's tongues, and I was asked why you are not married. I could feel John's anger, understanding this quiet man's feelings at such intrusive questions. Must make a joke of this and dispel the tension.

I tapped the young man in question, on the shoulder, asking, "Why are you looking for a wife?"

The young lady he was with was not happy and pulled him away to the dance floor. So many people still locked in the past, girls get married and have children.

A quiet start to 1964, John now working for his last exam, the endorsements for his engineering qualification completed. This included higher maths, and all aspects of mechanical engineering, leaving him with one exam, an O-level English language paper. I saw less of him during the week, promotion at work and trying to get to grips with this paper, taking his time and energy.

Eventually, one evening he brought past examination papers with him. Admitting he could not get his head round it. Complex designs for engineering projects, estimating costs and obtaining the work in the sales department, no problem. Not this area though. He sat with me working on the paper, whilst I did some sewing.

Somehow, that lack of schooling in his teenage years must have affected him, his confidence at a very low ebb. He was really asking for help. Step by step we went through several papers, until he realised that this is the language he uses every day. Nothing new, nothing to worry about.

One question related to reducing the number of words in a given paragraph, he was removing some of the words. Me being me, used a more practical approach. Read the paragraph, happy with that. Good, and I took the paper away, handed him a pen and paper, now write it in your own words. Come the spring, John was ready for this exam.

Mother wrote to me asking for help, it seemed father had applied for a job back in Oxford, would I please put him up for the night as he had an interview, the following week. They could afford the train fare, however, but had no funds to cover a hotel bill, of course, he would sleep in a chair.

I thought to myself, *it is more likely that his reputation in this city was so bad he could not let anyone know of his plans.* My mother was in trouble asking for my help, I had two sisters to consider, so I wrote back saying I would help but for one night only, he would most certainly be sleeping in a chair.

It transpired that he had fallen back on his experience in the merchant navy and applied to run the kitchens at the Radcliffe Infirmary hospital. The chaos that ensued following the Second World War was gone and order restored, father no longer able to move about in the co-operative, his reputation caught up with him, having been caught in some form of skulduggery, he was fired. Taking on a small public house in a small Cornish village, being moved on after trying to do a deal with the draymen.

Desperate times, hence, the mother's letter asking for help.

Somehow, he managed to obtain the employment, the family on the move again, one sister working and the other still at school. No choice for either of them, let alone mother. Falling back on an old friend, accommodation was secured in an old cottage in a village outside Witney, almost back to square one, sink with cold water, no draining board and an old bathroom with an immersion heater. Peter and Susan went to visit them, and shocked at the situation, helped clean the place and install, at the very least, a draining board.

Another letter came from mother, Wendy needed help. Could I help her find a bedsit please, in the city? This is my sister, of course, I could and did help. I found somewhere for her near enough to my home, so if she needed any help, I was in walking distance. Wendy being Wendy, grabbed the opportunity standing on her own two feet, no holding her back, another one flown the nest.

One day, she will tell me what really happened, during that time when it was just her and Carole at home, remembering my mother and her agitation when accompanying Wendy to check out the bedsit, at the very least, bullying and harassment had been meted out.

Exam time came round, once taken it meant freedom from studying for John. Work, cricket and golf at the weekends, squash with Keith during the week. I was busy building a sewing business making wedding dresses, managing to make enough to cover my annual holiday. A time of adjustment, which came to a crashing holt that May.

I was asked to tea at his parents' house on a Saturday afternoon in May, this was unusual as his father went to the Liberal Club each Saturday without fail. Arriving around 3:30 pm, well, I was asked to tea, not lunch, to be met by a curt, we thought you would be here before this from his mother. John's Uncle Cyril and his cousin Susan were sitting in the little sitting room together with John and his father. I was sat down on a stool in the corner.

His cousin, Susan, was a legal secretary and had drawn up a will for his father. In the event of his father's death, his estate would be left to John. What about his mother, she would have nothing, absolutely nothing, such humiliation and having me there to witness it.

Oh dear, the old cold white anger all-consuming kept me quiet. The will duly signed by his father and uncle, off to the Liberal Club, Susan remained for tea. John said, "We will drop my cousin off, then you can change, ready to go out."

By now, he knew something was wrong. Susan stands back so I have to climb into the back seat whilst Madam proceeds to sit in the front, all pumped up with self-importance.

Arriving at my place after dropping her off, I opened the door, turned to John. I am disgusted, how could you let this happen. Your mother has nothing, absolutely nothing, her one sanctuary, her safe place has been taken away. Go away I do not want to have anything more to do with you, go.

I learnt from one of his friends later, he crashed his car on the way to cricket the next day. In collision with another car at a crossroads, I was not the only upset person.

Late August, he called at the bank to see me. Exam passed. Would I like to go out for a meal at the Trout Inn Godstow as a thank you?

I have always enjoyed evenings at the Trout Inn, as he knew, of course I would.

September, our original holiday plans having been cancelled, John went on tour with Reading Cricket Club, in Devon and Cornwall. I visited Peter, Susan and the girls in Cheltenham.

Autumn evenings, walking, time to talk. To discuss the reason for my reaction to his father's will. As he pointed out, there was not a lot he could do, the decision was not his.

At the time of the will signing, I was incensed at the treatment handed out to his mother, how one woman, "John's cousin Susan," could treat another in such a way, this is 1964 for goodness' sake, this disgusted me. His cousin had drawn up the paperwork and this was signed in front of his mother, cousin, uncle, John and me. I have never seen such misery on anyone's face in all my life as I saw on his mother's that day.

The house was her sanctuary, the place she felt safe, where she worked all her married life, virtually taken away at the stroke of a pen. John's father was not bright enough to have thought of this procedure, it was his cousin's work, working as a legal secretary in Oxford.

The actual implications in the event of his father's death, would be John owning the property, he would be liable for the utility bills and council tax, in other words, he was responsible for his mother, as his parents lived from hand to mouth, no savings, so in the event of her husband's death her income would be very small and John would have to support her.

Another thing sticking in my throat, why was I asked to be there, I thought I was coming to afternoon tea. The only reason we could think of was they were all still living in the 1930s, having never moved with the times. Women's lives were changing, but not in this household, I had to be made aware of the position a woman holds in this family.

They still had no idea of my employment, working in a bank, what did that mean to them, a typist, come secretary, probably, I would give up this employment when I married, as his mother had. Poor John looked resigned, I am glad you realise this, can we carry on seeing one another, with that big grin of his, let's see how it goes was my reply. As normal, John had a rejoinder, what were you going to do if I had not got in touch? Just as quick I told him, either go train to be a teacher or join my friend Yvonne in Canada.

All he said was, "Should not have asked."

I cancelled my application for employment in Canada a few weeks later.

Winter came, just us two going about our lives, enjoying one another's company. Walking in the evenings relaxed and talking of our friends and their families, how they had all moved on into a sedentary family life.

One evening, he asked me what I thought about something that happened during the summer after we broke up, a female member of the cricket club tennis section, asked him to walk round the cattle market with her, they had known one another for some years.

I said, "Well, of course, you went."

A bit sheepishly he nodded, then proceeded to tell me what transpired. She was single, not in a relationship at that time, but looking for a husband who could provide her with the lifestyle she aspired to. John had a very good job, in return, she would have his children. I asked him how he felt. He replied, it felt like I was being put out to stud. Laugh, I nearly cried.

This made me think of a movie from America, which came out in the UK called the Stepford Wives, based on the book of the same name, where this sort of proposal was seen to be normal, the meal ticket syndrome, provided a lifestyle to which otherwise they would not have.

Some women in the 1960s were looking for more material things in life than their mothers, looking for a meal ticket, someone to provide for them, still not seeing that this is just a continuation of the old way of life, subservience in another form.

Later in November, I was asked to Sunday tea at his parents, however, not quite the normal greeting, instead, a more welcoming greeting, it transpired that nobody else had been to visit them since May. John had told them how disgusted I was with the treatment his mother had received, so his father was nervous, dragging on his woodbine. A truce of sorts, it seemed, at least I knew how he thought the future should be, dumped his responsibilities on his son, instead of providing for his wife. Contempt was what I felt.

Another change of events occurred around Christmas, this year I was invited to stay with John's parents on Christmas Eve, we were due to join a few of our friends that evening, and normally John would drop me off at home. My staying overnight would mean John moving from his bedroom into the one over the tunnel between the houses, mainly full of the old furniture from his parents' bedroom. I was surprised, but I was invited, so I said, "Fine, as long as he was happy with it."

Christmas morning, it was very cold in the house, I could see my breath steaming in the chilly air. Luckily, I had come prepared with my winceyette pyjamas, John slipped into the room, knelt down on the floor beside the bed, whispered, "Happy Christmas scamp, will you marry me?"

"Yes," I whispered back.

Then the door opened wide, his mother, what is going on in here, as I am in thick winceyette pyjamas under the blanket.

"Not a lot," says John, with a big grin on his face.

*Everything,* I thought, *just about everything.*

Christmas is a very special time for us both for ever going forwards in our lives.

# Chapter Four
# A Wedding, A New House, A Mortgage Forging Ahead in a Male-Oriented World

Forefinger to the lips indicating keep it quiet, was easily understood, as mother-in-law to-be would take to her bed.

Christmas morning came to the Lucas household. I had bought presents for John's parents, wrapped in Christmas paper which surprised them both—a small instrument for cleaning and filling a tobacco pipe for his father, a smoky coloured specimen vase in a modern Swedish design for his mother which echoed her colour scheme and a leather document case for John.

From John, my favourite perfume, with that big smile of his saying 'Mine' came ready wrapped. Christmas carried on as normal, lunch at 1.30 pm, John and I taking our leave as his parents settled down for the Queen's speech at 3 pm.

Parking the car in North Oxford, we walked around the university parks, just happy being together and started making wedding plans; simple to make for us—two questions: when and where.

One Friday, January 1965, saw me on a bus, travelling to Peter and Susan's home in Cheltenham. Followed by all five of us, Peter, Susan, the two little girls (Katherine and Elizabeth) and myself, travelling to Plymouth, in Peter's mini, which was great fun, we were off to another family wedding.

Trevor was getting married to his first wife Pat, strangely, this is a wedding I have little recollection of, probably wrapped up in my own happiness. During the reception, Susan and I went outside for a quiet cigarette, social smokers the pair of us, as ever, straight to the point, Susan wondered if there was going to be another wedding this year, my reply, "maybe."

Trevor and Pat remained married for several years, having a family of two daughters, Nicola and Karen. Eventually divorcing and Trevor remarried twice, Vivien and Dianna, Di as we know her, being with him to the end of his life.

John and I both knew that making plans for our wedding would have to be carried out very quietly if we wanted the wedding to be the way we wanted, due to John's mother but the best part was that even though we would have to tiptoe around her we would have our wedding, and this was very important to us.

Over the years, we had been to evening carol services in Oxford, when the weather was bad, we went to St Michael's in the Northgate church carol service, and this is where we decided to marry. September would be the month as this would be easy for me to book holiday time as it was outside summer season, and I would not have to give a reason for a certain date and as the cricket season was still in full swing, a morning ceremony would be the best time. The wedding ceremony and reception, for me to organise, the honeymoon was John's domain.

My joy of list making, always a strong means of organising and prioritising, came into play. September 11 soon established itself as the best date, church available and booked, reception to be held at The Clarendon Restaurant within walking distance of the church.

Guests to be close friends and family only. Meanwhile life continued with us both working and talking about our days when we got back to my apartment in the evenings or when we were out walking, happy times, driving around the local villages, calling into the local pubs to try and establish where we would like to live at some point in the future. The decision was made to start our married life in the apartment, which was a no brainer, as this would allow us to save a deposit for us to buy our first home.

April 1965 and the beginning of the cricket season meant John was busy, weekends becoming time for me to finalise our wedding arrangements. Wedding dress fabric was to be obtained, and a dress made, as well as a going away outfit, well maybe not, as the wedding reception, church fees, flowers, bridesmaid dresses, all had to be paid for. I would become a married woman without a penny to my name, but did John mind not a bit of it?

"That is great, Scamp, just my wife."

One Saturday afternoon in May, Susan arrived unannounced bringing my two little nieces, as ever straight to the point, well if you will not come to the mountain, the mountain will have to come to you, are you or are you not getting married, friends as always, I was able to explain the difficulties we had encountered and the answer was yes, September 11th at 11 am, would she allow the two girls to be bridesmaids. That was a big affirmative, out came the dress designs, and what size shoes do they need?

Peter and Susan would buy their shoes, no argument allowed. Being able to talk about our plans was such fun, having someone to check over everything, an enormous help. Final plans began dropping into place, the bridesmaid dresses were easy, simple white cotton. My dress was a different matter as my design needed heavy silk to hold the simple lines and the only place I could track the material down was in France, costing much more than I had hoped.

John knew something was bothering me and assumed it was to do with our honeymoon, which he steadfastly would not divulge anything about. Something must have made him think maybe this was not the reason and when he saw the bridesmaid's dresses sitting in my work box, he asked after mine, I explained my dilemma, being unable to decide upon a cheaper fabric and lining the dress or send for the silk, his answer was immediate, this is our day we will remember it all our lives, order the silk I will pay for it.

This became the essence of the strength of our married life, this was our life, we will live it well, together. Late June and a visit from an old friend occurred, Yvonne had returned from Canada to visit her family. I think her return was to check to make sure she had been right in the decision to emigrate, meeting with her old boyfriend, the two-timer, certainly sorted that out.

We had many lunchtime chats, and she requested a couple of dresses to be made and would I help her buy a new coat, winters in Toronto are bitterly cold, all to be bought and made during those two weeks, before her return.

After she returned to Canada, a letter arrived from her, telling me she had been met at the airport by Ray, the man she mentioned in passing, the trip home made her realise what a great person he is. Her sweetie, as she called him, another wedding was on the horizon.

Arrangements for our wedding were well underway, dressmaking always such pure joy for me. I was left with just flowers and bridesmaids' presents to consider. Regarding the going away outfit, I still had my Prince of Wales check two-piece from our Ibiza trip, no problem there then or so I thought.

John had ordered a new three-piece suit from Austin Reeds, so I asked what colour buttonhole he would like, red. What colour was my going away outfit, you have seen it, I wore it to Ibiza, wrong answer, what was he planning, I had to get another outfit made. Around this time Reverend MacDonald Ramm called into the bank and asked me to join him for a coffee at lunchtime.

"Things to discuss, Joan," he said, when the wedding bans would have to be called, and there is going to be a second wedding on September 11th in the afternoon, would we mind if the mother of the afternoon bride decorated the church with flowers. One answer was simple, it would be my pleasure for the bride's mother to decorate the church, as this was beyond my budget. I asked what the latest date for calling the bans would be, and I would discuss it with John.

July saw his parents take a short break to Brighton, leaving us free to go shopping. We needed to purchase an engagement and a wedding ring for me, not for John, as rings can be dangerous for engineers and a going away outfit for me. We had decided to tell his parents of our wedding plans at some point during August, which also gave me the timeline I needed, in relation to the invitations which needed to be written and posted and my parents needed to be told, as well as advising Reverend Ramm of the date for calling the bans.

My rings remained with the jewellers to be altered to the correct size. John had a plan in regard to informing his parents regarding the wedding and one Sunday lunchtime he simply placed my engagement ring on the table and said, "Joan and I are getting married."

Congratulations or when the reaction? No, his mother simply said, "I always wanted a pretty ring."

How sad in so many ways. Although John never mentioned how difficult the next few weeks were, I knew they caused him to be upset and exasperated. I didn't escape the drama and upset of course the following Sunday I received the afternoon tea invitation, John and I were joining our friends in the evening after the cricket match, he would come and collect me from his parents, I advised him I was a bit busy and would join them around five.

As I walked through the tunnel to the backdoor, John's father spoke, no hello, just, "there you are, have a drink with us to celebrate."

"No," I stated as I do not drink alcohol because it affects me very quickly. I have always had a bad reaction to alcohol, leaving me with not a nice feeling at all, let alone the enormous hangover, tea, a small wine or a small gin and tonic, maybe. Despite my protestations, an almost neat gin was thrust into my hand, and what followed was a lecture about my forthcoming marriage and what was expected of me.

John's mother sat there with a smile on her face, she must have gone through the same lecture years before. Dictatorial tyranny by her husband. Well, as I said, alcohol and I are not a good combination, so I sat patiently listening to this tirade, with the glass of gin in my hand, and when he had finished, I asked, "Is that it?"

John then walked in to pick me up for our evening out and it was just as well, as I had had to hold my tongue, I quickly escaped and, in the car, we looked at each other, I laughed and so did John. This was just a small example of what was to come.

"Food please, just feed me," I said to John.

Full of laughter, the evening after, he held out the jeweller's box, do you still want this then? Yes, so long as you come with it.

September saw him taking his mother to the same shop where we had bought my going away outfit to purchase a wedding outfit for her, she chose a dress in a strange brown colour, which I found difficult to understand, but I suppose it was not a time of celebration for her, just fear of what her future now held. John continued to face several weeks of his mother's unhappiness, whilst I went to work the next day wearing my ring. I shall never forget the joy with which this was greeted, and the interest in what I would be wearing.

Did I need anything? I still needed shoes and a head dress and veil. What size did the reply come in, borrow mine. These friends of mine, so kind. All set then, the parents to tell and the invitations to post left to do. Saturday found me on the bus again off to Shipton under Wychwood, to visit my parents and youngest sister. We all sat in the kitchen come living room, with a cup of tea when I told them John and I were getting married this coming September.

Mother was pleased but tearful, we cannot afford to pay for it. Father left immediately to go to the pub. After reassuring my mother, that all was taken care of, she simply had to turn up on the day. This was met with more tears, I would like to buy you a wedding present, something you will enjoy every day, we need some matching dinner plates, I replied. A simple present, but I really appreciated what she was really saying, dinner plates with matching side plates is what she bought me, some of which I have to this day.

Wendy, Mother and I met in Bakers the Baker's Department store where my sister worked, during the following week. Choosing dinner plates to match the coffee set already purchased by John's working companions. Afterwards, mother and I visited John's parents, a very thoughtful thing to do, as meeting at your children's wedding could be very awkward. To this day I am unsure what John's parents expected, the only comment ever made was by his father, she is so young.

Just one thing to overcome, a car to take me to the church, no problem, one of the bank customers congratulated me on my engagement, when the wedding date is set, let me know, I would like to drive you to the church.

"Amazing, how about September 11," I replied, laughing.

He said, "Consider it done. What time and where, this is on me."

People so kind.

Saturday, a week before the wedding, mother-in-law came to view our wedding presents, I mentioned this to my sister Wendy and how I dreaded it. Worry not, came the reply, I will help. Help she did, and within an hour she had the place shining and orderly, arranged all the presents on the table and ironing board, making a lovely display.

To this day, I do not know what my mother-in-law thought, let's just say she never visited again. Wednesday night before our wedding day, John's stag night. Friends, cricketers, golfers, work colleagues descended on the Eastgate Hotel. A very good night had by all, Keith called into the bank next morning to tell me if this is anything to go by, one hell of a wedding coming up, that was with a hangover. The whole branch was agog with gossip, wedding of the year, that's what is going on. I knew John was well known and well liked but this was the first inkling I had of just how popular he was.

The following morning on my way to catch the bus into the city, a woman I had never met jumped out of a car as I passed and starting shouting at me, "You are not good enough for him, I know all about you and your family, I know what your father got up to and what he and his cronies got up to in that flat."

Adversity having been a part of my life for a long time, the rejoinder was swift and cutting. "You know more than I do, how come?"

Leaving her standing there with her mouth open. I wondered who that was, I thought and mentioned the unsavoury episode to John that evening, he immediately knew who it was, a female cousin from his mother's side of the family, and it came to light that this woman had visited his mother the day before, say no more. Just what did these people think I would do, run away from such abuse, hardly.

That Friday morning in the bank, the day before the wedding, everybody was smiling and happy, such a great team to work with, thank goodness I did not have to choose who came to the wedding or for that matter who did not. My colleagues covered me that Friday afternoon and I was free to go home, giving me time to pack my case, check the bridesmaid dresses and my own, pack away our wedding presents and clean the apartment.

The evening soon came around, and John arrived to collect my passport, his own key to the apartment and my cases, one for our honeymoon and one containing my going away outfit, to be taken into the restaurant in the morning. We had a big hug as he left and he simply said, "See you tomorrow, Scamp."

On the morning of my wedding day, I awoke early after a good sleep and had a bath, changing into underwear and a tee-shirt. I quickly tidied the rooms and made the bed, followed by coffee and some time for me. This was the most important day of my life, and I intended to enjoy it to the best of my ability.

Susan and Peter arrived with the little girls, Peter left immediately, off to collect flowers and my father. Susan and I sat with a cup of coffee and talked to the little ones, who were very excited. Finally, it was time to prepare, hair done, make-up done, two little ones into dresses, both with newly washed shiny hair, so adorable.

Lastly, Susan helped me into my dress. All ready. Peter returned with my father and our flowers. Wide-eyed little girl, Elizabeth, stating, "My plant mummy," a perfect start to a wonderful day. We arrived at the church, the first thing I wanted to know was, Is he here? It was reported back that yes, Affirmative. Into the church I went, with the little girls standing with Peter and Susan, wide-eyed.

It was just wonderful, the music started playing as I started down the aisle, John stood at the end, a big grin on his face as he beckoned me with his arm, come on, remember there was a cricket match later! Everyone was smiling and laughing at him, setting the tone of the wedding. John's response simply, yes, I do loud and clear. I have to admit that the word obey had been removed from the declaration, we agreed, but certain other members of the congregation were very shocked.

Out into the sunshine we all went, photographs taken, church bells ringing, a nice surprise as I had not been able to afford this, amazing how kind people were. We all walked across Cornmarket Street to the reception, people in the street smiling and clapping. We had a simple buffet with the cake on a stand in the middle of the room. Room full of chattering people, John and I mingling.

My mother was beaming, I am going to introduce your sister to these cricketers, so funny. John's parents, Uncle Cyril and Aunt Addie, sat together and did not move throughout the event. Speeches, cake cutting over, there was a tap on my shoulder, "Come on, Scamp, time to get changed."

All my friends from the bank joining me in the ladies changing room, dress off, shoes and head dress returned. Into my suit then they loaded me up with box after box of confetti stuffed into my dress, Susan giving a bit of a helping hand here, such fun what a day. John had hidden the car in plain sight, his friends had spent the morning looking for it, in an attempt to decorate it, he had literally parked at the end of George Street, no tin cans tied on the bumper.

Figure 8—Top left is me and John on our wedding day. Top right is Peter and Carol with Trevor and his wife Patricia, middle bottom is John and I, with my parents on the left and John's on the right, with Katherine and Elizabeth the bridesmaids.

Figure 9: John and I after we were married

Figure 10–Myself with the Bridesmaids

Farewells made almost unable to bend with the amount of confetti pushed down into my dress, I stepped out to join him. "Ready scamp, let's go!" Both of us talking about the morning and how much we had enjoyed our day, how amazingly well-behaved Kat and Elizabeth had been and the fun of walking from the church across Cornmarket Street, into George Street and the reception venue, morning never to be forgotten, almost perfect, John remarked.

The only issue is it had transpired that his mother had been given the task of collecting buttonholes for John and the best man, and true to form she spent almost half an hour in Brown's Café in the covered market drinking tea, John's uncle was despatched to locate her, photographs of John and his best man are devoid of button holes, nothing new there then.

As we were chatting away, so much reflecting on the wedding, I hardly noticed the direction we had taken out of Oxford, on our way to the airport, I assumed, well you know the saying, never assume. We drove right into the centre of London, pulling up outside The Cumberland Hotel, near Hyde Park Corner, the luggage was swiftly unloaded, and the car taken by the hotel staff to be parked.

This husband of mine had started in the way he wanted us to live our lives. We were shown to our suite, and I glanced back as John was laughing, oh my, a long line of confetti trailing behind me, newlyweds, no argument about that.

Confetti banished and into the bin and we left to walk to Hyde Park Corner, listening to the people on soap boxes telling us about this and that, walking happily around, then we travelled on the underground to Leicester Square, for dinner at the Angus Steak House. A couple from America joined us at our table, very interested in our day and what we were going to do that evening.

I had no idea what we were doing and this was when I learnt that we were going to the Drury Lane Theatre to see Camelot but not just any seats but seats two rows from the front of the stage, so close you could see the beads dropping off the costumes, it was a wonderful and spectacular show and above all a wonderful end to a day that we would remember all our lives.

The next day, we had an early start, no luxurious lay in, a quick breakfast, and we were off. I quickly repacked the bags and they were taken to the foyer ready for our departure. The car was brought round for us and away we went off to the airport, as we were flying to Majorca and on to Cala Milor, doing all the things we enjoy, walking on the beaches, visiting villages inland, exploring on the local buses, evenings spent outside with music playing, wonderful atmosphere. Just very happy.

After two weeks, which had soon flown past, as time does when you are enjoying yourselves, we were back in the apartment, very tired, no food in so back to earth with a bang, fish and chips from the chippy it had to be, always such fun eating them out of the paper with our fingers.

The local shops were luckily open on Sunday morning, so an early start again, breakfast and evening meal purchased. To end our honeymoon, we went off around the local villages for a pub lunch and a look around. We were keen to live in a village close to Oxford, away from city life, we wanted peace and quiet and had great fun eliminating those we did not like.

We had spent time during our honeymoon discussing money and how we were going to save a deposit for our first house, none of our parents were in a position to give us a hand and this was something we needed and wanted to do ourselves, not be beholden to anyone. We decided that we would continue to live in the apartment and live on my salary, saving John's, very much working together.

Monday quickly came around and it was back at the bank for me, to be greeted by the other members of staff, all talking about what a good time they had at the wedding. Very much a normal day for me, time to organise student account opening, but lunch time no longer spent chatting and browsing the shops, as I had dinner to purchase, as we had no refrigerator in the apartment, so this became a daily occurrence.

I used to really enjoy shopping in the covered market, in the centre of Oxford, as it was loud and busy with a huge variety of stalls and always lots of characters, I shopped for fresh vegetables and fruit there being a butcher and fish monger's shop all under one roof, that is where we got our food, as we were saving hard, I always looked for the cheapest options and became very creative with especially minced beef.

Even when John was in his 80s, when asked what he wanted to eat, he always said beef mince. John used to telephone me to say if he would be working late any evenings, which brought a new depth to our relationship. These were simple but happy days.

Newlyweds enjoying our time together, one would have thought this would be an easy transition, we had known one another for a very long time. The first argument arose when I was delayed at the office, daily balance a few pounds adrift, all the staff involved stayed until the error was located. I stood back, leaving the administration staff checking entries in ledgers and sheets of numbers, trying to locate the error, and concentrated on finding a different solution. I checked carry forward figures, nothing wrong there. Tempers began to fray as everyone wanted to go home.

Could this be a simple reversal of numbers, such as £51 for £15, or even two such things, a poorly written cheque. I began to check through the actual input of cheques to the entries. Other members of the group began to follow suit and two such errors were located. One reversal and one badly written cheque. Well, of course I was late getting home, John wanting to know about food, he was used to it being on the table at a certain time ready for him to consume.

The rubbish had not been put out. I was tired, nearly three hours of checking through poorly conducted administration work is unpleasant. Tempers flew as simply stated is my name written on the rubbish bag. The fish and chip shop is just across the road, are you off to get some?

He was steaming that his regimented life had disappeared. Sharing of domestic work, a totally new concept. Something he had never considered. I have a temper when provoked, especially by injustice, but cool down very quickly. Taking the rubbish with me, I went for the fish and chips, leaving him to think. Food on plates, we sat down to eat, as ever, we just looked at one another and burst out laughing. Both of us learning to adjust.

Mornings with John were very different, the routine of who uses the bathroom first, who makes the coffee, added to our life together. What intrigued him most was the start to my day. I put my underclothes on in the bedroom, this consisted of knickers, tights and a bra petticoat, this was literally a bra with a thick shift style petticoat attached and walked through to the sitting area.

The wardrobe was in this room, which had a large mirror on the inside of one door, reflecting the morning light, enabling me to brush my long hair into a French pleat and put on my make-up in. Finally, on goes the dress and shoes. This fascination never left him, buying me face creams and new underwear became one of his ways of showing me how much he cared. Thank you, Aunt Joy, a lesson well learnt.

Later in the week, John's Uncle Cyril called into his office with a message from his father. John's mother was in a bad way; he would have to come and see her as soon as possible. Poor man up to his eyes in work, juggling different time zones when telephoning clients, and now issues with his mother again. We chatted and decided to visit together, which would be Saturday, after I finish work and when John had played a few holes of golf. This situation, with his mother now and in the future, we would handle together. As our lives evolved, this proved to be a very wise decision.

Saturday straight after work, we drove to his parents' house, passing his mother as she turned the corner carrying a bag of shopping, she was trudging along, head down, her coat which had once been green, was now a pale shade of grey around the shoulders and looked threadbare, the boots she was wearing were cracked at the toes and the heels were completely worn down. I just looked at John and said, "We will buy her a new coat and boots, this is dreadful."

He just smiled that smile of his, "love you, Scamp."

I climbed out of the car and walked towards my mother-in-law, taking her shopping bag and walking into the house with her. John immediately walked his father down the garden path where they talked together, his mother put the shopping away and set about making a cup of tea.

No greeting, nothing, just pure misery. Someone must do something here, looks as though it was going to be me, so I set about finding out what was wrong; firstly she had had to ask John's father for more funds, he was not giving her enough to pay bills and cover the cost of food, the loss of John's contribution to the family budget leaving a huge hole for them, so not only was he not giving her enough for her personal needs, but also the running of the house. This would have to be something John and I discussed together.

The two men came back into the house and his father slunk off into the sitting room. John sat down in front of his mother, as I fetched him a cup of tea. What can we do to help? Being his first question, "I want to continue washing your shirts," she stated.

"Fine by me," I replied.

John asked if she would like us to come to tea on a Sunday and I asked her if she would like us to find her a little job, so she has some money of her own. She just nodded with tears running down her face.

I stated, "Well, in that case, you had better have a new coat and boots, we will take you shopping next Saturday."

It transpired his father had ranted and raved at her about having to pass over more cash because it meant less for him to gamble with and fewer pints to enjoy with his mates at the club. Needless to say, the garden path conversation had been explicit, his father had been told a few home-truths. Mother-in-law set about getting his father's Saturday high tea, a ritual event before he went off to the club.

John suggested I stroll up to the shopping centre for our groceries and I gave him a hard look, getting me out of the house, I thought, but I agreed, leaving them to speak. I do not know what was said whilst I was out, but upon my return, his father was missing and his mother smiling again. This was to be a repeat story of the years to come, but we would deal with this situation together. All I had to do was find her a part-time job.

The following Sunday, John's shirts were delivered, and we sat down to afternoon tea. Tinned salmon and tomatoes, bread and butter, with a bought cake, very thoughtful, well, I thought so, although John smiled and asked what's for dinner very quietly, minced beef was the reply. A recurring joke between us, finding out how many ways one can dish up minced beef. I had asked around in the city during the week and heard of an afternoon job in the canteen of the local newspaper, would John's mother like to do that?

She just stared at me, what would I have to do, make tea, sandwiches, things like that, do I have to apply for it? Obviously a concern, no, just call at the front desk and they will take you around the canteen, then you can see if they offer you the job or if it's what you want. We had taken her shopping, as promised and purchased her a new coat and boots, so she was already.

John's chat with his father must have pricked what conscience he might have had towards his wife and the neglect he had shown, as he had handed over sufficient for her to purchase wool to make herself a new jacket and hat.

Then my nasty mind thought, *he might not have to hand over money for her personal things, if she gets this new role and this gesture makes him look good, thinks he is on a winner.* How badly women were treated, this is 1965, and this poor downtrodden neglected woman, had lost the one person she felt she could rely on when her son married. How unimportant she must have felt.

John and I talked about this situation, and he emphasised that our relationship would always come first. His parents would have to be a part of our life, no matter what transpired, and he would call in once a week to check on his mother. The simplest way for him to achieve this was to leave his sports equipment and golf clubs at their house, it would not be obvious that he was looking after her. John was such a kind man, with a great sense of duty and we looked after her, until she died.

In October, we were invited to a party at the home of one of the cricketers, not someone John liked very much and upon meeting him for the first time I could understand why, a pompous type, who found it hard to swallow that John had been invited to join the prestigious Frilford Heath Golf Club in the previous year, as it was obviously, something he aspired too. John remained a member of this golf club until he could no longer play, in his 80s.

The party started very civilly with everyone talking politely, then the alcohol set in and the noise level rose, during one of these almost screeching times, the wife of this cricketer comes across to me saying come and meet my friend, she had a date with John Lucas a few weeks ago, she stated, "I asked you two to the party so we could check on this after all you had only just got married."

I replied calmly, after all I had not been drinking, "Well, we have been joined at the hip, since our wedding, so him having a date would be a little difficult," and walked away, preferring to speak with John and not become involved.

Talking to John on the way home, it appears that some people will go to huge lengths out of spite. Her husband had not been invited to John's stag do, as the cricket team didn't like him and they had not been invited to our wedding, that everyone has been talking about for weeks, and he was not a member of a prestigious golf course, which John was.

The conversation was so loud, other people had also heard it, including John, who had gone over to the so-called friend of the cricketer's wife and asked exactly where we went on this date? Spluttering on her drink, she could not answer. John, so incensed, dealt one of his cutting remarks, "Let me introduce myself, I am John Lucas, I have never met you in my life and would not come near you, as I would not know who you have been with."

We left after that.

After such a fantastic year, life came crashing back to reality with a bump and that Christmas 1965, brought a big, unexpected change in my life. Peter, my eldest brother, had been enamoured with aircraft ever since his days in the Fleet Air Arm, upon hearing of an opportunity for engineers to join Boeing in Seattle, the decision was made to follow his dreams. Did this affect me, of course it did, did I let anyone know how I felt, of course not. Another of the three girls from Milham Ford School off to pastures new.

February saw all four of them sailing across the Atlantic Ocean to Ellis Island, through immigration. Peter took Kat up on deck so she could see the Statue of Liberty, Elizabeth and Susan below deck, as Susan had previously broken her arm, then they went across America by train to Seattle, in Washington State. Did they embrace their new life, very much so, and they and their daughters never returned to live in the UK.

Eventually, John and I visited them in 2004 to celebrate both Susan and my 65th birthday, and recently I visited them in November 2023 with my daughter and son-in-law, which was brilliant, and now due to the miracle of mobile phones and technology we are all in contact daily.

Life for us two was busy and exciting, spending time with our true friends. John still playing sport especially golf in the winter months, as I still worked full-time with alternate Saturday mornings, leaving him free to pursue his love of all things sporty. We spent the evenings reading and talking, planning for the future, arguing as we always had but above all enjoying one another's sense of humour.

John had attained a high-ranking position within the company, which afforded him several benefits, one of which was a company car and another a company card allowing discounts with businesses trading with the company. Perfect for his sporting equipment.

Whilst in the office during the spring of 1966, he received a phone call from his friend Keith, asking why an invoice had not been paid. John had no idea and told Keith he would come over to the administration block and have a look. A business trading in floor and kitchen tiles, John's a very astute man, was suspicious, took one look at the invoice and realised someone was using his name and discount number. An address in Cumnor Hill being quoted for delivery.

A quick check by Keith confirmed who the individual was. Leaving Keith to work out how he knew John's number. John went to have a quiet word with the individual's father, a member of the company management team, who soon sorted the problem out.

A person using John's card number was a married man with three young children, John confronted him in front of the whole department where he worked and asked a question the individual was not expecting. Have you been having dates with women using my name and background? Got it in one. That situation came to a close and so did the discount system. How the number was attained, simple, the individual had been dating one of the girls in the administration office.

John was still attending the motor shows at Earls Court, London, and I would take the train up to London and join him and go to the theatre. We both enjoyed the theatre, standing up in the gods at Oxford's New Theatre had been a highlight during those early years, when money was very short. Off to the theatre we would go, Harry Secombe in Pickwick Papers, during 1963, that was memorable, as was watching Ginger Rogers, a Hollywood Star, performing in Mame, we were so lucky to have seen such an iconic star live.

Our holiday in 1966 was a trip to Devon and Cornwall, with John showing me where he played cricket when on tour with Reading Cricket Club. We stayed in bed and breakfast establishments as we travelled around, making it a holiday with a difference. John really enjoyed showing me the places he had visited.

I became an auntie again in 1966, as David's wife gave birth to a baby girl, Jane.

We were still hunting for a house at this time, not easy as there was so little building of new houses being carried out, but eventually we found some houses being constructed in Abingdon, they would be completed in spring 1967, and one of these houses became our first home. This was a semi-detached house, with a sitting room, dining room, kitchen, three bedrooms, a bathroom and single garage, with a small sloping rear garden.

Saving for the deposit by saving John's wages and staying in the apartment had worked, however, we would still need a mortgage. I knew that my position in the bank meant it was possible for me to have a bank mortgage, so I asked the chief clerk if this would be a possibility, amazingly the answer was yes, a minimum deposit of 10% and the property was to be in joint names, a percentage rate of 2.5%, on a repayment basis over 20 years.

In the present day, this would be seen as a normal situation, a woman being on the title deeds of a property and named on a mortgage but I was only able to be on the mortgage as it was in joint names, with John acting as a male guarantor, it wasn't for another 8 years, in 1975, with the Sex Discrimination Act that women didn't have to have a male guarantor when applying for a mortgage or credit card and women had to be served equally at banks, this act also meant that women could finally open a bank account in their name and banks had to treat women equally, also women could finally own property in their own name, incredible when you think about this and being only 50 years ago.

Nowadays, women don't even think about anything holding them back in relation to having a bank account, credit card and mortgage, and thankfully this is the case. The application we completed swiftly, and some of the people working on the application were shocked, as they discovered how much John's salary was, even more shocking when the amount of deposit was noted more than 25% of the purchase price. We were on the property ladder and all the saving and eating of minced beef had worked, we were beyond happy, we both had a home, were not dependant on anybody and were secure.

The bank officials inspected and valued the property, with no charge (today you would need to pay for a survey) even better and all we needed was a solicitor, oh yes and some furniture.

So, the hunt for furniture began and in the autumn of 1966, we travelled up to the Design Centre in London, to see a furniture exhibition. We found the furniture we both liked, and it was all made by a factory in Nottingham. As no orders were taken at the exhibition, we needed to visit the manufacturers and place the order.

We both took a day off work and went up to Nottingham and placed an order, which consisted of a three-piece suite, settee and two armchairs, a round teak table, six chairs and a sideboard, bedroom furniture and chair and yes, I still have most of it here at my current house in the 21st century.

In the 1960s, all purchases of furniture were bought to last, the thought of regularly replacing it to keep up with modern interior design trends was not even remotely possible. There was no such thing as the company DFS, for example, flat pack furniture and self-assembly were unheard-of, it was purchase it new, as we did at the manufacturers, or buy it second-hand, as most people did or hand-me-downs.

1967 New Year's Eve, we went to a party hosted by one of the cricketers and his wife, a great time was had by all, and we welcomed the New Year in the time-honoured manner. To my surprise, one of the cricketers' wives, Sue, took me to one side and asked if we would consider going on holiday with them that year, this was 1967, we had talked about our holidays driving to Spain with them, and they said they also would like to do that type of holiday. I simply said I would talk to John and let her know, and judging by the reaction of several other wives who were there, this was not going to be a foursome.

At that time, in the late 1960s, a new kind of vacationing was emerging, booking a villa, rather than a hotel. This appealed to John, but his only concern was that it would be less of a rest for me, as it would mean I would be cooking, cleaning and washing. At the time, I thought there was no harm in trying this idea, let's give it a go.

So, I telephoned the inland revenue, the next day, where Sue (the cricketers' wife), worked and she sprang into action, organising a get together the following Saturday at her home.

I was right, there were four couples in attendance. We made the decision to return to Calafel as we knew the area well, we would travel in two cars, this left just the dates to agree. Sue just loved to organise things, taking into account everyone's doubts and aspirations. Organise it she did, and I was delighted to discover maid service had been included.

Being able to continue to live in the apartment, once we had bought our first house, made the move much simpler, as we were able to have the carpets laid in the new house before we moved and the furniture delivered and put in place, as well as the refrigerator and cooking stove all connected.

We took the decision to order new bed linen and blankets, as we were still using the ones that I had bought in the market all those years ago and as we were at work we had these delivered to John's parents' house, this obviously caused another episode of her being upset but this was to be expected, as the blankets were thick and satin bound, my mother-in-law could see, once again what life could have been like for her, when they moved in the future we made sure she had new bed linen and blankets.

The last thing to do was put the bathroom cabinet up and we were ready to move in. Sunday saw us ferrying our personal belongings from the apartment with a visit to the supermarket to stock up for the week. Oh my, we were tired, and going upstairs to make the bed and hang the curtains, to our absolute dismay, we discovered that we had forgotten about curtain rails; whoops, back to the war years and we stuck newspaper on the window frames, not exactly blackout but sufficient for privacy—not that we noticed, as we just fell into bed.

The next day we started our new, daily work routine, up very early and at the same time, with John then dropping me off at a bus stop on the edge of the city and me journeying into the city by bus to start my day with coffee in the covered market and an early start at work. It was a revelation as to how much I could get done in an hour with no interruptions.

We discovered that buying a new house had its problems, some self-inflicted like no curtain rails, and others far more difficult to deal with. The driveway leading to the garage was two paths of concrete, not a problem one would have thought, but the curve was so tight that the car could not be driven into the garage, as the angles were all wrong. We had to call the builders in, and the driveway was promptly ripped out and replaced, with the rubble stacked in the back garden. I was a bit shocked when arriving home one day to find the pile of rubble all over the back garden, not John though, and he proudly stated, "I am going to build a rockery with steps going down to a lawned area, with trees and a small flower bed."

Rather you than me, I thought, but this was the time I discovered my husband was a keen gardener, he loved pottering about and found it relaxing.

One spring weekend, I had my orders, "Off you go for the weekend, go see your family or something!"

He had organised for a large group of his friends to spend the weekend building the rockery, levelling the soil ready to seed the lawn, planting rose trees and a rotary line base inserted. I came home and I remember being completely amazed.

The next-door neighbours had been involved, keeping all the workers supplied with tea and beer. The Saturday evening had been spent next door, where they all had food and a few games of cards, a good time was had, and this became a regular occurrence. John had done all this for me, to say thank you for all the good times we had shared, I was very happy.

Vacation time came around again, all packed and ready to go, with two cars and four adults in each. Luckily, there were five people able to drive, so we shared the long drive. We stopped for the night at a typically French hotel and the others were somewhat shocked at the toilet facilities, as in France it was still a hole in the ground with a place for one's feet either side, for women, in those days.

For the men, it was no problem, but there were quite a few squeals from the women, as peeing over a hole does take some getting used to. I remember John finding this very enjoyable and laughing. The next day was very long and arduous, with not everyone enjoying the changing scenery or driving into the mountains, especially. We arrived at our destination that evening, the atmosphere of the seaside town embracing everyone, calming anxiety, and fatigue.

During the day, everyone went off to look at local interests and different areas. Unfortunately for us, this was where the difficulty of not having our own car became obvious, since John and I were unable to explore with a baguette, fruit and cheese for our midday meal, in the back of the car like we were used to. We were unable to travel into the mountains and experience the incredible views of the road we had travelled, curling back around the mountain side, with the hairpin bends and almost leaning over the side of the road, not something the other members of the party wanted to do.

It seemed sitting in the bars on the beach during the day and eating out in the local taverns at night was their enjoyment, much less adventurous. So, in the future, our precious, annual two-week vacation became more focused on what we liked and enjoyed, it was a lesson well learnt, the time was not something to be taken for granted.

Did we enjoy ourselves? Of course, we did. We had early morning strolls to watch the sunrise, with a cup of coffee in the little tavernas, walking along the water's edge. We adapted to the needs of the others by sitting around a swimming pool rather than on the beach, with the other wives sitting watching John swimming and diving, as a tall slim athletic man he was in good shape and they used to discuss how to get their own men to shape up, this used to make me smile.

It was an enjoyable two weeks with friends, helping them navigate a holiday abroad, with all of them travelling abroad for the first time. They left Spain with their lives altered by those two weeks. In the future, one couple was to retire early and move to France, one couple never to venture abroad again, and the other starting a family nine months later. As for us, these precious holiday times had started to evolve, with adventure and exploration at the centre and would continue to do so well into our retirement.

October came around and brought with it a letter from my mother, her sister Gladys had passed away, my mother would like to go to her funeral and would I go with her. As the funeral was to be held in Tring, not too far from my home, I agreed to go and took a day off work. As John was away at the motor show, this made it even more straightforward. My mother met me at work, in Oxford, and we travelled home to our house in Abingdon, on the bus together.

Our new home surprised my mother, and to this day I have no idea what she had been expecting. The following morning saw the two of us travelling to Tring by bus and train, arriving at my cousin Mary's house in plenty of time for the funeral. My cousin Mary's sister Marjorie was there, together with her husband and family, having travelled down from Manchester. The funeral was a quiet affair, I remember thinking how small my aunt's coffin was, as she had been a large lady.

This was a sad time for my mother, but this sadness was offset by Marjorie's youngest still being a small baby, my mother did after all love babies. She had to burp the little one, after feeding him, and the baby promptly regurgitated the baby milk all over mother. The journey home, with mother deep in her memories and me nauseated at the smell of baby sick.

That winter, we continued with our love of the theatre and went off to the Prince of Wales Theatre to see Juliet Prowse in Sweet Charity, which was an incredible show.

Christmas lunch continued to be at John's parents, to avoid upset, with us on our way home before the Queen's speech, as always. The difficulties encountered in their marriage in relation to money had settled down, having a job to go to several days a week helped his mother greatly, as it meant she had friends, a purpose and spending money for herself. Although she seemed to resent our home and lifestyle still.

Our lives continued to be busy with us both working full-time, John travelling with his work, playing cricket and golf, gardening in the evenings, card evenings with the neighbours, playing cribbage for pennies and eating out at local restaurants, happy together, as always.

Life was not boring or humdrum, a simple lifestyle that included everything we needed. We were still taking long walks in the autumn evenings, as this was a time for reflection and contemplation over the future, as well as discussing all manner of events going on in the world.

New Year's Eve that year, we spent with our next-door neighbours playing cards for pennies, unfortunately I have always been very competitive when it comes to card games, scrabble, monopoly etc and admit to avoiding them, if possible, this competitiveness probably comes from playing with my brothers all those years ago, they were expert cheaters.

But not this New Year as my husband egged me on, yes, I won. John loved it. "Never seen that side of you before, scamp. Remind me not to play Blackjack with you." So much fun.

Johns: Uncle Cyril and Aunt Addie's youngest daughter Lynda returned from America, in January, as she was getting married to an American also called John. Her wedding plans were going very smoothly, except there was no best man, as John was an American, and his friends couldn't make the wedding. Lynda came to see us to ask John to be best man at her wedding.

After the wedding, they went back to America to begin their married lives, although they didn't stay there once, they had children, as they wanted the children to have dual nationality, so ended up settling in Reading but with John continuing to work in America, to maintain his citizenship and look after the home they had there in Fort Lauderdale.

Life settled into a steady rhythm, my work busy and enjoyable, meeting people every day, helping with their needs, listening to the stories of their lives, working with my friends, many of them now married and starting families, new employees to help train and become part of this amazing group of people.

One young member who had been at the bank several years, and whose wedding dress I had made, became pregnant with her first child, this brought such obvious happiness and pride, but these feelings were dashed with the baby being stillborn.

The obvious total devastation she felt, opened my eyes to the loss of my sister Christine, all those years ago, and the pain my mother must have felt. Giving me a clearer understanding of her need to travel with my father to New York on The Queen Mary, following Christine's death.

Our holiday in 1968 was once again travelling by road to Spain, just us two this time and taking an apartment in Denia, which was further south than we had previously ventured. Once again, we had our early morning strolls, venturing into the central area of Spain which was so arid.

We also discovered that the further south we travelled, the roads became flatter and much to John's disappointment, here there were no mountain roads clinging to the mountain side. Denia is a port city on the Spanish eastern coast, full of history, the Moorish castle overlooking the city, it was once a Roman port, and Mount Montgo looms in the background, a very interesting spot, and we had a wonderful two weeks exploring this area.

John was working in the sales department of Pressed Steel Fisher, still, visiting France, Germany and Sweden on several occasions. We used to talk of the different approach these countries had to car manufacturing, with the contrast with the way British cars were made, striking. Pressed Steel Fisher made body parts for vehicles, which were then shipped across to the car assembly plant.

It was in the assembly of the cars that the contrast was so vivid. Pressed Steel Fisher still had plenty of work making tools for other companies, so John was not too worried at this time, but he did not forget what he had seen, and it started the seed of concern about the future of the British car industry.

That autumn and our theatre trip saw us visiting Drury Lane, in London, to watch Ginger Rogers in Mame. What a privilege, a mega Hollywood Star. I kept the programme for many years to come.

Christmas was, again spent with his parents, this ritual, although was beginning to wear thin. New Year's Eve again saw us with the next-door neighbours, nibbles, wine, chocolates and cribbage. Not as competitive as usual as I had a very small glass of wine. I was a funny drunk, hilarious according to my husband, and as I only needed half a glass to push me over the edge, a cheap date. Everyone was in tears of laughter, as I was, quickly, fast asleep on his shoulder.

Spring 1969 and life continued in its pleasant way, eating out occasionally, meeting friends, although the group was much smaller now, with most of the couples having had families, which changed their lives, as babysitters had to be organised and going out planned, meaning it was no longer spontaneous.

People dropping in to say hello, no longer easy for them, the women unable to meet for coffee, or shopping expeditions. Life evolves and families become all-consuming.

John and I were still happy with our life, work taking up a large part of our lives, with sport and walking. Although I noticed John becoming more introverted, quiet. Still himself, still great fun to be with but more subdued. His father, due to retire in 18 months, had booked to go to Spain for the last time in July and his mother had already retired, being 61, so they weren't a worry.

We had lunch at the golf club to celebrate John's thirty-fifth birthday, and it was time to ask what was bothering him, his response as always was one of deep consideration, talking of how what he was considering would impact on my life, my career, my freedom, every aspect of the life I had built since branching out on my own, our annual holiday would change beyond recognition.

My reply was whatever it is, I will make the decision, I knew this could be only one thing, he wanted a family. Had I considered this well, no, after being the eldest female in a large family, babies were the last thing I was thinking about.

This was a massive step to take, I would need to really consider this, at the time I was a bit shocked, which shows how selfish I had become. I told John, let me think about this, please, let's carry on as usual for the time being.

We continued to book a holiday for September, no matter what the decision, we would fit this in. Somehow, I knew that the decision about having a family had already been made by John and it was what he wanted, so this was up to me.

Thinking time for me, did I want children, as such, not really, did I want John's children, that was a different thing altogether, did I want our children, that was an easy decision, and it was a definite yes. My main concern became that we had to have two, there was no way we were having one child and no way we were having more than two and most importantly, should we be lucky enough to have a daughter, she would be given equal opportunities as men in all things, especially education.

My other thought was, income, how would we manage? My salary had been going into the mortgage account, luckily John's income was more than sufficient to cover our needs, after all, with us putting down a large deposit, the house was almost paid for and very reasonable to run. My only doubt, the complete change in my life, the interaction with customers, colleagues and friends would disappear overnight.

If I thought John was quiet and preoccupied, it was nothing to my own deliberation. Sometimes too much thinking is not a good thing and sitting in the garden next to the rose bushes, planted for my enjoyment a few years before, the answer was simple, this incredible man who asked so little of life, who gave so much, simply asking me to start a family with him, I walked inside and said, "How do you fancy being a daddy next spring?"

A few days later, I was in the supermarket, walking along the washing detergent aisle when a wave of nausea hit me. Baby number one on its way. Just smells setting my stomach in a spin at this point. John took one look at me that evening, what is it, you are going to be a daddy, that's all I can say as I threw up.

Early in August, we travelled to London to meet his parents at the train station, his father was dressed in an old pair of shorts, kept up by a belt around his waist and an old shirt of John's, his mother in trousers and the inevitable woollen cardigan, John just stared and later stated to me "she is bandy, her legs are bowed, please tell her never to wear trousers again." What a sight.

The summer passed with warm evenings, with us just talking and hoping that my early feeling of being pregnant was correct, we agreed that the burden of being an only child, still formed a part of his life and if possible, we would have two. I was feeling nausea all day long was making life a bit difficult, and my appetite had disappeared, I thought, so be it this morning sickness is supposed to be a phase.

Holiday that year was off to La Manga in Spain, to a hotel right on the beach, flying this time as driving would take up at least 5 days. It was a wonderful hotel, a holiday of rest and lazy sunny days. Unfortunately, the sickness was becoming worse, and I was unable to keep solid food down and survived on drinking peach juice and water. John was very worried.

September came around and so did the confirmation that a baby was on its way, due in May of 1970, John was over the moon with delight, I was so very happy to see how much this meant to him, I just had to sort the sickness out. John told his parents when we went for Sunday tea, that week. Did we get the usual response, congratulations, not really, a simple "we have waited a long time for this."

*No surprise there then,* I thought. I tried to eat my tea, but it was no good. Off to the toilet I rushed. John's mother asked if she could make baby clothes, would I mind?

"Carry on," I replied.

The talk was all about the baby being a grandson, they were back in the dark ages of male descendants and the importance of the first born being a male. We left early, with my morning (all day) sickness a good excuse.

The visits for pregnancy check-ups were positive, the baby was just fine. Myself, not so fine you would think, somehow, I seemed to be strong enough for the first four months, controlling the nausea as best I could by not eating solids during the day, just drinking milk and orange juice together with iron supplements. Trying to eat dinner at night just the way of things.

Come January 1970, I had to give up work, my concentration levels were very low, John was very relieved, he had been a worried man, well, it cannot have been much fun watching your wife struggle so much. So, my working life, as I had known it, was over, baby making taking precedence, and I spent a lot of time sleeping and making cot blankets, etc.

I did find the isolation difficult, as there were no libraries or shops close by and there was little I could do at the time, but something we needed to address when the baby years were over. The thing I had learnt from being part of a large family was that the baby years were very short, and little children with minds and personalities of their own are interesting. My working life may have been on hold, but the coming years would be much more fulfilling, just four months of sickness to go, we three would survive.

The baby was lively, John's face was a picture, when the first kick caught him in the stomach, when he hugged me on getting home from work. Cuddling us both became a big part of his day after that. April came and went; no holiday plans were made as the baby would be too young. Early in May, and we had a sudden burst of warm weather, surprisingly, I was full of energy, I spent my time sitting in the garden chatting to the neighbours and the sickness had abated. I was finally feeling well for the first time in many months, with John coming home to his favourite dinner, laughing, I can only just get my arms round you two.

A thunderstorm blew in and unsurprisingly, my waters broke, off to the hospital we went. It was a busy night in the maternity ward, as thunderstorms and baby arrivals seem to go together. Our son was born in the early hours of the morning, John was there helping the midwives; I was busy panting about and with the baby, giving me a final kick, he emerged. John held him whilst he was still attached to his umbilical cord. The baby seemed a bit blue, I noted, but then he yelled, and boy, we discovered, he had a good pair of lungs.

Sleeping restfully at last, with no early morning baby jumping about, I was woken by activity on the ward, babies being brought from the nursery for their first feed, breast feeding is not for the faint hearted, it seemed but I was lucky and with one small tummy full and one spread eagled little boy, my son was so cute. It was then time for mums to be checked up on, luckily, I had had a natural birth, so no stitching or invasive devices, so I got to enjoy my days of being pampered, this was the nursing staff's message.

John arrived mid-morning with flowers and chocolates and a big grin on his face. "You OK, scamp." Immediately he picked up his baby boy, stating "what do I do?" as a little fist grabbed his finger, "Just enjoy holding him, obviously he likes to be held."

A strong bond already formed at his birth, father and son happy together. With John walking up and down with the baby in his arms, I asked what he had been doing, he had just gone home and crashed out, and he planned to go and tell his parents that afternoon. In those days, there were strict rules on the maternity ward, husbands were only allowed to visit in the first 24 hours. The baby became squirmy and fidgety, it was feed time, John immediately handed him back to me.

Off he went to tell his parents and telephone mine. I hoped this breastfeeding settled down. The following day was Friday, and the ward was closed for visitors, other than for husbands again, as more babies had arrived during the night. My parents had travelled to see us, on that day, but were not allowed on the ward, the nurses showed them their grandson, which seemed enough for them, a healthy boy. I was to let them know when we were due to go home, and mother would come and look after us.

With evening and visiting time almost over, John arrived with a magazine for me to read.

"Just in case you are bored, Scamp."

He had already seen our son in the nursery and had called into work telling everyone and into his parents to tell them he would be bringing them on Saturday with his Uncle Cyril and Aunt Addie.

Neither of us mentioned what name he would have as we had discussed this many weeks before. If the baby was a girl, I would name her, and if it was a boy, John would name him. We were just so glad he was a healthy little boy, with a strong pair of lungs.

That Saturday afternoon visiting time, all of us mums were told back into bed, ladies, to leave more room for visitors. As families began to arrive, this all made sense, so many people all admiring babies and chatting away. John walked in and gave me one of his bear hugs, asking how I am, he turned to his son, picking him up.

The mother-in-law sat down on the one chair beside the bed, obviously expecting to hold the baby, but John had other ideas, father and son happy together. John's father and his sister Addie both came out with, you will have to name him after his grandfather of course, Frederick Walter. I was taken aback, it had been a good few days up until that moment, how do I handle this?

One name John and I had decided not to use popped into my head, "I think we will call him Matthew."

Absolute uproar occurred, his uncle's face a picture of horror, you cannot call him that, they went on, John gave me one of his looks, grinning at me, saying, "His name is Duncan Jonathan, a strong name."

Well, everyone was so glad he was not going to be a Matthew, no further argument ensued. To this day I do not know what is wrong with Matthew.

Sunday on the ward and all was quiet, we mums decreed well enough to have our babies with us all day, as we were able to fetch and carry all we needed, clean diapers, water to drink whilst feeding, also being able to bathe and change them.

Having been a big sister, it all came back, and I automatically tested the water temperature with my elbow, I undressed him and low and behold as soon as the cooler air reached him, he peed a good twelve inches into the air, it was just as well I was about to bathe him, into the water he went. One happy little boy, no yelling, just a bit of a splutter when I washed his face.

Monday came and home we went, John being so proud. The carry cot fitted neatly on two dining room chairs, just right for a little boy and his dad, as they spent time together. John was reading his paper and DJ, as he became known, gurgling and inspecting his fingers and anything else which came into reach. Pram toys, mobiles, all manner of things, presents from family, friends, neighbours, all were waiting for his attention. My mother arrived that afternoon and shooed me off to bed, knowing that DJ would let me know when he needed to feed.

This was an important time for me to recover, those nine months of nausea left me very tired. Giving birth was a pretty natural process for me, other women on the ward had a much more difficult time. Mother looked after DJ, cleaned and cooked meals, it was amazing, with the baby getting as much attention as she could give him, she brought me water and cups of tea for the night-time feeds. My, she loved babies.

Saturday came around and with it a delivery, one baby's perambulator, a silver cross, a present from my parents. Mother left to return home a few days later, leaving John and me with our baby son.

Looking after a baby was very time-consuming, and it did not take long for me to realise that a routine was essential or my life or me as a person would fade into obscurity. So as ever I did things my way, up early for a morning feed, into bed with him to spend quality time with his dad, then into his carrycot whilst John and I had breakfast, quickly followed by bath time and his morning snooze, whilst I did the washing and housework.

The afternoons were spent outside in the garden whenever possible, with a full tummy and fresh air sending DJ off for an afternoon nap, whilst I did dinner prep. All this was to enable this little boy and his father to have time together.

My sister Wendy was to marry her fiancé, Mike, in July, of 1970, the sickness had left me quite slim, and my figure soon returned to normal. That amazing husband of mine understood the need for a new dress for this happy occasion, but just how was I to go shopping with a six-week-old baby?

Would need to be between feeds, with John most unwilling for his parents to be involved, I asked my mother to come and stay for a couple of days. With the problem solved, and whilst we were out shopping, my mother advised me to introduce the baby to bottle feeds, her experience and love of babies explaining why, the baby will sleep longer and be less demanding, and I was too thin, having lost weight since she last visited. We bought the necessary equipment and a new dress for me.

Arriving home to a crying baby boy, with his father pacing up and down trying to sooth him. Bottle feeding will make it easier; John could feed him, mother stated. So, breast feeding was over during the coming weeks, and this led to early morning feeds and quality time for father and son and sleep for me.

John's parents were invited to Wendy's wedding, which they accepted. It was a great afternoon as DJ was cuddled and admired by all and sundry. He even slept through the service. At the reception at the village hall though, disaster struck. Everyone was sitting at tables on the edge of the room, with a centre space for dancing. John's mother for some reason spotted a lone chair in a corner and picked it up, bringing it over to a space far from the tables, which were all set and decorated for the occasion.

John had DJ and I think she wanted to have the baby to herself, as so far that day she hadn't had a lot to do with him, crash down she went, the chair was broken hence its banishment to the corner. I went over to help her, not physically hurt thank goodness, but very upset and tore into me, apparently, I was keeping her grandson from her, not coming over for Sunday tea anymore, and a lot more besides, John's father simply lighting up a woodbine, it was obviously down to me again.

My sister came over to see if she could do anything, so I took my mother-in-law by the arm, saying, "Come, and sit here," on a table with four chairs. John came over, "all right, Scamp."

No problem, I explained, but could you ask the kitchen to warm up DJ's bottle, and hand DJ over to your mother, he gave me one of his looks and did as I asked. This would be discussed later. My, but John's parents thought the world should revolve around them, everyone dancing to their tune, a little boy only a few weeks old, enjoying the attention and reaching out to people, safe in his daddy's arms, handed over to two people, just staring at him and given his feed before he was ready for it.

John was angry, I thought it was with me, no, leave her to burp him and hope he regurgitates all over her, worry not, I replied, he will need changing shortly and you will be given him back. Well, I know my son by now, true to form, he needed changing.

After the reception, we dropped his father at his club, and his mother at her home. Little one was in his carrycot in the back of the car, sound asleep like most babies on a car journey. The discussion was straightforward, regarding his mother and her problems. The chair being placed as far away from my family as she could get it, expecting to have DJ all to herself. My method of placating the situation, understood, but not agreed with. This little boy, his son, of whom he is extremely proud, his mother making a scene to get her own way.

Fine, he had every right to be annoyed and maybe I should have walked away and left her to get on with it, or for his father to deal with the situation. Thinking time again, two months of putting ourselves and our family first, selfish, I do not think so, nine solid months of illness and still expected to carry on with the old routine. Did we consider them, of course. John called in to see his mother when he could, but his young family came first.

This discussion continued into the Sunday morning. Once we made our decision, John went to see his parents that afternoon, as it was clearly the time for some straight talking. What was said, I do not know, but something most certainly was, as Sunday tea would be at our home in future. With John fetching them whilst DJ had his afternoon nap. His family came first and that is how it was and how it remained. As always in these situations, there was a downside, and it was my job to prepare the Sunday tea.

John was concerned and looking worried, eventually, during our quiet time together, he told me about it. Since their marriage, John's parents, with his aunt and uncle, went to Brighton each year, to go to the races (Horse races). This was very much the thing to do during the 20s and 30s, ladies dressed up much as they do today. Men in cream cricket flannel trousers held up with a club tie tied around the middle.

John's Uncle Cyril had bought a new motorcar, and his wife wanted to go to the races in it. Well, what's the problem, I asked, only one driver and his uncle was very nervous about such a long journey, there and back in one day. His Uncle would like John, me and his father to accompany him and his wife to the horse races at Glorious Goodwood, with his mother looking after the baby.

How did I feel about this? I was not sure, really, did I want to leave our son with someone other than John or myself, well of course I did not, he was after all only two months old. John was in a pickle, what a situation to have to deal with this was a request from the uncle who had given him that first chance, he owed this man.

Feeling I had little choice really, as if I said no his mother would take to her bed, as she always did, and this would cause us more issues, in the long run and take up more of John's time. So, a compromise had to be made and DJ would have to be looked after by his grandmother, after all, what harm could occur in only a few hours.

As the trip was in a matter of days, I had to get busy to get everything ready for her to be able to look after DJ, as he would need, nappies, clean clothes, should he have an accident and all the other paraphernalia that babies need. I ensured the nappies were in plain sight, the bottles prepared and in the refrigerator.

I nearly forgot, food, I would have to leave lunch for his mother. This was at the same time as doing the normal chores around the house, looking after a small child, taking him to the clinic to be weighed, making dinner, etc. Would there be any point in setting out DJ's normal routine, probably not. John can do that, I thought.

The four of them arrived mid-morning his aunt in silk chiffon and a large hat dressed up to the nines.

I left DJ bathed, fed and sleeping in his pram next to the roses in the garden. I was getting changed and John explained the routine DJ was used to, to his mother. As we left, with John driving his uncle's car, his father laughed, saying to John, "Not sure she listened to a word you said."

"How tactless." I thought as leaving your child for the first time is never going to be easy, that stupid remark did not help but to be expected from the father-in-law. Did I enjoy the races, to some degree, looking at the horses in the paddock was a magnificent sight, so close to them, the races themselves, lasted for only a few minutes, but the actual venue was a delight.

When it came time to leave, having enjoyed the company of John's Uncle and Aunt, John's father was missing. They knew where he would be, at the jellied eels stand under the trees with a group of men, spitting the bones out onto the ground, said it all, I thought.

On the way back, we collected fish and chips for all, great as it meant no cooking. We were soon back home, John went straight in to find DJ, who was decidedly unhappy, making a right racket with his fine pair of lungs. Plates were quickly put out of the cupboard.

"Make yourselves at home," I stated. "I will deal with this young man upstairs and join you shortly."

With a towel on my shoulder, I picked him up, he immediately brought up his painful overfeeding on the towel. He was soon changed and comfortable and

I brought him back to John. Everyone ready for a cuppa, it seemed, so the refrigerator for milk and lo and behold, two bottles of baby milk left, she must have made his formula up herself, not surprising he threw up. *At some point, I would get to eat,* I thought to myself. Oddly enough, my mother-in-law never asked to look after him again. I had done all I could to make it easy for her, but obviously she was not prepared for the demands of looking after a small child.

Did I enjoy being a mother? Yes, I did, adjusting to the enormous change in my life took some time though, my body recovered quite quickly, and my mental state remained positive and relaxed.

When DJ was three months old and already trying to pull himself up to a sitting position, we sat together a little boy sitting on my lap as I turned the pages of women's magazines, looking at the pictures, he was completely fascinated and I learnt about new recipes and cleaning tips, clothes and hairstyles, keeping up-to-date.

Life was good just a couple with a young family.

Christening time came around, the ceremony was to take place at St Michael's in the Northgate, Oxford City, where we were married five years before. My family were out in force, just two brothers and their wives unable to attend. It was a lovely ceremony; our son's love of water making his baptism delightful as he drew in a long breath at the feel of the cool water on his forehead and then gurgled. The reception was at our home, with everyone milling about inside and out in the garden.

Christmas 1970 was celebrated in our home; this would continue each year from now on. John was getting into the mood, holding DJ as we decorated the tree. I sat him on the work surface as I iced the Christmas Cake, putting decorations on the top. I handed the little boy a small robin's breast decoration, thinking he might like to put it on the cake, no, he tried to make it fly after all that is what birds do.

John, laughing and saying, "You're in trouble, mate."

To me that was a wake-up call, time to ditch the magazines and collect books for little ones with pictures and words. Our afternoon tea and book time began. Being a firm believer in nursery rhymes and songs, I had been singing these to DJ for some time, books of animals and birds, cars and carriages with the name written in large letters, and all-important poetry for children.

These were the baby years which I soon came to realise were extremely important in a child's development, as mine had been. His first word was dad, at this age mum is just an extension of themselves providing all that was needed, dad coming home each evening the highlight of this little boy's day, dad was full of fun and games, playing cars on the carpet with him and teaching him how to go up and down the stairs. We purchased a baby bouncer, a harness which was attached to the door frame, DJ was strapped in and bounced up and down with great gurgling laughter.

He was quickly learning to crawl and investigated everything he could get to, Dad showing him how. DJ simply stood up suddenly one evening and looked at his dad with a toothy grin. Nine months old getting ready to walk. Mum was for serious stuff like food and drink, a clean bottom and learning.

DJ's first birthday came around, one cake with one candle. John's parents were brought over by John in his lunch hour. They had no real interaction with DJ, just sat watching his every move as he played with toys. I had tried so hard to understand these two people, so far beyond my comprehension.

This was a quiet period in our life with a simple routine, little boy running around the house, rough and tumbles with his dad and John still playing cricket at the weekends for Abingdon Town Cricket Club.

Late spring was a time of tragedy as, unfortunately, John's Uncle Cyril passed away suddenly. Lynda came back for the funeral, as she broke down as the last time she saw her father was in his coffin, a very unhappy day for all.

We had always said we would have two children, so it quickly became time to complete this family to enable me to get my life back on track. There was no need for any discussion this time, just me hoping for an easier pregnancy. I quickly fell pregnant again, which left John looking a bit smug and it was to be another spring baby.

If I had expected to have an easier time, I would have been disappointed, not the smell of washing detergent this time, just fish (and still fish to this day) The issue with fish arose when we were in the supermarket looking at the fish on display and according to John, I went a pale shade of green. So, it was back on the milk and iron pills, but no oranges this time, just cream crackers and soft cheese triangles (my daughter still loves cheese triangles).

We carried on as normal, as long as we could, with me sleeping a lot more with this pregnancy. John told his parents, one Sunday tea that September, the news being met with stony silence, which was not a surprise to me, as I had begun to realise John and I were expected to duplicate his parents' life and a second child was not part of their plan.

Was I overreacting? I am not sure, but something was odd here, whatever it was would arise at some point, John just ran his fingers through his hair in total exasperation.

Christmas was great fun being the first one when DJ opened his own presents. He had quickly twigged that as soon as the tree decorations appeared, good things were coming. He was car obsessed, so we made him a cardboard road to lay out on the carpet, to drive his cars around on, he spent many happy hours with his car collection. The new baby was kicking happily and so far, all seemed good, just sick again.

January came and one Saturday during a mild spell, John went to play golf. I was carrying DJ down the stairs, chatting as usual to him, and I slipped, damaging my ankle. The pair of us sat on the stairs, not moving, I was waiting for the new baby to move, DJ watching my ankle swell up. John came back around 2.30 to find us sitting there, he was very panicked. We rushed off to the hospital, with the hospital staff immediately stating, "We need to get the leg to be x-rayed."

I calmly replied that I was not sure about that, as I was pregnant, so I was wrapped in large heavy shields around my midriff and the leg was x-rayed. Luckily, it was just badly sprained, but I needed it plastered to keep it immobile, so what commenced was three weeks with my leg in plaster and a pair of crutches to get around, fun and games.

We all survived, but this accident highlighted for John how his life had basically continued as before, and that the children were an enhancement of his life, he needed to make some changes, and that was the end of weekend sport for several years to come.

Soon, the plaster was off, and my leg was as good as new, just a few more weeks of sickness left. The baby clothes were resurrected, and something stirred me to make cot sheets and a quilt cover embroidered with rabbits and spring flowers. The Doctors were more concerned with this pregnancy, as the baby had dropped ready for birth very early, the decision was made to induce labour, which was very convenient, really, and I went into hospital in the morning, and the procedure was carried out.

John went off to collect DJ from a neighbour and take him to his parents. The contractions started just after he left, much to his disgust, "I wanted so much to be there for you scamp."

My reply, "Do not worry, you have not missed much."

I went into the delivery room around three in the afternoon, luckily with John in attendance, this baby is smaller, I said and needs more help from me, as I panted through the contractions. I was right, a little one was delivered directly into John's hands; a small cry and then the two men were checking the baby over, which was so funny, talk about leave me to it.

At last, a more robust cry and John brought the baby to me, it was a little girl who was so small she fitted into her daddy's hands. This was one of the only times, in my life, that I had seen my husband cry. The baby was whisked away, almost immediately, to be monitored by the nursing staff, she was to remain in the unit for twenty-four hours, as she was so small. John went off to get our son and tell both sets of parents, sleep time for me.

The baby was kept in the nursery for 24 hours and I had a good rest, a breast pump provided her with the initial important feed. Come the next afternoon, I held her for the first time, and she immediately settled when held, with the sister in charge telling me she had been restless and crying a lot.

I thought she needed her mum and dad, as she started feeding and was soon full and contentedly cuddled up. John arrived during the evening, after looking after our son all day, apparently DJ had been fine all day, fascinated by a light flurry of snow, which had him transfixed, one baby born during a thunderstorm and the other baby during a snowstorm, obviously they were going to make a mark in life.

DJ was fast asleep when John left, the next-door neighbour was babysitting. John looked at me with his big grin, let me have her then, father and daughter, an enormous bond formed at the time of her birth, a tiny little girl laid in the crook of his arm, fingers grabbing him, one besotted daddy. The little one left with me that evening and during the night, enabling her to feed more or less on demand, her little face had already filled out and a healthy glow to her skin. Her brother had been a big, strong baby, this little one would need a lot of looking after in her first few weeks.

The next afternoon, John's parents arrived on the ward, John stayed outside with DJ, they had been warned that I had a more difficult time with this baby and came in looking very apprehensive. Mother-in-law sat in the chair by the side of my bed, she was asked if they would like a cup of tea, she must have looked worried in reception.

The baby was whisked away to the nursery, once they had seen her, as the nursing staff were very cautious, she was a tiny baby. Tea arrived, and father-in-law comes out. I always wanted a little girl, I would have called call her Ann, I just smiled, with no retort, hardly worth the effort.

Early afternoon next day, John and DJ arrived to take us both home, one little boy running to me and hugging me round the knees, totally ignoring his new sister. The men of the family had enjoyed themselves enormously, out walking and playing around in the snow flurries. Not so sure I appreciated all DJ's soiled diapers waiting in a bucket to be dealt with. John grinning, said, "Glad I don't have to do that anymore."

I lit my pipe up each time, so funny.

This was a long day for a little boy not yet two and he was soon in bed sound asleep. John and I curled together with our little girl in his arms, what are we going to call her, Tracy Michelle, such a lovely small name for a tiny girl. I asked, had you thought of the name Ann?

Answer straight forward, does not suit her at all.

"Totally agree," I said, telling him of my conversation with his father. That is not what he told me, apparently, I ruined his marriage. Just what is it about his parents that they think they could have a say in naming our daughter. So, entitled.

My mother arrived that afternoon and immediately took over, leaving John to entertain DJ. Two am feed, came around and mother and I were helping a little girl with her bodily functions, Joan you need to have these little feet checked out something is wrong, the sooner you see to it the better, she was right, the midwife and mother in deep conversation, it seemed Tracy had been born with clubfeet, a phenomenon, where the feet are not flat and are curled, making walking impossible, if not dealt with.

A referral was made to The Nuffield Orthopaedic Centre when the baby was four weeks old. My mother's love for babies and her knowledge helped this little girl live a normal life, John and I never forgot, what went on in my childhood, paled into insignificance.

So, the little girl had plasters on her feet up to her knees, one incredible physiotherapist who massaged her feet and applied new plasters every week, this continued for the first months of her life, John took her on most of these visits. Tracy was an amazing baby and did not once complain.

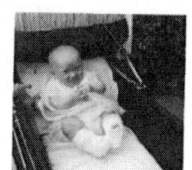

Figure 11: Top left, Duncan outside our first house. Top right: Tracy, Bottom left and right, the rockery John made and the final image is Tracy at 6 months old with her plasters.

Life was full with two little children and arranging the christening for September was fun. The family christening robe covered her little legs encased in plaster casts, as many members of the two families as could made it. Mother had made DJ a denim jacket to go with a pair of navy shorts, he looked very smart, well not for long as he was into everything.

During the early summer, I had noticed a helicopter circling over the fields at the back of the house beyond the stream. Thinking again, what they are doing. How do I access requests for planning permission? With the little ones tucked up for the evening, John and I were talking and discussing our day, when I asked if he knew how to access the planning permission request, after discussing the helicopter circling, he went quiet for a while.

He will ask Peter Roberts, one of the cricketers. It transpired that a request for a housing estate had been lodged with the council, just a preliminary request at this point. Our home was small, and with a growing family, we would need more space, it was time to look elsewhere.

John's contacts once again came to the rescue, two of his old sporting companions had an estate agency in Abingdon, I had to leave this to John as the children needed a lot of my time and attention. One day in October, he came home full of excitement. I had a look at a house in Dorchester-on-Thames today, I have made an appointment for us to view the house on Saturday morning. This was the village I had visited with the school cycling club all those years ago, which made it very exciting.

Saturday came and saw John impatient to be off, this man of mine so eager, we had driven around this small group of houses long before we married, it was an area he aspired to; this is what he had worked for. Was it perfect of course not, did it tick enough boxes, yes, could we afford it, that remained to be seen.

Monday, saw the beginning of a nerve-wracking time, our present house was valued far more than we expected but another mortgage would be required, this was not so simple, as women on mortgages was still not a normal occurrence and finding a financial company to accommodate our requirements proved difficult for a financial advisor working with the estate agents. No matter what, this property would be in joint names, John and I worked as a team, and this was the way it would stay.

My being on our first mortgage with the bank, sorted this out, and an old contact of mine from my banking days contacted me to ask if this mortgage request was for me, sorted, problem over. During all these transactions and people viewing the house, I was too busy to get involved in the financing of the property. Not a problem really, but an illustration of how women were viewed in relation to family and finance. The decision was made to have an interest-only basis mortgage for the lending offset by an endowment policy. Perfect.

However, the life insurance was only taken on John's life, in other words, the family house would be secure in the event of his death, in the event of mine no problem he would still be working, and payments made, just how I would continue to run the house and bring up two children not considered, and in the event of John having to bring up two children on his own, who would pay for childcare, cleaning, after school care, let alone do all the things that keep the family fed and well. How, undervalued women still were, this was 1972.

Early summer 1972, visiting John's parents had become a work of art. My reliance on lists coming to the fore. Two children under three and both in diapers, a baby and all the bits and pieces needed for comfort, a little boy needing toys to entertain himself. Not something to undertake on the spur of the moment. John was busy with bags and a little boy, after unbuckling him from his car seat, watching him run up the garden path. My job unbuckling Tracy and carrying her round to the rear of the house.

Both of his parents sat in the kitchen, John dumped the bags and reached for his little girl. I turned to see what DJ was up to, and heard my father-in-law, telling him that he would always be number one, they would see to it. Enough is enough, I simply said calmly, "You will treat them both the same or you will not see either of them."

John stood there and said, "You heard what my wife said."

Mother-in-Law made tea and we stayed a while.

Children in bed, both of us tired, two tiny children, some looking after, curled up together, we talked of the incident at his parents' house, and I had a surprise as John held me in his big bear hug, saying, welcome back, scamp. Missed you and your feistiness. Motherhood is all-consuming as you raise your small children, this is the danger time when a woman's personality, characteristics and needs can become immersed in the needs of others.

Putting aside time each day, just for myself, I found it very difficult. Sitting down with paper and pen early one morning, I listed exactly what I did with my day, noting how important evenings for John and me were, but still I needed some me time. Time to think, time to be creative, time to plan our lives, John and DJ were early risers, their days starting around 6.30 am, Tracy already showing signs that she would be an early riser. Afternoon activities and both children down for a couple of hours.

This became my me time. Bedtime for them an hour later than had become the norm, more play time with their dad. Just this short time to be by myself each early morning, enabled me to deal with the difficulties we encountered in our lives. Me time is an essential part of any woman's day if only to paint one's toenails.

October was not a good month to put a house on the market, and it was January before a young couple bought our house. No mortgage involved; his parents were involved in the purchase. Come the end of March, we left our first home and arrived at the Dorchester-on-Thames property.

The only key available from the estate agent was for the front door, nothing else to be found. This was strange, and as the removal men started to unload as best they could, we tried to locate the rest of the keys. The woman living in the house adjacent, arrived on her bicycle, so sorry I called into the property last evening and took the keys. Either plain nosy, or thoughtful.

John left to fetch his parents, to show them the house whilst the children and I inspected the garden. A large garden with a wall built in 1759 running along one side, with a gate at the bottom giving access to the lane leading down to the River Thames.

The parents-in-law arrived and stood in the front garden, mother-in-law grabbing DJ by the arm, this must have hurt him, as he squealed and pulled away, running straight across the drive; the man living next door arriving in his car, just missed him. I was no longer exhausted from the early years of motherhood and took command—DJ, inside and find your toys—to my parents-in-law: come inside and we will make a cup of tea.

John helped the removal men complete their tasks and worked with the electrician to install an electric cooker, at this point gas was not available in the village. Cups and kettle in a box together with tea and sugar, milk for the children already for the off. I remember thinking how strange, not a biscuit or cake, nothing, they had come empty handed. Moving day and no help, nothing.

Busy day for all, John took his parents' home and I set about feeding the children and getting them ready for bed. Both tired, no problems there, new rooms, but accepted as they were sleeping in their familiar beds. I had made curtains for most of the rooms, having learnt my lesson with our first home. John was coming back with fish and chips for us.

The next adventure underway.

# Chapter Five
# The Adverse Years

My husband's pride in his new home was a delight to behold. It was in a small close, with only 11 other houses, we had the corner plot, the house had four (well three and a box room) bedrooms, two bathrooms (amazing luxury in comparison to John and my childhoods), an open plan dining room/lounge and a large kitchen, it was an ideal family home and above all light and airy, it was everything we had aspired to and more.

The house was set in an idyllic location, in a pretty village, only a few miles outside Oxford and was surrounded by fields and footpaths, John absolutely loved it and especially the peace and quiet. The property had a garden big enough to keep him busy for literally years to come.

There were several large trees throughout the property, one large weeping willow at the end of the driveway, plus a cherry tree and acacia, but there were no flower beds at this point, no colour whatsoever, in the rear garden, which was huge, there was a herbaceous border the length of the wall, and more trees, three horse chestnuts, a hornbeam and a Scots Pine, with a large lawn for a little boy and girl to run around in, a side gate, which was lockable, so all safe and secure.

John had such a sense of pride in our achievement in purchasing this house, especially as we only needed a small mortgage to buy it and considering both our starts in life, all this we achieved on our own. The village also had a primary school and a couple of useful shops for convenience. Ladders were quickly brought out and he proceeded to repair window frames, repaint them and then fixed the rendering. To put it in a nutshell, sorted the outside before even considering the inside. Looking after his family.

Tracy's plasters were removed for good in April 1973, just after her first birthday, and John had her crawling on the floor, much to her delight and her brother's disgust as she played with his cars, up and down the stairs. Her favourite place to rest was on the rug in the hall, in front of the door, which had glass panels so made it a very warm spot. We set up the baby bouncer in the door between the dining room and kitchen, and she was a happy little girl, using her legs at last. She continued to have check-ups, when she was older, but the plasters had straightened her feet and she had no need for further intervention, which was such a relief to John and I.

Figure 12: John's pride and joy, the house and garden in Dorchester

Duncan was a very lively toddler, and it became evident that it was time for him to go to playgroup and interact with other kids and also so his sister could have some time with Mum, so I started looking at opportunities for him to release that energy. That Easter break we celebrated with an Easter egg hunt in the garden, Tracy with her dad pointing and telling him where to go get an egg she had seen, a little girl with a huge personality.

The grandparents watched on, I think they enjoyed themselves, but as always it was difficult to tell as they just sat and watched. John had a good time with his two children, this man was such fun to live with, life was good.

DJ was three in May that year, so off to playgroup he went, such a relief, as he was very attention seeking and struggled with sharing my time with his sister, there was a small weekly charge, but it was worth every penny, for a multitude of reasons. At the playgroup, I met many of the other young mothers who lived locally and in some of the villages nearby, this was great as it meant my life began to expand again, finally.

I had enjoyed the last few years of looking after the children as babies, but it was all encompassing and wholly focused on them and their needs and not much for me, especially with a baby who couldn't move due to her plasters and also had needed weekly hospital trips. I was also no longer tied to the house, as the children were older and I was able to walk out in the fields with them, looking at birds and flowers together. In the afternoons, after DJ had had a nap, being tired from playgroup, we would make rock buns together, at around 3:30 pm.

The other children living in the close soon got to realise what was going on, and as it would help my two learn to share, one evening, leaving the children with John, I called on the other mothers asking if it was alright for their children to come and eat rock cakes in the afternoons.

*Well,* I thought at the time, *you have to think of likes, dislikes and allergies.* The mothers had no problem with the idea and most afternoons, from then onwards, found a group of small people in my kitchen or on the front lawn, which helped with my children's, DJs especially, ability to share.

This is the time I began to understand just how intelligent my daughter had the potential to be. Terry towelling diapers, with plastic pants used to be very warm and uncomfortable, a hindrance to a little girl just learning to walk on her own, one hot afternoon I put her into knickers for the first time whilst playing in the garden. Nature being what it is, she wet herself, she didn't cry, but just a look at me and uttered one word, nasty, from then onwards she went on the potty. So, at 15 months old, she had potty trained herself, diaper life over for both of us, hooray.

As I waited to collect DJ at playgroup, I met one of the other mums, called Dawn, and we started talking about schooling, she had four children and her eldest two were primary school age, so had started at the local village primary school. Dawn and her husband had recently moved into the village, having returned from Australia, they were very worried about their eldest two, James and Justine, who had started at the local primary school.

It seemed all the children were taught in one room, Second World War style, when there was a shortage of teachers, and all age groups taught together. After the children were in bed, by 6.30 pm as normal, both very tired after a long day, John and I talked over dinner, both of us horrified at the local village school education that seemed to be being offered.

John was especially concerned considering his own educational experience and how hard it had been for him to catch up, having to go to night school and spend an extra year at school, as I had such a positive educational experience, I was more aware of what school could offer and wanted this for the children. As always, a joint decision, and we started by deciding to check the information that Dawn had given us and form a plan. Everything about the house move had been such a success, so neither of us had expected this old-fashioned education system.

The information Dawn had given us turned out to be absolutely correct. Dawn and Nick, her husband, an ENT specialist at a local hospital, at the time, took their eldest son and daughter away from the village school and enrolled them at a private primary school in Oxford, called Greycotes school. We had more time to think about this school, as an alternative option, as our two children were so much younger but for John there was no alternative, he couldn't let his children struggle like he had.

I wanted the same sort of education for our children that I had, so we set about putting a plan together, firstly to find out all the details of this school, fees for example and above all I would need be able to transport the children to and from school.

John loved to tease me, aggravating me until I reacted, this was a source of great merriment to him through our entire relationship, not sure about me. One day, after we had discussed this school as an option for the children, he calmly tells me, yes we will send DJ to this school, that's for definite, this was like red rag to a bull and react I did, stamping my feet and telling him, very clearly that both of them will go to this school and that no matter what our daughter will have the same opportunities as her brother, no matter what it takes, I will simply go back to work to pay for it.

I received a bear hug from this man of mine, wonderful scamp. Of course, she gets the same chance, look at what we have achieved together, and a lot of this is down to you. Appreciation at last.

My mother came to visit in late summer of 1973, that year, somehow this visit didn't make her happy and she seemed sad, at the time I thought that our new home and large garden upset her, because she hadn't had anything like this in her life but looking back now I realise what it was that first attracted me to this house, the garden, it was very much like my grandparents' home in Gosport, visiting must have been difficult for her as contact with my parents changed at this point, to birthday and Christmas cards only.

That year my Christmas and birthday presents were rolled into one with the arrival of a white mini, John had addressed the transport situation immediately by buying us a second car and car seats arrived for both children. I had transport, which was to prove to be one of the most important changes in my life, as it gave me the freedom I needed from living in a village.

I had started to learn to drive before DJ was born but failed my first test, the examiner being very concerned about my pregnancy. After Tracy was born, I attempted the driving test again and passed on my third time, so it all came together.

This was to be an exciting Christmas, as it was the first in our new home, we had a small tree in the hall, but a second Christmas tree, a much bigger one, in the lounge. We had great fun and games with the children as we crafted a snow man from boxes and tissues, there was glue everywhere and also hung homemade decorations everywhere.

Peter and Susan sent the children Christmas tree decorations, a small gold coloured baby angel for Tracy and Father Christmas riding his sleigh for DJ. (on John's passing many years later Tracy put her angel in his coffin with him) That Christmas morning, the parents-in-law were collected by John and the children, whilst I warmed up mince pies and prepared vegetables. Once they had arrived, we started opening presents and soon there was paper everywhere and two very happy children. Then the game playing began, with John on the floor with both the children, with his bemused parents watching, leaving me to cook Christmas lunch.

I thought to myself, at the time, I must be doing something wrong, not once had John's mother offered to help, I laughed and thought I must make it look too easy. Well, anyone who has cooked Christmas lunch knows the truth about that! It's a marathon. New Year's Eve that year we did not celebrate as we were both too tired.

It was soon January 1974 and playgroup resumed, I would drop DJ off and return home with Tracy, she was a very chatty little girl, always full of question's as we turned pages of books, with a little finger pointing at pictures to hear about the subject, curling into me sucking her two middle fingers as we read nursery rhymes and children's poems, these were precious times before her brother returned.

Later that January, the young woman running the playgroup called around to the house, about mid-morning, she asked if I would please come and help at the playgroup, as her assistant was ill. It didn't take me long to make a decision and I stated "of course, no problem!" I quickly put Tracy into the pushchair and away we went.

This became a permanent situation, being the playgroup assistant and was something I really enjoyed, as I was out of the house and using my organisational skills. There was no pay for my time but both children went to playgroup five days a week and we didn't pay any fees. Eventually I took over the running of the playgroup and this was something I did until Tracy started full-time school, in September 1976.

Following Tracy starting school, my time running the playgroup came to an end, which was a good thing, times were changing, and playgroups became nurseries and preschool classes, with a lot of rules and regulations, which was something I was not qualified for.

I reflect on those years running the playgroup and the cost of childcare today and think how simple playgroup was, we mothers all came together to provide childcare for the children of the village, each doing shifts on days when we didn't work, it was so simple and of huge benefit to the mothers, as well as the children, I wonder if bureaucracy has got in the way in the modern version of childcare, after all the children didn't suffer.

So, I was now home alone, with just the school run and the domestic chores. John, that caring man, understood that I needed an outlet from domesticity and childcare and suggested I find a Saturday job, he would look after the children each Saturday. I thought great and quickly found myself a job working in the cash office of a department store in Oxford, this was using my finance skills again, but on a much smaller scale.

This was a good time for me, time to meet new people, talk of life not just children, and use my brain and skills that I had learnt from the bank. It transpired that two other women, who lived locally, worked Saturdays in Oxford and so we formed a car sharing trip each week, which was great fun.

John cooking food for the children each Saturday had them in stitches at times but also in horror at other times, one time he cooked them liver and onions, well it turned out to be like lumps of coal! I remember that John was quite irate as Tracy refused to eat her dried burnt offering. We were simply just a normal happy family at that time, with the two children at school enjoying a rounded education just as I had.

The school we had chosen was a pre-preparatory school which educated boys to the age of 7 and girls to 11. This meant DJ would have to change schools in 1977, and we chose a small preparatory school, near the RAF base where John had finished his national service, where he had seen the children playing sports all those years ago, it had left an impression on him.

We had to make changes to the school runs when DJ started in September 1977, as DJ had to start school at eight in the morning, John would drop him off on his way to work and collect him in the evenings after the school day, which included time in the late afternoon to do homework, called prep. I took Tracy in the mornings and collected her in the afternoons, so it all worked out and our lives together were close and happy.

What could possibly go wrong.

The 1970s was a time of great hardship for many, with soaring interest rates and years of deep social unrest and blackouts as electricity supplies failed. Our years of working together and securing our home gave us a buffer against the financial difficulties which arose.

Luckily, our mortgage was small, and the increased payments were manageable but the cost of running a home grew, with the price of energy high and cost of food high, and we had school fees to pay, it was much worse than the cost-of-living crisis today, as inflation hit 8.8% in 1973 and by the end of the decade was at 12%, peaking at 14% in 1980. My experience in those formative years during and after the war helped me to improvise and feed the family well on little money, I made everything myself, including bread, and John took on an allotment, which I helped with by weeding and watering the produce.

We invested in a large chest freezer, and this enabled the harvested fruit and vegetables from the allotment to be frozen and stored and also helped as we were able to buy things like meat in bulk. Mushrooms, which grew on a field at the back of the house, I foraged, which I found an enjoyable pastime.

A big area of concern was our reliance upon electricity for cooking and heating the house, the boiler was oil fired, but electricity was needed to ignite and control it. Electricity was mostly made by coal-powered factories at the time, and in the 1970s, the government entered into a battle with the miner unions, over pay and conditions.

In 1972, the miners went on strike for 6 weeks, which led to a small pay rise but in 1973, they went on an overtime ban which led the government to impose a three-day week, with the aim to conserve coal stocks, TV companies were ordered to stop broadcasting at 10:30 pm, and people were told to heat only one room and keep non-essential lights off.

This led to a state of emergency in the country as thousands of people were made unemployed and, in some pubs, people had to drink by candlelight and in shops workers used headtorches. This triggered the high inflation and the unrest continued, with power cuts still occurring in 1977. In response to this electricity unreliability, and with such a young family, we installed a wood burning stove in the lounge which heated the whole house.

John had great fun foraging for wood in the coppices around the fields, behind the house. It was amazing what one can achieve with a partner like I had. We saved a fortune, and we were always warm. We continued to have a log burner and use it all the time, well into our 80s, but had the logs delivered.

Retirement age in the 1970s for women was 60 years old, my parents-in-law received old age pension payments from the state, not a large amount, but enough to live on. I was surprised when John's mother gave up her afternoon job when her pension commenced, as she really enjoyed it, she gave no real reason, but unfortunately, this brought a recurrence of her unhappiness, with her taking to her bed. John was asked to call in and talk to her by his father, who was also in a bit of a state.

It seemed that their neighbours who had been living in the close for many years, as had my in-laws, were moving away to live with family or to homes for the elderly. This meant changing times, in the area of Oxford they lived in,

Cowley, new neighbours arrived from very different ethnic backgrounds and culture to them, the smell of curry cooking floating in the air, dogs barking all day, young children kicking balls into their garden, noisy chatter as they gathered together and spoke in a different language, this was more than my mother-in-law could cope with.

This once quiet oasis to the east of Oxford City had become part of the sprawling housing developments that occurred after the war, the influx of people with different ways of living, drove the original population to move to pastures new. Cowley is today a thriving part of Oxford, an area that celebrates social diversity and has undergone a great rejuvenation.

Also, they were complaining that as winter was drawing in, their house was cold, the kitchen very cold first thing in the morning, and neither of them was able to do the grass cutting and weeding.

John came home and we needed to have a discussion, once the children were in bed.

*Just what was this litany about,* I thought, *what were they asking?* They obviously wanted to leave the close in which they had lived for many years, what had sent the mother-in-law to her bed, there must be more to this, we needed to discuss some more.

So, we quickly organised an afternoon discussion with the parents-in-law, it transpired that they wanted to move but could not face selling and buying another property at the same time, with all the stress this can cause. They had been looking at properties for sale in the local paper and had not yet seen anything that suited. My mother-in-law presented as deeply upset and highly agitated.

In the end, I had to step in and ask the question, what is it that they would like to do? Father-in-law replied that they would like to sell the house they currently lived in and move in with us and the children whilst they looked for another property, I was not at all surprised by this request.

John and I talked long and hard about this situation, the impact on our lives would be huge, but he was very worried about his mother, and I wished I understood her deep neediness. In the end, there was no alternative, as the situation deteriorated over the next few weeks, and the mothers-in-law's mental health deteriorated further. The parents-in-law's house went on the market at just about the worst time ever to try and sell a house, as we were in the 1970s and inflation was huge and mortgage interest rates high, so buyers were rare, and it was not wise to try and sell a property empty.

With the decision made that they would come and live with us until a new property was found, it galvanised my mother-in-law into action, and she quickly cleared the house. The property sold a few months later at a much-reduced purchase price, which would bring its own set of problems.

So, in 1977, we adjusted to the in-laws moving in and living with us but it was not easy. Firstly, the two children had to share a bedroom with bunk beds, they were happy enough, as they both had busy lives and were ready for bed at the usual time but the full extent of the impact was felt by John and myself, as his mother tried to return to the days when he lived at home, with her and the similar routines. This put a huge amount of pressure on John's time, and the time he spent with his children really upset her, she began demanding his attention as soon as he returned from work.

I noted him managing the situation by escaping to take a shower each evening, so did the children, they knew what to do and joined him, to chat before bedtime. Eventually it all became too much, and he had to tell her that his wife and family came first, life could never revert to the way it was, when he was younger and lived at home, with her.

For me, the change was huge, first thing came the dictating, the mother-in-law did not want to cook the evening meals, which really meant she did not want to do any cooking at all, the ironing was also vetoed as the electric iron frightened her. In other words, they both expected to be looked after, this took some getting used to, with the weeks drawing into months and as far as I could make out, not a lot of effort towards finding a new property.

One winter morning after dropping Tracy at school, I went out walking to Wittenham Clumps (a historical old Roman fort, which is now just a hill and popular with hikers) giving myself thinking time and that all-important me-time. I tried to look at the broader picture of the life we were now all leading, to say John was angry and frustrated was putting it mildly, his family time was gone during the week and at the weekend.

On Saturdays, he was expected to drive his father into the Liberal Club in Oxford and return late in the evening to collect him and his mother as ever very demanding, all this responsibility had dropped on his shoulders and he was close to breaking point, balancing work as well. Taking a long look at the change to my life, during this time, I could not believe how they viewed the role of daughter-in-law, it was obviously my job to look after them, to make their lives comfortable. I also reflected that this could be about the increase in the cost of living, which was spiralling out of control at that time, and they only had their state pension, as she had given up her afternoon job.

The state of their personal belongings, bedding towels etc. was poor, sheets turned side to middle, blankets very thin and warn, no warm eiderdowns just cotton candlewick throws which covered the underlying truth, they had been struggling to cope whilst living in the house in Oxford, on their own and could see the only option was to live with us and for us to look after them. John and I needed to talk, urgently, there was a real imbalance, yes, we were financially well off and had put strategies in place to cope with the huge rate of inflation, but we did also have two young children.

From my view, the issues were the complete lack of input to the daily running of the house, the demands to ensure their life continued in the normal pattern of things but worst of all was the treatment of the children, I had overheard my father-in-law telling DJ about how he had been a high-flying cricket player and how DJ had to do better than either him or his dad, sport was what mattered and how his sister was not as important as DJ.

I could no longer let matters lie, this was the last straw, I would not have my children affected like this and potentially damaged and above all, he was a liar, as it was John who had been the high-flying cricketer and definitely not him. I told him what an appalling parent he had been, and if I ever heard him talking to my children in this way again, I would tell them the truth about a man who kept his wife and child short of funds whilst he peed it against the wall.

So, what was the solution, I reflected, as I walked up the hill. I knew money was always a factor when dealing with the in-laws, so this area had to be considered, John and I had accepted funds to cover the increase in food bills, but not for anything else, the state of their bedding, towels and personal clothing could be very quickly addressed but obviously not something they were willing to undertake.

Just how much effort was being made towards finding another property, next to none, was what I could see. Arriving back home from my walk, I found them both in the kitchen making a cup of tea, was the washing done? No, ironing, no, dusting or anything for that matter, no.

I was very aware that getting annoyed would get me nowhere, so a cheerful 'oh good make me one' was all I said as I put the washing on and went through to the lounge to light the wood burner, then collected more logs from the store and in no time they were sat in the room drinking tea, they had obviously been waiting for me to sort everything out to make them comfortable.

John sensed the change in atmosphere as soon as he entered the door, that evening, with just Tracy and I to welcome him home, normally he would come home for lunch but had not that day. He just handed me details of a property for sale in the area around the Liberal Club, I saw the property price range was a lot lower than we had been told the in-law's house had sold for, this is when I learnt a lot more about the sale of his parents' home.

Their house had been sold for a lot less than the asking price, but they had not considered the cost of agent's fees and solicitor costs to buy a new house, so they simply could not afford to buy the type of property they aspired to. John and I discussed this and decided, no way could they continue to live with us. We sat down with them and discussed the lack of funds from the property sale, and discussed the type of property they could afford.

The winter was not a good time to buy a property as most people are waiting until after Christmas and the New Year before selling.

The state of their personal belongings was also discussed, I made sheets for our beds, and it was no problem to make new sheets for them and John was happy to buy them new eiderdowns, blanket pieces could be purchased from a shop in Oxford, which could be edged with ribbon, this we would also undertake. However, we drew the line at personal clothing and suggested they took the bus into Oxford and sorted this out.

They toddled off to bed whilst John and I curled up for one of our chats. Discussing, talking, and teamwork were the strengths of our marriage, working together.

John undertook the research into the price of property, in the chosen area, whilst I thought long and hard about funding this situation. What could I do, which would facilitate school runs, school holidays and my Saturday job, I had coped easily with working at the playgroup five mornings a week, household chores and enjoying my children and whatever I decided to do must fit in with my family's needs.

John and I needed to talk, but his parents' presence in the house had put a stop to our time together, which had been so carefully planned. We overcame this by taking the children out walking in the local area, so full of history, so they could run free, and we could talk, being careful to put them and all the questions about the iron age fort, dyke hills, Roman settlement as well the importance of

Wittenham Clumps through the ages first, leaving them to bask in their imaginations of times gone by. Giving John and me time for one another and the ongoing difficulty of his parents.

One grey winter afternoon, walking down to the river, we talked of the property type his parents could almost afford to purchase, houses were out of the question, especially the type envisaged by my mother-in-law, an apartment could be a solution. We discovered a new complex had been built close to one of the university cricket grounds, not far from the Liberal Club.

John and his parents were of the impression these had been built by the council, now I had to admit that I had been studying the local paper to peruse the local property market, one of these apartments was listed in the recently sold section. Big bear hug time, both children racing back to join in, family hug time, these two were very tuned in to John and me.

So, a possible solution, in the option of one of these apartments, they had just enough money to buy one but we still had to deal with the insufficient funds for the purchase and paying agents and solicitors to buy one of these apartments, I was unwilling to jeopardise our own financial situation and came up with a suggestion, I would look for work to earn enough to cover the expenses which would be involved, banking training came into play once again as I explained the outgoings involved in purchasing a leasehold property.

John's cousin Susan had been involved in the sale of his parent's former home and I asked that a different person be involved, John was more than happy with that, then asked what work can you do after all there are the school runs, food shopping, cooking and everything else, so, I answered, firstly, there are four adults in the house, some of the jobs can be allocated to the other three, secondly, I am already viewed by your parents as an unpaid cleaner come housekeeper so I might as find a job doing this and get paid for it.

I had not heard him laugh so much in months, he grinned at me. We walked home with the children, Mum and Dad were happy again, all that mattered to them.

John dealt with his parents regarding my going back to work, but did not mention the possibility of an apartment, as there was nothing for sale at that time. Also, he told his mother that she could do more around the house, whilst he undertook more of the work immediately.

Next morning brought one of the saddest days of my life, busy cleaning our bedroom, John's parents stood in the doorway, his mother very agitated, her words very revealing. "You won't put me in the workhouse, will you?"

I was emphatic in my reply, "No, of course not, never in a million years."

So afraid all these years, as I took them both downstairs to make a cup of tea and asked if she wanted to talk about it. No, saying she was fine, father-in-law just sat smoking his woodbine.

Maybe this is the only window I will find into my mother-in-law's torment. Information needed, poor John once again having to fill me in with his family history.

What a history it was, his mother was born just before the start of the First World War, the youngest of thirteen children. The eldest sibling was 22 years old when she was born. She experienced terrible loss with the death of three of her brothers during and after the First World War and the death of her father not long after. The main breadwinners having gone, living with the fear of having to go into the workhouse for those remaining at home.

John was told that his grandmother ran a laundry, and I did not disillusion him, this was a euphonism for taking in washing to earn money, university life meant a lot of domestic work was carried out by local women, the younger members of the family including my mother-in-law had to help with this chore. She also lost her mother, when she was 15, and she had to go and live with her sister Hilda, yet another traumatic experience.

Living through the times of the great depression in the 1920s, when going into the workhouse was the fate of so many. So much suffering, the effects of which coloured the whole of her life, she suffered from total and devastating insecurity, we have to remember there was no benefits system in the UK, at that time.

The workhouse was where people went who could not support themselves, in return they got accommodation but had to work, the workhouse became where the infirm and elderly ended up. Conditions were very poor and the regime harsh, with long hours, malnutrition, beatings and neglect.

In the 1920s, how difficult life must have been during this time, reliant upon one's children if you reached an age beyond fifty, no old age pension or benefits, nothing.

Time for action, and I quickly put an advertisement in the Oxford Mail, offering my services as a cleaner, charging a very high hourly rate, well if you do not try you do not get, I thought at the time. A week later I received two invitations to call and discuss what would be required, one in a local village requiring three days a week for three hours a day and the other in Oxford one day a week for three hours. Perfect I thought.

Life was a little less stressful with John's mother trying to help, but still refusing to cook, John took on vacuuming the floors and washing the kitchen floor and learnt how to work the washing machine. A change in our lives but working together in the evenings was good fun.

One evening, Dawn called round whilst walking her dog and asked if I would like her husband Nick to take Tracy to school each day, he already took his children into Oxford, and she would be very welcome, such kindness, occasionally you meet people through the journey of life, who lift one's spirits with simple acts of kindness.

This was an affirmative yes to Dawn as this enabled me to take on more work and I began working almost every day. This called for Christmas preparations to be well organised that year. List making linked to a time sheet certainly worked and this would become the template in future years.

A life too well organised can be stifling, spontaneity a part of our lives was now needed to be rekindled. Christmas Eve and my father-in-law expected to go to the Liberal Club as he had for years, John was not happy, this is his family time, the time he really enjoyed. A simple question from me to my father-in-law, who will bring you back, no reply, would a couple of hours in the afternoon suit you? John gave me one of his; what are you up to scamp looks.

Then the penny dropped. Before the children arrived, we spent Christmas Eve walking and shopping in the Oxford Covered Market, then afternoon tea in the Eastgate Hotel, with the father-in-law slightly mollified, the old Christmas Eve ritual was revived, with three others in tow. Yes, we included John's mother, and we had tea in the Mitre Hotel, much to her enjoyment.

The spring of 1978 came at last and the property market perked up, an apartment came up for sale at the complex near the Liberal Club, with John being one of the first to be contacted about its availability, he quickly arranged to take his parents to view. I was working so it was down to him to take them, some sought of trauma took place at the viewing and a very angry husband awaited me when I arrived back from work ready to shower and fetch Tracy.

The phone rings with the estate agent asking why they had not kept the appointment, as I had no idea, this was a bit awkward, could I get there for 4 o'clock, you bet I could. John was standing there running his hands through his hair, it must have been bad. I took the details from him, turned it over to see a map of the complex, right swap cars, I will see to your parents whilst you pick up Tracy.

Father-in-law was in the lounge, and I went through pointing out that the apartment overlooked his beloved cricket ground and was full of sunshine, it also had a garage, just what more did they want. John left and the father-in-law had words with his wife, and we went apartment viewing.

As we drove along, I explained to them both that this is not a block of council flats, a small section of it was set aside for council tenants but this was nowhere near the apartment we were going to view.

As it transpired, the flat was lovely, and all they really needed was a new television set. Well, having lived with us for so many months, they could probably afford one, I thought. This situation was getting to me, I had to not lose my patience, the area suited them both and gradually my mother-in-law relaxed.

That she would revert to her old routine was obvious, life would be warmer and far less work, the wide-open view from the apartment reminiscent of the time they first moved into their former home. Hooray the decision was made, and we had an apartment to be purchased.

John and I covered the difference in purchase price and paid the required fees. My income was making a difference, but I would need to continue to work to replace our financial outlay. Order was quickly restored with the children back in their own rooms, and I admit to cleaning the house from top to bottom, trying to irradicate the smell of woodbine cigarettes.

Once again, evenings curled up together, just quiet, listening to music or watching sport on the television, we had survived and I had a better understanding of John's parents, and his loathing of his father.

A perk of private schools was that they had longer holiday breaks than state schools, which made it possible to take the children on holiday during September. Into the car went buckets and spades, wind breaks and raffia mats for sitting on sandy beaches. A few changes of clothing but not a lot.

Off to Hayle in Cornwall to a chalet on the beach. Total freedom from dusk to dawn, two young people running around in the sand dunes. Down on the beach we all went, swimming, beach cricket, sleeping in the sun. Cool evenings sitting in the car eating fish and chips with our fingers. Blissful days.

John's parents settled into the apartment and seemed happy with their new life. Taking them to the supermarket, weekly, was undertaken by John, simply because I had enough to do. Sunday tea at our house became the new ritual, with homemade scones, cream and jams, becoming a firm favourite.

Family life returned to fun and games with both children being early risers and the morning greeting resumed, a little girl lifting my covers and slipping in for a big cuddle, one much larger son taking a flying leap onto the bed between John and me. Life settled into a warm, loving time.

In the late 1970s, the British car industry was in deep trouble with deep unrest in the workforce. This impacted on the company John worked for. The ramifications of Thatcherism affecting manufacturing, mining and thus almost all industry in the United Kingdom. Pressed Steel Fisher, the company John worked for, joined forces with the local car manufacturers, causing times of great change and insecurity. New management was brought in to address the dire situation, within the company and redundancy looming in all areas.

John now worked in quality assurance and was called to the assembly plant to sign off a batch of cars. One of the major problems with cars built by Morris was the unreliability, or to put it another way, poor workmanship, sloppy work. The philosophy was just getting the cars out of the plant, numbers not quality. John's job was to inspect each car and in relation to one specific batch, refused to sign off any of the cars due to the poor workmanship, he listed every defect of which there were many, a huge argument ensued, with the person in charge, culminating in John telling him that if he wanted the cars out of the door, he could sign them off himself.

This was very courageous of my husband, and he was no fool, he knew that if he signed these cars off, giving his expertise and qualifications to cover this mess, the repercussions would be allotted to him. These were dark days, for John, as one by one the other engineers from Pressed Steel Fisher left the company, off to pastures new, Sweden, Australia, Canada and America and this gave John the same idea, why not go to pastures new?

John and I talked each evening about this situation, Australia being his preferred choice, the only employment fitting his experience and qualifications was in the Northern Territory, would I go with him? Yes, of course, I would. He just grinned saying I will look into it. That Sunday teatime, and the children were talking to their grandparents, who told them we might be going to live in Australia, my mother-in-law just stared at me, you would go with him, and take the children, she cried. This met with an affirmative reply from myself, and total silence occurred at that point. It was not the same whilst being taken home, mother-in-law hysterical, father-in-law told John he was selfish. Poor man, as if life was not difficult enough.

Normal reaction, mother-in-law took to her bed, but much worse this time, and I suggested calling the doctor, to find out what was wrong. No need she was up and about next day, damage done, we would not be going to Australia to live. It was many years before John, and I eventually spent time in Australia.

The difficulties for John, at work, increased as department after department closed, and he ended up travelling between the various plants, across the UK, troubleshooting as he termed it. He came back from his destination each day in time to collect Tracy from school. He was often late, though, but Tracy thoroughly enjoyed sitting on the wall outside the school, with her friends or going back into the school and reading.

These pickup times were a great time with his daughter listening to her chatter and the events of her day, on hearing she had been told to read a book she had read months before he decided to go chat to her teacher. Tracy had read all the books and was very advanced in this area. He also saw her do her first solo flute performance to an audience and as Ratty in a production of Wind in the Willows.

One very proud father, and something to help him consider his next move in the months to come. Both children were due to change schools in 1983, which gave us just over two years to address our options.

Thinking time for me, what can I do, returning to full-time work at this stage, was not an option, as the children were still quite young, work more hours, but this was not really feasible as my life was full. I went through the ideas, start tightening the belt relating to income, examine our expenditure in detail, check our investments were earning the best rate of return, grow more food on a larger allotment, order wood for the burner in the summer when it was cheaper, cut back on unnecessary car journeys including school runs, sewing machine in good working order, no new clothes for me, necessities for everyone else. Making all these adjustments became a game changer in the future.

Christmas was as happy as ever, with presents limited for the children, not that they noticed and John and I happy we had one another. All the children remember was a pile of presents under the tree, even if it was just a packet of pencils, I took to hiding the presents as Tracy was very keen to find out what she got in advance! New Year of 1981, no big celebration that year, just John and I curled together, happy and close, we would weather whatever came our way together.

By Easter, our lives had changed, John had been offered a position with Jaguar cars in West Bromwich, Birmingham, when attending the interview, he had been unable to access the plant via the main gate, as there were employees standing outside demonstrating, fighting for their jobs.

On walking around the plant, he found the conditions old and antiquated, with car bodies still being manually pushed around on wooden dollies, very poor working conditions, attitude of management outdated, a very prestigious car, maybe, but at what cost. The job offer came through a few days later, Chief Engineer, what an achievement.

That evening's conversation was difficult for John, I can't take this on, scamp, it will be short-lived, that factory is not good. My reply at that point, sleep on it, see how you feel in the morning. The stress of the past months had taken their toll, so not a good time to make decisions.

The next morning started with our usual awakening, John looking very tired and stressed. I hugged him as he left, saying talk again this evening.

I was late to work that morning, as I spent too much time with lists, and studying our accounts. The day progressed as normal, although John was snappy with the children, they understood and went up to bed early without a complaint, Tracy happy to curl up with a good book.

John went into the shower, coming down to a cup of tea on the dining room table, giving me one of his what are you up to looks. Two blank sheets of paper on the table.

Firstly, we discussed the job offer based in West Bromwich. The ramifications for us. We could sell the house and move, take the children out of school, how would we manage the in-laws and visiting, my work being disrupted. Then came what I expected, John did not want to take this job, this company was in trouble, as no investment had been put into improved working practices.

Looking at the company's finances had left him staggered, and he knew it would take an enormous investment to update this plant, these funds simply were not there. By turning this job offer down, he would be made redundant, all this was noted on one blank sheet, I then turned to the next and added a heading Plan B.

Question one. What would you like to do?

Question two. How do we achieve this?

Question three. What is the monetary situation relating to redundancy?

My husband was no fool, he had already worked out what his redundancy package would be, but needed confirmation, he had been working for them for 30 years. He slept well that night, off we all went next morning getting on with our day. John and I will gather information to aid this decision. Discussion time that weekend, as we went walking with the children, John had thought long and hard, we could buy a small hotel and run it together.

Friends had joined Abbey Life selling life insurance, Keith (John's childhood friend) had simply gone to work in the university administration department, but he was a single man with few aspirations. All possible answers, John selling life insurance, maybe not. Administration is not using his skills. Hotel life, I had witnessed this first-hand when my father started his employment in Oxford years before, this is a full-on occupation, affected by the economy and people. Still very frustrated, we continued our walk.

After dinner and putting the children to bed, John came into the lounge where I was watching television, running his hands through his hair, he said, "We will have to sell the house and downsize."

Enough, time for serious talk. Reminding him of the early years when we were friends, we talked of his attempt to move into the oil industry, how he was successful until the lack of qualifications held him back. Now he had the qualifications, why not try again? He sat down next to me, just how are we going to manage that?

Into the dining room we went, paper out of the draw and figures explained, redundancy money, pension contributions refunded, our savings came to a tidy sum, the next page showed our monthly outgoings to run the house, food etc, with insurance marked as a point of discussion, details of school fees, last, but not least, necessary expenditure.

Far too messy for John who immediately picked up on it being a monthly sum not annually, irritating man playing for time. Looking him straight in the eye, I told him there is a reason for that. Still not sure if he was excited or irritated as I went on to explain, I will go back to full-time work which will cover the monthly outgoings, that he would need a car and to pay his fees for the golf club, writing a CV and applying for jobs is hard work and he would need an outlet. That would leave enough funds to pay for two years of school fees, it will be tight, but gives you a two-year window. Tall man pacing around the rooms, exclaiming; You would do that.

I just grinned at him. He was up very early the next morning, going over the figures, having re-calculated them on a yearly basis. I learnt a lesson that day, always do two sets of figures, one for me and one for John. He asked if I had a Plan C, grinning at me. Of course, sell up, send the children to state school, no problem. It was so good to hear him laughing again. That was the day he refused the job offer, to the amazement of the human resources team.

Unfortunately, the woman involved argued as Jaguar had been impressed with his interview and knowledge, not wise but he did something very unusual for John, forcefully telling her that he was not going to sell his house in Dorchester-on-Thames or uproot his children from their private schools to go live and work in West Bromwich just to make her life easier.

So, all I had to do now was find a full-time job, unfortunately, the banks were not taking on new staff, as a lot of women had looked for employment as the factories gradually laid off the male workforce. I encountered an amazing bias at this time, women trying to return to the workplace were treated as though they were incapable of rational thought or holding down any form of employment, which involved thinking, only suited for working at home or maybe a job in a supermarket filling shelves.

During an interview for a position with the water board, I was asked if I could write a letter, as a lot of the work envisaged involved interaction with the public by letter and telephone, good customer relation skills were essential. Most importantly of all, he would have to be able to work with this person. I wondered if this man had even bothered to read my CV, probably not, would I be able to work with him, that was a question. There was something very seedy about him, talking to John that evening, soon sorted it out. No way are you working for him, keep trying.

As it turned out, a job was already available in the department store where I worked on a Saturday, and I was able to commence work in customer services after Easter, full-time. Handing in my notice to the gentleman I worked for, as his cleaner, was a sad moment, it had been 5 years after all, but he understood and handed me a cheque for a large amount. Such kindness. The other job was more difficult, the woman involved becoming emotional. Time to move on.

The cheque was unexpected, and John suggested we have a short holiday over Easter, as it was unlikely we would be able to afford such a thing for a few years. A simple break, renting a holiday cottage, taking the food with us, keeping the costs down to rent and fuel. So, we had a week in wet and windy Wales, two happy children running around and two happy adults embarking on the next phase of their lives. Just one hurdle left, telling John's parents.

The biggest fear in my mother-in-law's life, was John being out of work, as the past fears of the workhouse would resurface, taking a risk not the supposedly easy way out of going to West Bromwich, as I thought the fall out was as traumatic as we expected, John told them of his taking redundancy and changing industries, which made me smile, such a positive response changing not trying to change.

No offer to help if needed, nothing. We left them to get on with the trauma, I would be starting full-time work the next day and had no time or patience to deal with his mother taking to her bed.

Oddly, the following year was not difficult for me, John and I worked as a team, splitting up the jobs which gave me more time to relax. Allotment work, watering and weeding done by John, cooking dinner and ironing was about all I did for a few months. John completed his CV and began the task of applying for employment.

Joining agencies and finding out the best way to approach this difficult task, and difficult it was, sending out CV copies and introductory letters with nothing but negative replies is soul destroying. Curled up close and tight, I tried to reassure him, "John, one, that's all you will need. John, it will come."

Summer months came, golf during the week, children to look after during the holidays.

John honed his skills with letter writing and learnt to adapt his CV to each job application. The New Year of 1982 brought the breakthrough, an interview with a company in Reading, part of a team, design and procurement for oil rigs, the area John had been concentrating on, how he felt, I do not know. Hug from me with a wish for good luck as he left to take DJ to school before going for the interview.

Two days later came the telephone call, I arrived home to music playing and a husband who grabbed me in his bear hug, I got it, scamp, I got it. Swinging me round. Wonderful day. Sobering up over dinner, he looked worried again, I smiled and said, "Plan C."

He laughed, you are too much, scamp, tell me later.

After the children were in bed, we talked about the problems of school lifts and school holiday coverage, or Plan C. DJ's school had been recommending he became a boarder for some time, financially we were secure, managing just fine with my salary covering expenses and John securing a job much more quickly than we had catered for, so boarding fees would not be a problem, one problem left Tracy, and her afternoon pick up.

Another family in the village had children at the same school as Tracy, I volunteered to approach them to ask if they would bring her home in the afternoons, Tracy would be fine with them and could have a key to let herself in at home. A massive yes, of course, but leave her with us until you get home from work, that will be good as she gets on with our daughter who needs some female company, with two brothers. People can be very kind.

Only the half term in February, the first school holiday problem to solve, an elderly couple had moved into the close a few years back. The husband walked the dog past our house every day and knew that John had been at home for several months. His wife stopped me in the village and asked how things were, I told her of John's success, that the school runs had been sorted out, but not the vacations.

Oh, let them come to us each day for this coming half term that will give you time to sort things out in the future, I shall enjoy feeding them. It is at times like this when you find who your true friends are. They remained friends until they passed away in 2020.

Covering school holidays was a huge issue at the time for working families, requesting time off at specific times to fit in with school holidays was not understood and frowned upon by many men, who though that women should be at home, many women were unkind as well and very judgemental, stating women shouldn't work and should be caring for their children. It was very difficult to balance working and the children, at the time.

This is an issue I still see for many women today, the juggle between being a mother and also having a career, some women make a clear cut choice to have their career and not have children and suffer the social stigma this involves and others try and manage it all or happily get married and have children, choosing not to work again, it still surprises me how unsupportive women are of their individual decisions.

The early years of John working contracts rather than a full-time employment, had their ups and downs, but once his reputation was established, he did not look back. Contract work was precarious, I had only intended working until he resumed work, but my bringing in a steady income gave John the freedom to pursue contracts wherever they led him. Travel the world he did, having to undergo training for being on an oil rig, great fun, jumping into water from several feet in the air did not seem to worry him, neither did landing on an oil rig in a helicopter.

Our lives were beginning to take a new path, but not so for another branch of my family.

My brother David's son Mark, born in 1963, was a happy-go-lucky young man who joined the Royal Marines at the age of 16, in 1979, a life he really enjoyed. The Falklands War broke out, between Argentina and the UK, in April 1982 and Mark was deployed with his regiment to go to the Falklands.

The Royal Marines were involved in many of the battles, and unfortunately, Mark was killed in the Battle of Goose Green, a young man 19 years old, at the start of his life, his parents never recovered from this devastating loss. He left his younger sister Jane, at the age of 17 years, to deal with their all-consuming grief.

My parents were in shock, my mother having expressed her fear for David to Wendy, but the wrong person was worried about. Mark was buried with his compatriots in the Falklands and in 2023 Jane went out and laid the ashes of both his parents with him, peace at last. Terrible sad days followed, John and I remembering wartime years. There was nothing we could do to help.

That year, I started thinking about resuming my career, which I left in 1969, fine but a high-flying career taking up most of my days and energy, perhaps not, with two children about to change school and the teenage years on the horizon, this was not the time to put oneself first.

Taking the local paper each day, to scan the situations vacant. *No harm in doing that*, I thought, *as you never know what opportunities arise.* Looking to see what opportunities there were out there, and also me thinking about what I would do after the children had left home, I knew I would like to go back and have a high-flying career and was keen to look for any opportunities in the world of finance and especially mortgages.

DJ was due to move to a public school, which involved an exam to be taken in the spring of 1983, his school reports were good, and the school envisaged no problems for him, which school he would attend was the decision. I felt that this one was for John and had a surprise as it transpired that he had relations who had gone to a school in Oxford, the connection being his paternal grandfather's brother. The connection with his grandfather was as strong as ever.

DJ was enrolled at St Edward's School. Tracy was a different kettle of fish; we went to an open day at Oxford High School for Girls. Very much like the Milham Ford School where I had attended. English for Tracy was, and always has been excellent, mathematics a little weak. Talking to the teacher for this subject annoyed me, let alone Tracy, she had some sort of trick question she asked all prospective students.

As I said, Tracy's weak point, she just shrugged her shoulders. In the car on the way home she asked if she really had to go to that school, as she would rather not. My reply, we will look at Headington Girls School and see what you think. Big School with several houses dotted around the grounds where the boarders lived, big playing-fields and large light classrooms.

Academic status not in the same league as the High School for Girls but good for all that. Dropping in at the supermarket on the way home, we treated ourselves to apple cream turnovers and sat in the car to devour them. Ever astute young lady asked if we could afford this school, yes, if it's the one you like, it transpired that a few of her school friends were also going there, so she would prefer this school. Problems gradually ironing themselves out, just me left to consider.

Time and patience were not really a strong point for me, but it paid off, an opportunity to join the mortgage department of a building society office in Oxford City was advertised in the local paper, how exciting I thought. I applied immediately, but heard nothing for several days, so be it, I thought.

Working at the customer service desk one morning, in the department store, an acquaintance of the bank manager I had worked with previously, approached the desk. Talking, remembering former days when he visited the bank to see the manager, both members of the local business group.

Smiling, he went on his way. I received a request to visit for an interview at the building society, where I was greeted by the office manager and members of the mortgage team, most welcoming with no reference to how I would manage having a family to consider. An office of women run by a woman. The job was mine, having been vetted by the manager, the friend of my former boss.

Full-time work with Saturday working on a rota.

I was beginning my new employment in June, half term vacations having been managed with help from friends in the close, but the summer vacation had to be addressed. John and I would have to cover this as best we could. This is the first and last time we asked his parents for help, they travelled over on the bus, bus stop being close to their apartment Monday to Friday for one week.

They had an old-fashioned way of thinking, I should be at home looking after the family, men should be earning the funds, John should not have taken redundancy. All this came out when John was driving them back on the Friday evening. There was no pleasing some people.

Asking my parents for help would have been a possibility, however, my youngest sister, Carol, who had two children at this time, a daughter, Kate, who was autistic and needed a lot of care and a baby son, James, she was also going through a very messy divorce and had to return to work, she was a primary school teacher, so my parents were needed elsewhere.

The next week of the school summer vacation, we split our holiday entitlement. Two weeks each, and, for the remainder, we enrolled the children in a summer camp. We all survived, and the children had immense fun at the camp, undertaking all sorts of outdoor activities, from pony trekking to canoeing.

September quickly came around and both the children started new schools, DJ boarding at *Teddies* (nickname for St Edwards), Tracy starting at Headington Girls School, with her good friends. School runs with friends also changed.

Tracy and I travelled into Oxford together and this independent daughter of mine caught the bus and travelled to school on her own, taking the bus back in the afternoons, with her friends. She would go walking around the shops with them before joining me in the office, she absolutely loved it. Working with women helped a lot as they understood my predicament.

Tracy made herself useful, when she wasn't walking around the shops, clearing up in the staff room, stamping leaflets with the branch address and generally helping out. Half term was a testing time for me as I left the two of them at home with instructions to go see the neighbours if anything went wrong. They were just fine, going out and about on their bikes, making their own lunches.

Hopefully, this was the way forward, but it was not an easy decision to make, and I rang nearly every hour to check on them, I was also aware the close had a great group of people who they could ask for help if needed and my daughter was very sensible.

Christmas came around with a new dimension, help for me, as Tracy made the mince pies and sausage rolls, DJ as ever on tasting patrol, teenage young man eating well and growing fast, beginning to catch his father up in height. John and

I on vegetable duty, both of us smiling at one another, shared memories of days gone by. The parents-in-law picked up in time for lunch, a lot later than usual. The children, John and I, went out walking after lunch, leaving his parents to snooze in front of the fire, television on for the Queen's speech.

Boxing Day as ever fun and games, outside in the countryside around our home during the day, with a cold supper, then card games around the dining room table. Scrabble, my forte, a winner. Everybody rolling around laughing, as I cheated. Well, they now had a better idea of spelling and English than I did, and as I was so competitive, it was the only way. Great times.

New Year 1984 was seen by all four of us, for the first time, I remember thinking the children were disappointed. With all the hype on the television, they expected more, I think, one of life's disillusionments.

John's reputation within the industry had grown to the point that at the end of one contract he was able to step straight into another, so there was no agency involved and the companies he worked for no longer had to pay commission, John therefore became self-employed. As well as a demanding job dealing with projects worth millions of pounds, he undertook his own accounting and tax affairs.

I cannot say that I had any knowledge of taxes at that point, not something I had studied. It came to light that money was owed to the inland revenue, a good place to start I thought, and I spent one lunchtime in the manager's office telephoning the local inland revenue, not exactly helpful, they told me that they would have to see the accounts, nothing more.

Logical thinking, having spent several evenings reading about tax, I had a pretty good idea how much was owed, this needed to be separated, and I duly trotted across the road to another building society to open an account and invest the money.

Back in the office, I chatted with the manager and asked him to recommend an accountant, he suggested, Aubrey, of course, why did I not think of him, another acquaintance from my banking days. One phone call later and the paperwork was dropped off during the evening, it all seemed simple enough, but a phone call from Aubrey a few weeks later indicated a problem.

The inland revenue was looking to fine John, and goodness knows what else, I told Aubrey of my previous telephone conversation with the local tax office, did I make a record, he asked, no, but I knew exactly when it was. Transferring the funds into an investment account that day was wiser than I thought, as it was enough to stop any further problems, my knowing the exact date of the phone call indicated an attempt to pay outstanding funds, we were lucky. Aubrey took over the accounts from then on, so one less job for me, simple record keeping and filing of receipts, etc, from now on.

It was a busy year for all of us, John now working for a company in London, commuting each day by train from Didcot Station. An early start catching the 7.15 am train and working his lunch hour enabled him to miss the evening rush hour and return home before 6.30 pm. Around half an hour after, Tracy and I arrived, giving me time to light the wood burner and start cooking dinner, whilst Tracy watched her favourite TV programme, the Australian soap *Neighbours*.

John was home, a bear hug and off for a shower to wash off the travelling grime. I was not able to use the hot water whilst he showered as it cut off the supply to the shower, giving someone a cold-water shock; well, of course, I forgot at times and the shout was probably heard 5 doors away. Life with this husband of mine was still great fun despite the adversity we faced.

DJ was very busy at school studying and he had started the Duke of Edinburgh award scheme, which kept him very occupied; this is a great scheme, as it teaches a lot of life skills, like resilience and leadership, you have to do some volunteering and expeditions, camping overnight. He also started rowing and this took over playing cricket, which John found difficult.

This year, we tried to change the school holidays problem; by taking my holiday a few days at a time, I could be at home for a few days during the three half terms, Easter, Christmas and summer long breaks, taking the children out and about, just having some quiet time at home.

John took a two-week break in the summer, taking the children to Tintagel, in Cornwall, whilst I stayed at home. This worked well, and during the evenings and weekends, they were all away, I decorated the hall, sounds a crazy thing to do, but I enjoyed the painting and the peace.

That Christmas with two teenagers was great fun, they no longer needed to spend time with John and me, although they were still happy to go out walking with us. They were very patient with their grandparents and just as happy to retire to their rooms with books to read.

Computers and mobile phones were still a way off. Sport on the television was not aspired to and board games were old hat. Card games for pennies ahh, now we have it and we played cribbage, New Market, and John's book of card games came into its own. Christmas suppers and family talk. Lovely times.

1985 and the children seemed happy at school, Tracy having a large group of friends, who she had sleep overs with, going home on the coach with them after school, one friend having ponies and she learnt to ride and a never ending cycle of parties, singing in the school choir and amateur dramatics where she shone, one particular memory was the production of pirates of Penzance, which she sang in and performing in the choir at Christchurch Cathedral.

When DJ started at Teddies, his father promised that if he no longer wanted to be a boarder, he just had to say. This was the time he asked to become a day boy, there were two other boys in the village who attended the school on a daily basis, and this was what he would like. I had my worries as to why, but this was man to man stuff, not for me to get involved.

It turned out that DJ was being badly bullied and John witnessed one particular incident where DJ was being pushed out of a window, all a lot of fun apparently, DJ had developed a way of coping by laughing and being funny, but John obviously thought that things had gone too far. I just had to start my day earlier, dropping DJ at school in North Oxford, Tracy at her bus stop, before parking the car and going to the office.

One of the mothers whose son also went to Teddies, asked if I would take her son to school each day to enable her to work full-time at the local GP practice. Remembering how much help I had received over the difficult years; I did not hesitate. Although the young man in question seemed to feel it was a bit demeaning to be seen going to school in a mini.

Evening runs were late, all schoolwork being done on school premises, prep time was spent at school, no homework involved, John undertook this run, picking DJ up at nine o'clock, man to man talk on the way home. Food needed to be provided as soon as DJ walked in the door, quickly followed by sleep. Another boy from the village attending Teddies joined the rota, his parents taking over the morning runs and John bringing all three boys back in the evenings. This worked well, taking the pressure off me, meaning I could do more in the mornings and balancing the household chores, taking more from John.

As ever there was a snag in the arrangements, John going abroad with his employment, when this occurred the evening pick up would be down to me, three strapping young men plus the driver, into my mini would not go, luckily the current contract in London did not require foreign travel, so not an immediate problem, but when the contract ended in 1986, this would have to be addressed.

DJ was working hard, starting to prepare for his O-level examinations, some of which he took a year early, a young man now living his own life, independent.

I was progressing in the mortgage department, at the building society, I now had my own cases to evaluate before referral to the mandated officer, better known as the underwriter. A lowkey job compared with my previous career, but enough to keep me busy.

Times were changing, young women leaving school with better qualifications than some of those already holding positions of authority, causing challenging times for some. The chief cashier came under attack frequently, not surprising as organisation was not her strongest point, and the younger generation ran rings around her. The new generation of young women, better educated, confident young women, no longer viewing marriage and babies as the sole reason for their existence, with the contraceptive pill, giving them freedom earlier generations could not have dreamt of.

Tracy came to the office each day after school, chatting with them and listening to their latest exploits, this made life easier for me, in relation to being accepted by this younger generation, as I was simply accepted, as I was never judgemental or critical and of course my banking qualifications had something to do with it.

My difficulties came with a member of the mortgage staff who had worked there longer than I had, and, in the end, I had to tell her to back off, as I had no intention of taking over the department, my life was full enough. It transpired I need not have bothered, when the manager heard of the goings on, he simply took this woman into his office and explained she would not be considered for any management positions.

Life settled into an easy pattern everyone getting on with their lives, no summer holiday this year, but all being well we would take a trip in 1986. This seemed to be enough for the two children, they are an astute pair, looking after themselves, as there was plenty to entertain them in the village.

Autumn came, and as we knew John's work would be changing, and he would be abroad more, we bought me a new car, so there was no longer any need to worry about the three boys being cramped in the mini, when I took over the evening pickups. We kept the mini though, and DJ wanted to know if he could learn to drive the mini when he was 17, well, it was not something I had considered, but one look at the grin on John's face told me a bit of forward planning had been going on.

That year, I thought Christmas would be as normal but I thought wrong, the Christmas lunch preparation as normal with Tracy and I baking, John and DJ cleaning vegetables, the two men fetching the grandparents, walking in the afternoon and taking John's parents back, but after a request from father-in-law, they wanted to spend Boxing Day with us, join us for supper and cards. This was very unusual as he normally went to the Liberal Club, not a problem, just a bit more fetching and carrying.

That night, as John and I curled up in front of the fire, we tried to figure out what the change was all about, we decided that the children must have told them of our supper evenings, and they want to experience it. Next afternoon they sat in front of the wood burner snoozing happily, afternoon tea and cake supplied, supper on the table, we four working in unison as we filled service plates and opened bottles, lemonade and lime for the teenagers, much to their disgust and wine for the grandparents with a small drink for John and me.

I have a problem with alcohol and John would be taking them home, hence the small glasses, even this affected me. Cards on the table, and the evening began, apparently, I am a funny drunk. Great time was had by all, John's father really enjoying himself, mother-in-law tight-lipped as ever. John and I wondered why now, after all these years, he decided to spend time with us rather than his mates at the Liberal Club.

New Year's Eve 1986 was welcomed in by all four of us. An important year in DJ's life, as he had his O-level examinations in the spring. Over the years, boys being boys, DJ had a few accidents. Three visits to A&E departments had left a lasting impression.

Messing about with John, he had cut his head on a panel of glass in the lounge door, a lot of stitches that time, running around the house he slipped and sustained a greenstick fracture of his right arm, and thirdly, playing with Wendy's two daughters, Julie and Susan, he managed to kneel on a darning needle dropped on the floor, which went straight into his kneecap, the orthopaedic surgeon had a difficult time pulling this needle free—these visits to A&E was where his dream of becoming a doctor started.

It was a stressful time for him, and he worked diligently, needing to obtain good grades in physics, chemistry and biology. As ever, John thought a reward for such an endeavour should take the form of a holiday, which he organised. He booked the last week of August and the first week of September, with us driving down to a small fishing port, Vieux Beaucoup in Southwest France, near Biarritz, a holiday destination made famous during the late 1850s-1930s. Travelling, with the children, this way was great fun, as they experienced the French roadside toilets, which Tracy hasn't forgotten to this day, and we went through Paris and stayed in Tours. This holiday was very different to the 1950s trip, though, we stayed in a mobile home situated under pine trees on a large campsite, within easy walking distance of the beach.

In the centre of the local town was a square with shops and restaurants on each side. One day, whilst we were visiting to get provisions, a circus came to town with elephants and acrobats, men climbing a greasy pole, it was an amazing experience, which left a real impression on the children. The weather was fantastic all holiday, the food was delicious, and they could swim every day in a warm sea, they loved it.

The history of this area was a surprise, the forest had been planted after a law was passed in 1857. Prior to the forest being established, people managed to survive mainly by herding sheep, the terrain so poor that one hectare would support one sheep. Shepherds had to travel up to 20 kilometres a day to supply sufficient grazing. They used stilts to travel over the rough ground and to keep their feet dry. Also enabling them to supervise their flocks from afar. The planting of the forest brought stability to the region, and new industries came from the wood products. A glimpse for John and me of our holidays in the future.

DJs exam results arrived in mid-August, and he achieved 11 O' level passes with high grades, these were more than good enough to continue into the 6th Form, at Teddies and study for his A levels, one step forward towards his dream of being a doctor. That September, Tracy chose and started her GCSE journey, she was to be the first year to take GCSEs in 1988, these were a replacement for O-level standard, a kind of guinea pig cohort, personally I couldn't see much difference, apart from the exam paper questions were shorter.

This is also the time when John's contract came to an end, luckily, he obtained another contract straight away and this was working for an American company in their London Office, which overlooked the Buckingham Palace gardens. It was a huge contract relating to oil rigs for use in the Mediterranean and the Middle East.

Some of the oil rig frame was being manufactured in Germany and John's on-site inspector expressed deep concern about the welding techniques being used, so off to Germany John went to personally inspect the product, refusing to sign it off for use. Once back in the London Office, he received a visit from three

American men, complete with Stetsons and cowboy boots, feet lodged on his desk, trying to intimidate John, no way. After a short time of John proving just what the problem was, they left, with their onward journey to Germany. The welding problem was quickly taken care of. John's contract was due to complete in October, but the company offered him an extension to work in their Milan Office to oversee work being carried out there.

The work he enjoyed knowing that it was for a few months only, and he also made new acquaintances, which was always important if you were self-employed. The company complex had a shop on the ground floor with a bakery, he certainly enjoyed that, and the gym provided for employees, but hotel life, not so much, although walking to local bars and restaurants with his new friends in the cold evenings suited him. At a reception given by the company, he met several of the Italian employees' wives, each and every one, saying how hard their husbands worked and such long hours.

John having witnessed these same men jumping into cars and driven off by a female immediately after work, he just smiled and agreed. Much to the relief of a few stood by. The end of his contract in Milan was December 23rd, and he was given a very pleasant send off, his work input very much appreciated. He was given gifts of a book relating to Italian Architecture, a silver magnifying glass with a cockerel embossed on the lid, chocolates for the family.

The flight home was a nightmare, the direct London flight was cancelled, so he rerouted and flew to Germany and then into Amsterdam. On the 24$^{th}$ he flew into London, travelled by train to Didcot, with a taxi home, this being the best Christmas present we could have had. Staff on the flight to Germany had handed out boxes of Ferrero Rocher to all the passengers, this was the first time we had seen or tasted them, they were very yummy. So good to have him home.

Christmas morning and a very late start all round as we had spent the evening talking to John, I volunteered to fetch his parents, Tracy and DJ worked in the kitchen leaving John to rest in front of the wood burner. Not having seen my parents-in-law for several months, I noted how thin his father had become, still smoking his woodbines and visiting his club, nothing had changed, but something was amiss.

Christmas lunch over, walking for us and snoozing in front of the fire for the in-laws. John had also noted the change, he would talk to them both when he took them home, meaning a late evening for him. His father sat in the back of the car, mother-in-law became carsick if she sat in the back, so talking to his father had to wait until he came to our home the next day. Boxing day, we two up and about, teenagers still snoozing.

Boxing Day supper on the table, DJ and Tracy pouring drinks. John talking to his father in the lounge. Cards immediately after, clearing the table, leaving the clearing up until later. A really good time of laughter and leg pulling with music in the background. John took his parents home, both seemed reluctant to go, which in itself was unusual, leaving us three to clear up. Retiring to the lounge for more music and drinks, tea for me. John came back and collapsed into a chair, stating his parents want to spend New Year's Eve with us. Alarm bells rang, this was so out of character for them.

Calmly, I told him, it was no problem, but they will have to share a bed (they slept on two singles in their apartment). DJ was a tall young man and had needed a larger bed some time ago, he had a large double in his room for them to share and he seemed fine about moving into a single bed in the spare room. No more was said until the next morning before I left for work.

When John asked, would I please make an appointment for his father to see his doctor as soon as possible because his father was having trouble with a stomach upset which kept recurring, he would have to be taken and brought back to the apartment.

*Let's hope I can do this in an hour,* I thought. The building society office was still very quiet, after Christmas, with only a few customers out and about, upon explaining my predicament to the office manager, she advised that it was not a problem, just make the appointment, use your lunch hour, the other members of the team agreed, no worries if you are late back.

A hospital referral was the outcome of the doctor's appointment, it seemed an operation had to be undertaken.

New Year's Eve, the building society office closed at lunchtime, allowing me to arrive home in time to put a meal together, roast beef and all the trimmings, a starter and a couple of desserts, did I have a premonition of things to come, possibly. Tracy and DJ set the table for our special meal, with John having left to fetch his parents whilst all this was going on.

Later, the older generation sat in front of the wood burner and watched TV whilst we all cleared up. A time well spent as we chatted together. Watching TV together, we saw in the New Year, 1987, had begun.

1987 turned out to be a year of hospital appointments for check-ups and investigations, more extended lunch hours for me and time off to accompany his father, John working in London and travelling with his work, he helped when he could. Any further promotion to being a mortgage underwriter had to be put on hold, as somehow the welfare of my in-laws had become my responsibility, there were difficult years to come.

Luckily, John's father rallied after surgery and life returned to something near normal, with just regular check-ups. They needed help with shopping, refuse collection and tasks around the apartment, so I collected the necessary medications during my lunch hour, and Tracy and I called in on our way home after work to help if needed.

Travelling on the train each morning to London, John always read the paper, one day he noted a complex being built in Florida, USA, for retirees aged 55 and over, houses in villages with golf courses surrounding them, thinking to himself at that time, I will have some of that when I retire and said no more, but never forgot it, storing the ripped out piece of newspaper for safekeeping.

This time of travelling was used for reading and catching up with trends in engineering, and he saw a contract job being advertised for a quality assurance and certification engineer, taking the nothing ventured nothing gained approach he applied and was successful. He continued to work in London but travelled to companies to carry out inspections, checking to see certification standards were met and adhered too, this included a lot of working on oil rigs. Most of the time he was based in London, though, with inspectors carrying out the work, and then he undertook a site visit for the final signing off.

Aubrey, the accountant became involved at this stage as the responsibility could leave John in difficulties if his judgement led to an accident, so John formed his own limited company and took out appropriate insurance. This reminded me of the query I had marked on the lists we made when thinking about John taking the leap into the oil industry several years before, the mortgage was insured in John's name only, a throwback to women not normally being named on a mortgage, after asking just how he would manage in the event of my passing, was enough to set that record straight.

Women were still having to fight to prove their worth in society, financial advisors at the time completely ignoring the role women played. The changes in the lives of women had been gradual until the advent of the contraceptive pill, enabling them to marry later, to enjoy the freedom on an ever-expanding field of experiences, and interaction with the opposite sex.

The situation in society had changed for young women, no longer willing to accept the old ways of thinking. Shops began to stock food which had been prepared ready to put in the oven, ready meals, automatic washing machines which worked with the push of a button, drying machines to complete the laundry chore, fabrics developed that required no ironing, all manner of kitchen and cleaning equipment to make life easier, hair dryers so light they could be held in the hand, hair colouring could be done at home, no longer having to spend hours in the hairdressing salon and the contraceptive pill enabling choice, starting a family when they wanted to, meaning more disposable income, freedom to change jobs if they wished.

Leaving older generations of men and women to struggle with the transition from post-war Britain to modern times. Working among these young women every day was amazing, just to listen to them each morning talk of their evenings, doing things which would have had been seen as scandals in my own youth. There was me, who had never gone into a pub with a group of young women and ordered drinks, listening to young women 20 years younger who met in wine bars during the evenings. Every single one of them eventually married and as far as I remember only one ended in divorce.

I embraced as many of these changes as I could, an automatic washing machine a must, a chest freezer in the garage, ensuring I could produce a meal quickly, especially as the demands of my in-laws increased.

John's new contract was based in the centre of London, once again travelling the world, certification relating to certain types of imports was required before they could be shipped to the UK, this covered many aspects of engineering, including the oil industry. Aberdeen was a frequent port of call for John, as he inspected oil refineries. One trip which stood out was a visit to Thailand to inspect a manufacturing plant just outside Bangkok, making gas cylinders.

The language barrier made it difficult for the interpreter to explain the problem John was pointing out, so, off came his jacket, tools in hand, he showed them exactly what the problem was. On returning two days later to see how they were getting on, he was greeted by the owner and entourage, who treated him like royalty. Reinspection proved the cylinders were now up to standard, which doesn't sound like much, until you realise that the product could be exported all over the world.

John was held in great admiration, he was taken out to dinner and handed a gift to show their appreciation, a small orange box containing a gold necklace and bracelet, this gift is symbolic, bringing luck, protection and blessings, an amazing gift. This may sound like an ideal job, but the reality was a long grinding day whilst based in London, often working his lunch hour to enable an earlier train in the evenings, unable to help with some school runs, and of course his parents.

Whilst at home he helped as much as possible in any way possible. As ever, teamwork, communication now so strong we could convey our thoughts with a smile, tuned into one another, understanding that I needed to rest, he suggested me having a rest or sleep on a Sunday afternoon.

The Sunday tea ritual had stopped as my father-in-law's health deteriorated, but evening drop-ins to the apartment became daily as John's mother was having difficulty coping. I remember being in the office when a call came through from her one day, can I come please, as father-in-law had fallen out of bed and could not get up. Other members of staff asked what was going on and I explained about my father-in-law's health and the evening drop-ins.

Everyone being very supportive as I left to go pick this man up off the floor, cleaned him up as he had been unable to control his body functions, dressed him and settled him into a chair in the lounge, remaking his bed and collecting soiled bedding, making them both tea and toast, all my mother-in-law could say was "You won't put us in a home, will you?"

I cannot imagine the fear. I had to be honest because they needed to be reassured that if the worst came to the worst, they would be looked after. "John and I will look after you as long as we are able, should your health deteriorate meaning you needed one-to-one specialised care then you might have to go into a nursing home, this would be whatever is best for you; if it was a private nursing home, funds would be found to pay for it."

I left saying I would call in that evening with Tracy to collect the washing. Needless to say, there were further calls for my help, the support of the other members of staff, amazing. One incidence had them all in stitches. Father-in-Law made several trips to the bathroom during the day, this irritated my mother-in-law as he kept slipping off and she had to stay beside him, just in case.

One morning, she tied him to the toilet so that she could get on with her work, then could not undo the knots in the scarf as he had slipped and tightened the knots, can you imagine the laughter as I told the others of my latest adventure, if it was not so sad I would have laughed until I cried.

Summer came a little different this year as DJ had a job at the local garage. We spent two weeks in Southwest France, again driving down and staying at the same place as the previous year, we travelled into the Pyrenees and surrounding villages more, so it was a more rounded vacation as we read maps and devised journeys, with both children now young adults, with inquisitive minds looking out into the world getting ready to fly the nest.

John and I, participating and enjoying their company, knowing this was probably one of the last family holidays of this nature. Just a happy family.

Christmas time, with my parents-in-law staying at home, John's father's health having deteriorated. Great fun for us four as we cooked and chatted together in the kitchen, after lunch, John and I went to see his parents. Making them a cup of tea, I left John with them, as I set to clearing up the kitchen, changed bedding, tidied the bathroom and ran the vacuum cleaner round.

John's Aunt Addie and his cousin were calling in on Boxing Day, I knew that this would make John's mother feel better. Tracy and I had packed a parcel of food to help the next day, and I received a pat on the arm from John's mother. A small token but appreciated, the first time ever.

New Year's Eve, the family had received an invitation to a party, this was really for the two younger members of the family, as this came from the parents of DJ's friend. I knew who they were, and so did John. A good party full of fun and games. I found DJ's friend Alex somewhat unpleasant, looking down his nose and sneering.

I knew his father was an Oxford solicitor, and I also knew that John's Susan had an affair with Alex's grandfather, but I think this is the first time he realised who DJ's mother was. The pompous idiot asked me why we had chosen Teddies for DJ, well, hit a snob where it hurts, "It's the family school, Ivan and Ivor went there."

*Chew on that one,* I thought, *go look them up.* Did Tracy enjoy the party, apparently not, as Alex, his brother and DJ spent the evening annoying her, as they were being immature boys, apparently. Maybe we will spend next New Year's Eve at home, I thought.

# Chapter Six
# Finding Our Winter Home and Dealing with Mental Illness

1988 was an important year for the family, with DJ having undertaken his mock A-level exams in the autumn of 1987 and received high grades, he had immediately started looking into medical schools. Teddies was very helpful, with John taking him to visit several medical schools and universities, including Liverpool, St George's and Charing Cross in London.

He received offers from two establishments pending achieving the right A-level results. So, all he had to do was get the high grades they required. Upon undertaking his driving test after the exams in May 1987, he had passed first time, typical and the mini became well used, as expected.

Tracy had GCSE (O levels replacement) examinations in the spring of 1988. After attending several parents' evenings over the years, at Headington, I was concerned about Tracy remaining at Headington for her sixth form years.

I knew that this was a very intelligent young lady but her form teacher telling her that she was not really a university candidate was not a helpful comment and made me angry and Tracy lose confidence in her academic capabilities, she needed motivation and encouragement, as she wasn't as driven as DJ, having not discovered anything she really wanted to do.

A very big discussion for us all, we would have preferred her to move school and took her to look at other sixth form options, knowing full well that Tracy would be the person to decide.

Both of our children had taken part in the Duke of Edinburgh Award Scheme, attaining their bronze, silver and gold awards, since they were fourteen, DJ being encouraged by Teddies, as it added to his medical school applications and Tracy because she enjoyed being outdoors and hiking across the wild areas of the UK. DJ had carried out his expedition training and final expedition with his peers at

Teddies, a different story for Tracy as only two girls participated in the gold award scheme from Headington, so she had to undertake the training and final expedition in conjunction with other girls from a local school called Rye St Anthony School.

This scheme gave young people confidence and a strong sense of independence. At Teddies, nearly every student did the gold award scheme and it was seen as an integral part of the curriculum, to aid university placement but at the girl's school these values were still not seen to be an asset for young women and only a handful did the bronze and silver and in Tracy's year only two, another addition to our concerns about Headington as the right place for Tracy.

John and I were correct, Tracy decided not to go to the schools we looked at but to remain at Headington, even though a key friend left to go to a state school called Cherwell and after a year Charlotte, a key friend throughout the years at Headington, left to go to secretarial college, interestingly the same one as Susan attended all those years ago.

As ever in life, there are times when you regret not being stronger or more forceful. Headington sixth form at that time was not the place for Tracy. Try as one does to give guidance to the next generation, they stop listening during those teenage years, and we parents have to await the outcome.

Easter came, no big celebration this year, with both children working for their exams. John and I walking, talking and visiting his parents. My father-in-law having been diagnosed with cancer, our help and support become even more important.

Tracy and I called in each evening, which was an essential part of caring for them both. Their shopping was undertaken during my lunch hour, together with paying bills for household utilities and collecting his prescriptions and with nurses calling daily to attend to his personal care and helping my mother-in-law cope.

Exams were taken by both children in May and June, and after these school activities changed, more sports, drama and excursions. The terms ending with sports day, we parents were not needed on those occasions. No more school runs for me until September, so from June I was able to call into my parents-in-law before work as well as during the evening.

My father-in-law's health deteriorated daily. It was a very upsetting time for all of us, and we made no holiday plans for that summer, DJ took up his job with the local garage again.

Late June, just after his birthday, my father-in-law was transferred to a hospice, asking for John to go visit him, when he once again reminded him to look after his mother. His final question, "Had DJ passed his exams?"

John replied. "Yes," leaving his father to die in peace a few hours later. This was a kindness to a man who had made his life so difficult as the exam results were not due until August.

Funeral arrangements commenced, poor John. Nothing had been discussed between his parents, although a burial space had been purchased for his grandparents at a cemetery which had a further space for his father in the same plot. The only thing John knew was that his father did not want to be placed there. Mother-in-law preferred a cremation, so the decision was made, but everything else was left to John and me to organise.

This led to more time off work as we visited funeral homes, registered the death and undertook all the paperwork involved, including activation of the will. Mother-in-laws despair was palpable, the question of the apartment now being in John's name needed addressing, so in a matter of fact manner, he told her that she could remain in the apartment as long as she was able, there was no need for her to worry about the running costs, as he would see to this side of things and me doing the shopping and evening calls would continue.

The cremation took place with very few of his stalwart friends in attendance, just family but one surprise came in the form of a bouquet of flowers, written on the accompanying card was simply, in loving memory Ivy. I wondered who that was, mother-in-law knew *that woman* seems father-in-law had a past.

August came round, with exam results, Duncan passed two of his A-level subjects with the required grades, but one was just not good enough for the medical schools to give him a place. Understandably, he was a deeply upset young man, John and I asked him what he wanted to do, take it again in the autumn was the reply.

Teddies for one term was not on the cards, as they did not offer the ability to retake but we knew of a sixth form college which had opened during the past few years, specialising in retakes and recommended DJ consider this, to see if it was what he wanted, they had a very good reputation for teaching and results.

The outcome was favourable, and they had a place for the autumn term, for him. With his holiday day job given notice, he buckled down to work diligently for this last high grade and reapplied for the medical schools for the following year.

Tracy had been successful with 9 GCSE's with very favourable grades, so it was sixth form for her in the autumn. There was no longer a need for an early start to our days as we were calling into the apartment in the evenings.

A new manager arrived at the office, very clever and very astute, immediately instigating training for me to become a mortgage underwriter. On discovering that my name had not been put forward, for a training course and exam in mortgage insurance products, he somehow managed for me to take it without the training offered to the other members of the team.

Whatever went on between him and the office manager, resulted in a large salary increase and recognition for my work over the years. Well, the exam was not difficult, having set up insurance policies for John and me in the past and more recently pension plans for John, I already knew what I was doing.

DJ took his resit in November, and immediately set about looking for employment, telling us how he wanted to spend his gap year. This was very much his father's son, I was not the least bit surprised to be told he would be going to Israel to work in a kibbutz for a few months and then to work at a summer camp in the USA, called Camp America, planning to travel across America on his own and down into Mexico before joining Peter and Susan in Seattle, after working in the camp, with the American children.

Christmas was a little strained that year, with my mother-in-law making it clear that she expected to come and live with us. John was adamant that this was not going to happen, as we had two teenage children about to go out into the world, and most importantly I was not going to give up another career. No discussion, decision made.

1989 was welcomed with a noisy evening playing cards and a toast to a successful year to come.

DJ settled down to working to build a bank balance whilst waiting for his result, with the mini coming into its own once again. Tracy worked for her A-level subjects, but not as driven as her brother, she was definitely not stimulated by her A-level studies, but then the teaching turned out to be poor.

It seemed the A-level teaching at Headington just wasn't good enough, especially one history teacher, who never seemed to be there and a geography teacher who, as a deputy head, was busy elsewhere.

The results came in at the end of January and DJ had the grade he required, and therefore a place to commence his medical training with Charing Cross Hospital London, in September, of that year. He left home at the end of February, joining a kibbutz employed in the growing of avocado pears. All I can say is that he had a great time, parents ringing up to wish him happy birthday was not what he wanted, party in full swing, he was nineteen years old, after all.

I passed my exam, allowing me to recommend the basis on which a mortgage could be negotiated with life insurance products included, followed by the introduction of an insurance company agent to make the actual sale, with the branch benefitting from the commission earned. A course to officially become a mortgage underwriter was organised for a date in early June.

As the course was for a week, this caused a bit of a problem, school run for Tracy and calls into the mother-in-law. John and I were now able to stroll in the local village alone, out into the lane at the end of the garden, to the River Thames a short distance away, into the fields past Dorchester abbey, which dated back to Saxon times, past the dyke hills, across the River Thames and then up Wittenham Clumps, the iron age fort clearly visible.

An area full of history, and when a group of workers were working on a new heating system for the abbey in the grounds adjacent to the north wall, a grave was uncovered. It was the grave of a Roman soldier with full kit and armour, this was immediately recovered by archaeologists. The allotment area, which many locals used for growing produce, was central to the village, and a Roman villa had been excavated there.

Talking as ever, I discussed my dilemma, no worry, John stated he would organise his schedule to be at home for that week. Working together again, renewing the powerful strength of our marriage. On these walks we started planning the next few years when the family flew the nest. Still happy together after almost 25 years.

A week away from home on my own, the first time in many years, a strange feeling which I tried to identify, was it loneliness, or lack of confidence. Neither of those, was it simply having no one else to consider time to be myself, possibly. The course itself was not difficult as I had been assessing applications for some time. So, I used the down time back at the hotel to take a long look at myself. I had my 50th birthday in the autumn of 1988, how did I envisage the future unfolding?

What do I need to do, to retain my self-respect? John and I would be a couple again when Tracy left for university, how could I enhance our lives? Menopause on the horizon, knowing how pregnancy affected my body, this was a big consideration. One evening I realised that at no time had I doubted my marriage, not once, the idea of returning to those days of being a couple, filling me with hope and happiness. This was the area for me to consider and plan. To start building a life for John and me and tackle the menopause as and when it affected me. No delaying, hoping things will improve, immediate action. The power of positive thought and the whisper of the aunts, believe in yourself, little one. Moving on to clothes, beauty products, etc, anti-ageing creams, the telephone rang, John.

Asking how I was and how the course was progressing. I was so glad to hear his voice and the closeness I felt to him; we chatted for a few minutes. Have to tell you why I rang scamp, Tracy is staying with Charlotte Thursday night, so I will come and collect you Friday morning, what time does the course end?

Course finishes on Thursday evening and we will be leaving after breakfast. Working late Thursday night to enable the participants who lived in Manchester to make their train connections.

Great, I will be there in time to join you for breakfast. I was over the moon that would be great. It seemed a few days apart had rekindled something very deep within my psyche, just how deeply I loved this man. This was my way forward.

The course ended around 9.30 on Thursday evening, with the final piece of the qualification to be carried out back at the office. All the course participants gathered in the bar for a final goodbye. Nobody would be staying long as the journey home for some would be arduous. Packing for me to be ready when John arrived in the morning, soon dropping off to sleep.

Breakfast started at 7:30 am, so a knock on my door just after 7 was not a surprise, the person stood outside the door was. DJ complete with keffiyeh, one very sunburnt skinny son. John stood behind him grinning. Communication between John and me, just with a look.

7:30 on the dot, we three went to the dining room, John and DJ ordering continental breakfast, and for me a full English, my breakfast was part of my hotel reservation. Huge plate full, DJ was salivating, goodness knows when he last ate. Swapped around DJ the full English and I the continental. Waitresses kept bringing food, and DJ kept eating, they enjoyed feeding him.

After goodbyes all round, into the car homeward bound, snores from the back seat, not a word or movement from DJ all the way home.

Life on the kibbutz had been rough and ready, driving tractors, picking and packing avocado pears. He thoroughly enjoyed his visit and travelled to Jerusalem before catching his flight home. Buying me a present. A little handmade wooden box with a tiny, blue dried flower which I kept for many, many years, but unfortunately, the fish glue used to stick it together disintegrated and it later fell apart. Having run out of funds, he could not afford a meal, just an ice-cream, which gave him a very upset stomach. No wonder he was so thin and hungry.

DJ was home for about three weeks before setting off again on his next adventure. Back to the garage to earn some pocket money, Mum and Dad supplying much-needed tee-shirts and jeans.

With empty nesting on the horizon and our silver wedding anniversary in 1990, our lives were evolving in a different direction.

DJ left for America and Tracy began working as a temporary employee (TEMP) at the building society with me, which she seemed to enjoy. Problems for me, as I expected, once again the person who had made my life difficult before, could not contain herself when my course report and case inspection came in. Advising the whole office that she and the team had got this qualification for me, the cases I had sent in had been worked on by the whole team. Sometimes you have to fight back, this was an insult.

Straight to the ledgers I went, pulled up her record of mortgage underwriting. At least the last 20 cases I had prepared, assessed, checked references and all aspects of them. The quality of my work supporting her role. Slapped it down on the desk in front of everyone and asked who it is that has retained this qualification for you, oh perfect one. I shall be doing this for my cases now, not yours, now you might have to do some work. Coffee everyone.

The chief cashier was not coping with the new younger generation of women in her department, errors, shortages in tills, all manner of things were going wrong. They had no respect for the chief cashier, just a very unhappy crew. This unhappiness bubbled over, and she brought me into the mix to try and shift the blame.

On the way home one evening, Tracy let me know what it was all about. Insurance commission, my recommendations relating to the basis of mortgages and insurance related policies brought in around 80% of commission earnings. The unhappy crew had been told that this would all go to me. Spreading the unrest to the mortgage department staff.

A few years before, I would have simply walked away, family matters taking up my energy. Not this time, I asked for a meeting with senior staff, and proceeded to discuss the matter in hand. Asking how management viewed the situation, only to have it dumped back in my lap, I had earned it, this was up to me.

*Being tested,* I thought, *what weak management.* I made the decision and asked to address the whole staff at closing time. Many years have passed since I stood in front of staff and made a presentation, but the mind remembered how to go about it. I opened with the subject, direct approach, stated the amount of commission earned, noting the sullen faces and a slightly sneering look on the chief cashiers faced I asked who earned this, stating, we did every single one of us, the cashiers who meet and greet the customers, the staff who check the daily work.

No one person earned this money, a team of well-trained building society employees did, the commission will be shared equally between us all. The chief cashier's days were numbered, and I was back on form.

Summer came with lovely lazy evenings, John and I working in the garden, strolling down the allotment to harvest fruit and vegetables or simply walking in the village. Our relationship as strong as ever, talking of our future and what we want to achieve in the coming years.

DJ had a flight booked to travel back to the UK from New York, but he was on the west coast of America and would like to visit Peter and Susan. This would mean paying for him to fly from Seattle to New York and a hotel stay for one night. John just grinned, all we had paid out for was jeans and tee shirts, DJ had funded his gap year himself. School fees had not been needed since November, let him have the funds and finish his trip we agreed.

Early September, we picked him up at the airport, he came strolling through the arrival's hall, backpack in hand, surrounded by young women. John and I stood there like a pair of spare parts. Finally, he looked for us, living his own life, we were no longer needed. Medical School here he comes.

The success of working in conjunction with insurance companies brought a new era to building societies, selling of savings accounts, mortgage-related insurance products became a part of everyday work. Staff were asked to volunteer for a new course relating to selling. The manager called me in, this is the opportunity for you all you need to do is apply.

This is the way your career should go, think about it. John was away on business; I would have to make this decision for myself. Would this change affect the family? Would it be detrimental to my marriage. Would it benefit me. No extra hours to be worked. Still based in Oxford, school run no problem, evening drop-ins no problem. Possibility of a more interesting area to work in. Obviously, a big change is coming in this area, why not take advantage? I applied the next day. John came back, I told him of the opportunity and his immediate reaction was, go for it.

Another member of staff applied as well, and we both went for an interview in Swindon of all places. I really cannot remember most of the interview, just one question stood out, something about dealing with difficult customers, my reply, not everyone starts the day feeling happy. Seemed to be the right answer, as I was selected to join the selling course. Once again this was to be held in Brighton starting in the spring of 1990. No school run problem as it was during Tracy's half term break.

A selected group of branches, their participation based on insurance sales, sent a selected member of staff, and office manager to participate in the course. Not the backwater hotel this time but The Grand Hotel, each of us greeted by a basket of fruit and homemade chocolates. There must be a lot hanging on this I thought. Thus began a long week of tutorials in selling techniques. The idea being that we would return to the office and introduce the staff to selling techniques. Looking for new savings accounts and insurance possibilities.

The branch responded well, and our figures soon outstripped those of the other branches involved. One thing became obvious within a few weeks, other members of staff liked the idea of spending more time chatting to customers and recommending products. The disorganisation of working methods under the chief cashier, came under fire. The length of time taken to carry out simple administration tasks made it difficult to find the time for this idea.

I was surprised when a group of the younger women who had asked for this to be part of their work, cornered me over coffee asking for help in achieving this. I had a choice help or not help. If I helped my life would be made difficult by the chief cashier, if I did not, anarchy. In other words, no choice.

These young women were trying to improve the way work was carried out; I would encourage them and live with the consequences. Immediately putting the ball back in their court. I asked for a breakdown of the most time-consuming administrative tasks, what was the job causing most frustration. Any ideas as to how things could be improved enabling better use of time.

One of the more astute staff members asked me for an example. I mentioned an everyday occurrence, when issuing a replacement savings account passbook, how many movements do you make? Fetching new passbook from the safe at the back of the office, across to the right to register the name against the number, back to the left to alter number of books held, back to your till to carry out the transaction, print the detail in the new book and stamp the old one cancelled. I saw the penny drop, time management; the discussion continued.

I did not need to be involved; these young women soon had a detailed list of suggestions which they put to the office manager. Total resistance from the chief cashier, staff uncooperative, customers complaining. Anarchy indeed but not seen to be caused by me. Chief cashier into disciplinary measures and finally left to work elsewhere.

This took several months, a very unpleasant time for the whole office. All the staff suggestions were implemented in a matter of days of her departure, new working practices were in place. The position of chief cashier was advertised, and a new member of staff was appointed.

During the spring of 1990 Tracy took her A-level exams and basically finished school. Time to take driving lessons, the trusty mini sitting in the garage waiting for her, like myself, it took her a few attempts to pass the test.

Getting the family together for probably the last family holiday was no mean task, but we eventually decided on the last two weeks of July, this was also our silver wedding celebration. Travelling to Menorca together, listening to our two children talking of their lives, friends and ambitions.

Arriving at our destination, a sun-baked villa to the north of the island. Wonderful heady smells of herbs heated by the sun wafted into the open doors and windows. Two weeks of fun and laughter, as we visited remote bays and villages. Dinners out in local towns and taverns. Swimming in crystal clear water. Halcyon days.

Home to await A-level results, with DJ back working at the garage. Student grants covered the basics and not much else, so he needed some money. Tracy was finally ready to take her driving test, which was just as well, as John and I had expected her A passes were not good enough, pass them she did but without the required grades for a good university. John gave her a choice, look for employment or resit her exams.

Resits came the reply, now a very determined young lady, the poor results giving her the required push. She went to the same sixth form college as DJ had for his one resit, as she needed to resit all her three subjects, this would be for a year. Early September, mini keys handed over and our daughter started her adult life. She loved that year at that college, the teaching was high class and stimulating and the independence she had meant she gained a new set of friends and had fun. John and I could now see the light at the end of the tunnel, just one more year of school fees.

Topping up of student grants being far less money to find. Discussion around our future, what needed doing in the house and a new car for John being the short-term goals. Then more serious subjects, not being a burden to our children. Ability to afford private health treatment if required. Travelling where did each of us want to visit. Interesting and stimulating times in our marriage, and joy in one another's company, a delight.

Well, as with all things in life, there is a downside. My emotions became extreme, laughing with John one moment, turning to start the washing up and finding myself crying tears streaming down my face. Menopause, I had expected hot flushes and bad tempers but not this state of emotional instability. One very worried husband.

Drying my face, I asked, "Were my emotions like this when I carried the babies?"

"Yes," came the reply.

Well, we know what this is then, I will make an appointment to see the doctor and get this sorted out. Doctor duly visited and he had been reading my notes before I arrived, have all your maternity notes here, are you feeling sick now. That made me laugh which set the tears off again. No need for blood tests, immediately offered HRT (Hormone Replacement Therapy) with a warning to make sure I check for breast cancer and attend three yearly scans.

Strangely, my mother was also 52 when she entered the menopause. Talking to her about it a few months later, she told of her inability to keep her temper in check and taking it out on my father. No regrets as apparently this was the best thing she ever did. *Bit late,* I thought, *should have done it years ago.*

Dropping in on my mother-in-law every day helped her to remain in the apartment, but gradually her health began to deteriorate. One morning I found her on the floor unable to get up, having been there for some time, on helping her up, I discovered her incontinence and asked if she had been in pain. Obviously, something was very wrong.

The doctor called, and he would visit later that morning. Rang the office and explained the situation, then John, who, needless to say, was hundreds of miles away. Poor man, I told him I would stay with her, not to worry, take care, safe journey. Stayed with her, I did through the doctor's visit and waiting for an ambulance until the early hours of the morning. As is still the case to this day, no beds, we sat in A&E for hours. A young doctor came to tell us still no beds, so I asked if there were any private rooms available. A long look, and he went off to find out. Yes, there is a room available, and I set about filling in paperwork. Up to the private ward to be washed and changed, ready for tests and investigations the next day. I took a taxi back to the apartment, collected my car and went home for a few hours' sleep.

Next morning back at the office awaiting telephone calls from John and the hospital. Mother-in-law had a serious infection, which they began to treat. John arrived home late afternoon and was given an update. Tracy prepared dinner whilst I rested, and John went to visit his mother. There was a room available on a general ward the next day, and his mother would be moved during the afternoon.

John and I went to visit the next evening, she seemed a little agitated, but tired. I picked up my shoulder bag, which had been on the floor, it was sticky. The floor and under the bed were dirty. John saw my alarm. This elderly lady had a serious infection, and the ward was not clean.

No way, off I go to see the matron and organised for her to be sent back to the private ward. John sat with his mother comforting her and told her she was going back to the private ward. She just nodded. John looked at me and mouthed "love you, Scamp."

Social services became involved, and it became clear that my mother-in-law could no longer take care of herself. Telephone call from the nursing staff one morning, requesting I come to the hospital and talk to the people involved with her care. Luckily for me, the office manager understood, having recently lost her mother. Lunch hour utilised again.

Reason for my presence soon became clear, my mother-in-law wanted to be near to our home, for this to happen I would have to locate a nursing home, I understood immediately, a private nursing home. Places in care homes were as few and far between in the 1980s/1990s as they are today.

Discussion point that evening, would need a far more in-depth discussion than a telephone conversation would have allowed. I could see the distress on his face and understood then just how the burden of his parents had impacted on his life. I had already obtained details of nursing homes, which might suit my mother-in-law's needs and handed the paperwork to him. Left him reading and took some me time.

Well, thinking time really, these nursing homes would need to be visited as soon as possible. John would not be free until the weekend, perhaps we should simply pick the nearest. Time for a cup of tea and a decision, John said, "Take a look at this one, it is a couple of miles away, and I drive through this village on my way home from London, a very decisive man."

Phone call to the office in the morning, and I took a day's leave.

The nursing home was light and airy with a pleasant atmosphere, the staff were very accommodating. Showing me round and introducing me to some of the patients. A bed was available, and the manageress telephoned the hospital for an update on my mother-in-law's particular needs, which the home was able to provide. Costs of services covered, together with details of any extras she might need.

All agreed and I signed the financial agreement, transport arranged for that afternoon. Off to the hospital I go, to tell her what was about to take place, not easy to do, what she really wanted was to come and live with us. John had been emphatic; this was not going to happen. I explained that she would see either John or me every day, and the staff at the nursing home were far better qualified to look after her than me.

Leaving her with the nursing staff, I went back to the apartment to pack her clothes and personal things before returning to the nursing home. By the time I arrived, she had been taken to the sitting room with the other patients. I just left her with the staff, I could do no more.

John dropped in on his way back from London, she was happily eating her tea and seemed reasonably happy. Bear hug as he came through the door, just stood holding me tight and close.

I often look back on the time my mother-in-law was a resident at the nursing home, after an initial period of adjustment tempered by wanting to live with us, she settled into this amazing caring environment. Calling to see her one Saturday, I found her sitting in the garden. Took my hand and said, "So nice to have one of your own come see you."

We spent a couple of hours talking about the children. After all these years her pride in them both was a shock.

Just mixing with other people talking of their families, realising she had something to boast about. Before I left, I went to see the nursing staff, simply to say thank you for looking after her. This was when I learnt that they had managed to coax her into a walk-in bath and had washed her hair. This was the first bath she had taken in her life, might sound strange to modern-day women, but one has to remember, bathrooms did not exist in most houses in the early 1900s. Immersing oneself in water was unheard-of.

Unable to adapt to the progress of life, living her life the way she had before the terrible trauma caused by the First World War. Unfortunately, I also learnt that her health was deteriorating very fast, making it necessary for the staff to move her to a room on the ground floor, to facilitate 24-hour care. Was I upset, very much so. Talking with John that evening, we both thought how sad it was that after all these years she was finally comfortable and at ease.

My parents' 60th wedding anniversary was in early September; Wendy was organising a party for them. Gathering of the clan, was the expression, all six of us with as many of the grandchildren as possible. I had seen very little of them since my mother's visit so many years ago, which had upset her so much. A lot of snide remarks from both parents relating to money, the worst being from my mother, something like, "I can see the Jew in you."

John understood immediately, standing behind me arms round me for a hug, he whispered in my ear, "I have you, Scamp. Nothing to worry about."

Must have been that hard no-nonsense look, of his he gave them because my mother went red and my father white, when they realised that John knew everything. We left the gathering early.

The following two weeks were more difficult for John than me, I went to visit his mother every day whilst John was abroad again. Arriving back on Friday afternoon, calling in at the nursing home, he was shocked at how quickly his mother's health had deteriorated.

Saturday morning, he went into the garden and picked every red geranium flower head, making a large bunch, asking for ribbon to tie them with. All three of us went to visit his mother, DJ was already back at medical school, she just reached out and touched the flowers. We stayed with her until late morning, John telling her he would be back to see her after he had eaten his lunch.

During that brief time, she slipped away. John came home telling me his mother had died in the short time he left to eat his lunch, feeling bad that he had not stayed with her. I gently told him that all she wanted was for him to go home and have his lunch, the geranium flowers she loved had helped her to go peacefully.

John was due to fly out to Milan on the Monday, meaning he was unable to register his mother's death. This upset him, quiet and sad, he needed time to adjust, just walking and enjoying the environment. I asked if he wanted to be alone, no, scamp, I need you with me. A long walk that day, talking about the past and the life his mother had lived. Hand in hand, just together.

John left on Monday morning, and I rang the office to take another day's leave. Visiting the funeral directors, collecting the death certificate from the nursing home, then travelling south to Henley-on-Thames to register my mother-in-law's death. Strangely difficult day, a mixture of sadness, regret and anger.

Thinking of her life, that one mistake, marrying the wrong person, could impact a life to such a great extent, unable to divorce, having to make the most of a bad job. Living with unbearable loss, afraid of the future and what it might hold. Did I do enough to make her life richer, I did not and did not know. All I know is that I tried.

Funeral arrangements made and John's Aunt Addie advised of his mother's passing, time to concentrate on my family. Tracy was still at home waiting to start her university life; DJ would be coming home to attend his grandmother's funeral, and I would need another day's leave.

John telephoned that night, and I told him of the arrangements and the choice of dates for the cremation, he was still upset, and we talked a while before he simply said, "Thank you, Scamp."

Funeral day arrived, we four, together with John's Aunt and her daughter Lynda. Only difference in the ceremony was the music. A recording of Grieg's

Peer Gynt, and for the final piece, the Charleston music to remind us all that life had not always been hard for her.

Walking amongst the rose garden after the ceremony, Lynda was looking for her father's rose bush, John's Uncle Cyril, her father had died in 1971, this is a remembrance garden where relatives can choose a rose bush and have it planted, for a fee of course. She stood there for a while, a look so very sad. I asked what it was she wanted, one of the roses, I bent down, cupped a soft rosebud and said "This one," a nod in reply, and we picked it.

Tracy had chatted to her cousins (Wendy's daughters) during the day about going to university, having attained high grades at D'Overbroeks. Off to Salford to study project management, a four-year degree course, with a sandwich year and sponsored by Costain's construction, which she achieved herself, following an extensive set of interviews and testing. She also told her cousins about her grandmother and the arrangements I had made, just normal chat between young women. Neither of us thought much of it. Come the end of the week, I received a telephone call from my mother, deeply apologetic. Had not realised how ill my mother-in-law was. It would be a long time before I spoke to my parents again.

Come early October, John, Tracy and I travelled to Salford to drop Tracy off to start her university life. The request to drive herself there in the mini, given an emphatic no by her father. I am sure he was concerned for her safety, but I think it was more a case of the trustee car would not make it.

Empty nest time for us, time to talk about what we would like to do, where we would like to visit, what we're both interested in, what sort of holiday we would like. Finding one another again, whilst continuing with our lifestyle. University and medical school grant top-ups from John and I were considerably lower than school fees, we needed to build a good-sized slush fund to enable us to, and both set about achieving this.

Having found the history of Southwest France interesting, we embarked on vacations that we could treat as an adventure, but also research and learn of the area's history before we travelled. May 1992 found us flying to an airport outside Venice and taking a coach trip, encompassing Venice, Florence, Assisi, Rome, Pompeii, Sorrento and back to Venice for the flight home. Venice came up to expectations as we travelled into the city by water taxi, visiting Rialto Bridge, Doge's Palace, St Mark's Basilica,

Figure 13—Duncan and Tracy in their early 20s

bridge of sighs and St Mark's square. On to Florence after a one-night stay in a hotel, John was used to living out of a suitcase and I had a lot to learn. Leave the books at home and simply bring notes in future, for one. Florence is a centre of culture, a busy bustling place, wonderful buildings, one still clad in marble. We visited the Cathedral of Santa Maria de Fiore, Ponte Vecchio, soaking in the atmosphere as we walked on the bridge. Stared in amazement at Michelangelo's famous marble sculpture depicting the nude biblical character, David. Wonderful city.

Onward next day to Assisi, a hill town in central Italy's Umbria region. The birthplace of St Francis. A beautiful place, but I soon learnt that churches are not something John enjoyed. On to Rome, busy bustling city, standing by the Trevi Fountain, totally in awe at the incredible work carried out so long ago. Visiting the Colosseum and letting our imaginations run riot at the barbaric life of Rome in ancient times.

Visiting the Roman Forum and gawping at the size and magnitude of this undertaking. Finally, the Vatican, an experience of a lifetime. Standing under the ceiling of the Sistine Chapel looking at Michaelangelo's work. A guided tour throughout Rome was the end of our day, amazing. Dinner that night in Tivoli, famous for its gardens and waterfalls. This John really enjoyed wide-open views and interesting planting. Soft waterfall sounds on the night air.

Pompeii, still being excavated, is deeply interesting and moving. Narrow streets with ruts where chariots had driven centuries before. The ladies are a bit shocked when drawings on the walls are pointed out, indicating brothels and other forms of carnal pleasure.

Coach travel is a good way to view as much of the country as one can, but you are stuck with your travelling companions. This was many years ago, women venturing out in groups for security. A gaggle of nervous women all competing for attention from tour guides and coach drivers, not a pretty sight.

Suffering from culture overload, we arrived at Sorrento and a very modern hotel, food good and a night excursion to a night club which I admit we ducked out of. Neither of us liked the idea of inebriated English ladies chasing tour guides. Next day we sailed across to the Island of Capri, and John really enjoyed. A lovely island with fascinating streets and shops.

Taking a cable car ride from the highest point, views across the sea and local houses, a magnificent sight never to be forgotten. Feeling the residual warmth of the sun beating up from the streets as we walked down to the harbour for our return crossing, lights all around, quite stunning, a wonderful evening. Romantic, oh yes.

Next day, we journeyed back to Venice, spending several more hours in this amazing city before going to the airport. Once again to be joined by the nervous ladies, one came over and asked if we knew which flight to catch. John sighed, I will let you know ladies, nothing to worry about. These ladies were on an adventure, such a thing would have been frowned upon only a few years before, let us hope they continued to do so.

Our two children, as ever full of surprises, DJ attained his degree with an honour's degree in anatomy. A junior doctor and off to work in the hospital earning a salary. Tracy ended her first year at Salford, which had not gone as planned, as always, the dreaded maths had let her down.

Discussion time in the house, finding out what she wanted to do, but she had already decided and had organised to start Lancaster University to read geography in the October. Mini still in the garage, so a good summer vacation before she headed north again. Lovely university complex with high-grade accommodation.

Late 1992, John came home one evening to tell me of a timeshare for sale in the hills behind Puerto Banús, it was for very late in the year. We could easily fly down to Marbella, the cost at this time of the year was reasonable. I could see that he really wanted to do this, I asked him to tell me more. The complex had a swimming pool, bar and restaurant. They also had a golf team. Now we have it, I thought. I did not hesitate when could we go visit, no problem, scamp, it's now or never. That irresistible grin again, go ahead if it's what you want.

Go ahead, he did, and late November we spent a week in Southern Spain, days were sunny but definitely not summer clothes weather. As I guessed, golf was the magnet, John playing every day. Did I sit around, no, I walked the course with him, trying to understand the magnet that is golf. At this stage it was just a pleasant walk for me. A winter week away. A week away from the grey weather at home. Very enjoyable.

Time to consolidate our life, the apartment needed clearing and cleaning, ready to be put up for sale. One weekend and many visits to the dump sorted that out. Time for the mini to go. Sad day but we had been using it for a very long time. All good things come to an end.

Christmas came without a glimpse of DJ, hospital life he really enjoyed, John drove up on Christmas Eve to fetch him, promising to take him back for his next shift. Christmas was a short celebration that year, just eating and talking together. Each of us having plenty to say as we recounted the year gone by. Happy days.

John's working life was busy, and he seemed to be enjoying the work. Travelling about meeting new people and visiting companies he had been to previously, interesting and varied work. 1993 brought change in the financial industry with banks and building societies merging.

The person who hoped to take over the department, became very ill one morning. I only just got to her before she collapsed at her desk. Holding her close and tight, she whispered I am so afraid, Joan, so afraid. The building society offered a health check with a London clinic for all members of staff, and six of us, including this young woman, took advantage of the offer, which had taken place a few months before this incident. We all had clean bills of health. I asked her if I could do anything to help.

Apparently, she had an appointment with her optician that afternoon, would you cancel it, please? All of us knew the optician very well, being a customer, and when I mentioned the collapse. Neither of us liked the sound of things, so instead of cancelling the appointment it was brought forward to the next half an hour. I told the member of staff of our concerns and offered to walk around to the opticians with her, just to make sure she was safe. She just looked at me with tears forming.

"Come on," I said. "Let's go."

What a good job we went, the optician saw that there was a glaring issue, her skull was low down on the nape of her neck and cutting off the blood supply to her brain, and affecting her eyesight and goodness knows what else. Straight to the hospital for an emergency operation to remove part of her skull.

Returning to the office several weeks later, she admitted that stress and frustration working in a dead-end job was also a major part of her problem. Leaving a few weeks later to take a far easier job with the local planning department.

Retirement age was 60 for building society employees, and the office manager would attain this age in the spring of 1993. I thought about this and wondered how she would fare, her whole life revolving around the office, no preparations made for retirement, her husband would not retire for several years. When the time came for her to leave, I made a mental note of this. Retirement is something you hope to reach and planning how to enjoy it is essential.

The position of replacement office manager was advertised, and it was suggested that I apply. Probably to make up the numbers, two of the younger members of the staff also applied. Something about the interview told me that someone was already designated.

Questions were obscure and had little to do with running an office in a financial institution. I was already on a good salary having worked there for so many years, it would mean a lot more responsibility for little reimbursement. Something stirred, I really do not like being used, especially as a stop gap. I addressed the person asking the questions and asked if she had read my application. Slight splutter, and I continued, then of course you already know that I have vast experience of running a branch of a local bank, banking qualifications. A major part of my day is spent smoothing over ruffled feathers and encouraging all members of staff in relation to their work and enabling the office to benefit from the abilities of all members.

Did I expect to get the job, did I want it, no, not really. I was right, someone else was designated, some idiot at head office thought the branch needed a shake-up. The beginning of the end of the branch and the building society. The same idiot rang me asking if I would please apply for the job vacated by the chosen member of staff, in High Wycombe.

Simple answer, why would I want to take a job in a smaller office, increase my commute time and length for a small increase in salary? Thank you but no thank you. Perhaps I would like to apply for the same job in Swindon. Same answer.

High time I started looking after myself, already qualified in relation to mortgage-based insurance products, I might as well go the full journey and qualify as an insurance salesperson. That was exactly what I set out to do. Obtaining a training position with an insurance company.

The big draw of the passing of exams and qualifying with FSA (Financial Services Authority), had to be carried out in my own time. Exams to be taken in a branch of the insurance company, just south of the M4. So be it, I would take a few days sick leave, no way was I going to use up my holiday allocation.

My but did that new office manager try to make my life difficult, hearing other members of the staff talking, I was not the only one in the firing line. The adage sweeping with a new broom came to mind. Anyone within the existing staff, earning more than a certain figure, probably more than her, was being squeezed and bullied to get them to go elsewhere.

Cost cutting to a high degree, one such method left me laughing all the way home one evening, rationing the number of pieces of toilet paper used. Thwarted that one, my desk was at the beginning of the exit to the staff room, I placed a large box of paper tissues on my desk. The others soon cottoned on, helping themselves as they walked past.

The strategy worked as one by one the existing staff left for pastures new, very soon all the experienced personnel were gone, the staff were struggling to deal with the volume of work. I was working on reception at this time, a very young member of staff in charge of the mortgage section. Unable to cope, appointments not recorded, and people waiting to be seen. This office manager was more of a bulldozer than a broom. Obviously, I had stepped back and took no part in staff problems, interface confrontations. Unwilling to be party to these goings on. Also knowing that as soon as I had finished qualifying, I would be leaving.

My annual assessment came around, what a surprise, nothing like my normal standard, sat in front of the manager as he asked me what I actually did with my time. My desk was perhaps 10 yards from his office, and he had to ask. What a weak man he was doing the office manager's dirty work for her.

I simply said, "This assessment is the lowest I have received since I started working here, I can only assume that this not only reflects on your assessment of the situation but that of the office manager."

Leaving him with my thick file on his desk.

I took a couple of days off sick a few weeks later and passed two of my exams needed to enable my qualification, returning to the office the following day, he called me into his office again. Cards on the table, Joan, you sorted out the mortgage department, showed the younger member of staff how to handle difficult clients and organise the workload, I would understand if you wished to make a complaint.

I can assure you it will not happen again. I knew the idiot at head office would not support me, no point in rocking the boat, all being well I would soon be moving on.

John and I had discussed this situation because as he pointed out, I no longer needed to work. Now was the time for me to do what I wanted to do. Total support for whatever I decided. This incredible man found the opening for me, still reading the paper on the train as he journeyed to work each day, he noted an advertisement for a financial consultant with a financial institution, based in the Oxford area.

After dinner, the evening after he found the advert, he sat me down and gave me a pep talk. Telling me that I could do this job, I was more than capable. I was to apply for it, I had nothing to lose. I could see only one drawback; I would be 56 in the following October. Age discrimination was not banned until the implementation of the Equality Act 2010. Long look from John, if you do not try, you do not get. I applied there and then.

I received a letter inviting me to go for an interview in Northampton, well, I thought this is really going to take me out of my comfort zone, never having driven that far on my own before. Another sick day taken; I journeyed north arriving at my destination in good time. All the others called for an interview were men, some very nervous. The pressure of having to support a family, with commission-based income, was difficult, and was an opportunity for them to work for a company rather than having to look for customers as insurance agents. My scenario is a very different situation.

My appointment time came and went, the whole business was running slow. Some very disappointed faces as one by one the applicants left. I walked into the interview, with a smile and a handshake. Apology from the interview team and a strange question, did I know of any reason why they would not employ me?

I answered after a little bit of thought, my experience over the years meets with the requirements detailed on the application, I am already taking exams to attain my FSA qualification. I have been dealing with people and their money for many years. Understand the need for discretion in this respect.

Only thing I can think of is my age, so I will understand if you wish to terminate the interview at this point. The whole interview from that point was like an easy-going chat. I drove home thinking to myself that's the strangest interview for a job I have ever had.

I had not heard back after my interview, which was not a surprise as it had been explained quite clearly that my references and status under my insurance qualifications would need to be checked. July saw John and I off on an adventure, and what an adventure it was. Flying into Hurghada Airport, on the Red Sea coast of Egypt and boarding our cruise ship. This was an educational cruise with lectures in the evening relating to the next day's excursion.

Our cabin was simple but adequate two single beds and a bathroom, shower being a douche which had John in stitches. Being a very tall man, this led to a bit of a mess as he tried to rinse off the body wash whilst the water sprayed everywhere. Think I will shower first next time.

Dinner again simple, fresh, tasty and plenty to eat, followed by a lecture, situated in the lounge come bar, relating to the next day's excursion. First night's sleep on board listening to throb of the engines, took a long while to go to sleep. Dawn found us docked at Sharma el-Sheikh, still reasonably cool at that time in the morning, and everyone boarding an air-conditioned bus.

At this point, we had no idea how hot the day would become. Travelling northwards along the coastal route before turning into the mountains. Travelling in the mountains to the foot of Mount Sinai and St Catherines monastery. This amazing place came into view the walls and building reflecting the sunlight giving an impression of peace and calm. Built between 548 and 565, this is the world's oldest continuously inhabited monastery. Walking in the chapel everyone quiet and respectful. The wooden seating glowing with many years of polishing, smell of beeswax on the air.

A lasting impression on a day never to be forgotten. Outside the hot air drying your lungs as you breathe, into the bus. This climate took some getting used to. St Catherine's Monastery and its history did little for John, but the scenery and the mountains thrilled him. This is going to be an amazing adventure scamp. Back in the bus for a packed lunch, John was in his second heaven able to see across the desert for miles and miles.

Back on the cruise ship for a shower and dinner, lecture that evening relating to our visit to Jordan. Very tired and all the throbbing engines in the world would not have stopped us dropping off to sleep, as we sailed to Aqaba.

Very early start to the day, whilst it was still cool, off to the place I had mentioned months before, Petra. Leaving John to sit by the window, the open desert scenes for him to enjoy, we pulled into the parking area, to be met by a string of camels, saddled and ready to ride. The colours of their saddle blankets rich and warm. The opportunity to ride through the Siq, a rock canal that measures 160 metres in length and 3 to 12 metres wide) on a camel was offered, but John and I preferred to walk. This was a long stroll through an opening in the rocks with shafts of sunlight breaking through.

The narrowest part of the walk making us both smile, very glad we walked riding a camel through that bit would not have been pleasant. On we walked turning a corner the most impressive sight in pink glowing light, Petra. Living up to its name, Rose City, so-called because of the colour of the sandstone from which it is carved. Famous for rock-cut architecture and water conduit system. It was also called, a rose-red city half as old as time.

Sounds of people's voices resonating in the heat of the late morning. Walking on further into Petra we found the Roman area so distinctive with its straight streets and buildings reminiscent of Pompeii.

Unfortunately, this is where I learnt to drink more water and wear a hat, as the hot sun made me sick and dizzy. Back to the cooler air in the shade we went. Wadi Rum (Also known as the valley of the moon) some 60 kilometres away was our next destination. A short time spent here gave an idea of the history and geological importance of the area, not enough time to explore the rocky caverns and steep chasms or look at the prehistoric inscriptions. This is one of the world's most breathtaking desert landscapes with enormous red, yellow and black mountains and sand dunes.

Swirling whirls of sand easily visible as they rose circled and eased. Visiting a Bedouin camp, marvelling at the ingenuity of these people, the colour and culture of their lives, leaving me in awe. A bit off putting though was the sight of three large vehicles parked to one side. It was not until 2011 that this became a world heritage site.

Off to Aqaba that afternoon, the bus being cool and comfortable, everyone talking of the day's excursion, thrilling. Pulling into the port to return to our cruise ship, we could look across the water to Aqaba itself, scene of the battle for Aqaba in the First World War led by Sherif Nasar and Auda Abu Tayi advised by Lawrence of Arabia. Now a famous film.

Dinner on board was noisy and air full of excitement as people related the day, all ready for the adventure as were John and I. Lecture tonight but we opted to watch a film in the lower deck of the ship, surprisingly quiet as we watched Peter O'Toole in Lawrence of Arabia. The ship left port during the night, and we sailed to Safaga on the west coast of the Red Sea, our gateway to Luxor and the experience of a lifetime.

Karnak Temple in the morning light, magnificent. Walking passed statues of sphinxes on both sides leading to the entrance of temple, the entrance itself awestruck at the size and ability of the people who designed and constructed these amazing statues 2000 years ago. Into the temple itself completely amazed by the sheer size and height of the columns. Walking through the and marvelling at the ability of this ancient civilisation.

Tall columns depicting the vegetation of the area. The pillars two of Thutmose, elegant reminders of the importance of upper and lower Egypt at that time (the lily and papyrus). The Obelisk of Thutmose, colossal, with three sides having vertical lines of inscription. One of which I remember was a depiction to Thutmose. Finally walking beside the sacred lake. This part of our trip was the one I had done a little research for.

Did I regret not going to the lecture the evening before, no, our tour guide was full of information. I was concerned as we headed back to the coolness of the bus, maybe John had been bored. Discussion relating to ancient Egypt, an area we had not covered, he looked at me in amazement, how could I be bored, how did they do it? How did they design and make all of this. How did they transport the sandstone and granite, remember the lake, how did they manage that? Different viewpoints on everything, which somehow seems to make a broader view of so many aspects of our life together.

On to the Luxor Temple, walking into the entrance way flanked each side by enormous statues of Ramesses the Second, I remember a obelisk of pink granite standing tall, a colonnade depicting closed papyrus buds, standing statues of Ramesses, which originally had crowns. They were on the ground having fallen off. A lasting impression of respect and admiration. Much shorter time spent here as we had a time schedule, onwards we travelled across the bridge over the Nile to the valley of the Kings with an armed escort in front and behind our bus. Something to do with a shooting in the area.

Bus dropped our party off, and we walked into the valley, so small, everything close together. Several burial chambers were more than a few as the pharaohs changed tactics when the pyramids were no longer deemed safe, being open to tomb raiders.

Unfortunately, the tomb of Tutankhamun was not open for viewing and we all descended in to the tomb of Ramesses 11, the paintings and hieroglyphics still clear and sharply defined, the tour guide explained that workers cut a large space and painted a red line on the ceiling to ensure straight paths for the stone cutters, this also served as a central point to ensure parallel walls and corners.

The tour guide became hushed in his reverence, which had me thinking I was sure his mummified remains had been removed because of looting, we were near a sepulchre made of stone, which stood alone, surrounded by drawings of the afterlife. As we walked back up to the tomb entrance, I was drawn to one drawing of Ramesses standing with a staff in his hand, civilisation had come a long way, but our roots are here in this ancient land.

Back on the bus, deeply moved by this experience, a gentle reminder from my husband not to think too deeply. Perfect day for me so far, and now it was John's turn as we journeyed north along the bank of the Nile River. Witnessing the rural life and noting the lush growth of vegetation all around. Seeing the small boats sailing on the river, called feluccas. I know we ate by the river and the air was cool, so we had shade but as to where I am not sure.

A long day but not over yet as we were ushered into our seats to watch the Son et Lumiere at the pyramids. Clear skies above with stars so close overhead, the sphinx in the foreground with the pyramids standing majestically behind. The lights came on and behold an amazing scene, golden stone glowing in the night with the moon as stars as a backdrop. Beautiful. Richard Burton's voice telling the stories and the three great pharaohs, Khufu, Khafre and Menkaure.

Time to rejoin the ship at Ain Sokhna after a very long day. So tired sleep was calling, and we were not sailing that night, no engine throb. Late breakfast and a light lunch on the upper deck, lovely Greek food. Most enjoyable. Into the bus we go off to Cairo a bustling metropolis and a night club to be visited. Passing a bar on the way had both John and I smiling.

The meeting of the generations, a donkey, a camel and 4x4 parked outside. Ancient and modern in every sense of the word. To say the nightclub visit was not the best part of our trip would be putting it mildly. Belly dancing is an acquired taste.

Next morning we grabbed a couple of seats on deck for our journey through the Suez Canal. Just a slow sail through the straits passing huge ships at certain points where it was wide enough for two vessels. Pulling into other areas to allow the free flow of ships, like sidings on a single-track railway. Very relaxed and comfortable in one another's company talking of what interested us or just quiet together. Our life at home on hold as we simply enjoyed our time together.

Long day at sea, and a good night's sleep engine throbbing more of a lullaby. Waking at dawn to a new day in the Port Haifa Israel.

Nazareth is the first stop for this part of our tour, this is a city of faith and religion, very spiritual and a feeling of holiness. As to my memories of Nazareth they are related to feelings and awe, the city itself busy and at that time modern. So much history in one place. I think I was overcome by emotion, John not very enthralled. Back on the bus neither of us talking very much. Very moving experience.

Bethlehem, the birthplace of Christ, was so moving and I was emotional again. Everyone ushered into The Church of the Nativity. The birthplace marked by an inlaid silver star in a grotto under the church. Walking through the church and into the grotto, everyone felt the feeling of reverence, amazing. John not moved; I think a little bored. Maybe, a bit of cultured overload.

Ushered out and into the bus, the tour guide seemed a little anxious. This is in Palestine; we are tourists and maybe just not very welcome.

On to Jerusalem a beautiful city, walking the four stations of the cross, streets so narrow, strangely moving walking us back in time. The wailing wall witness to so many prayers, wishes and hopes. In itself just a grey wall, but so much more a place of deep belief and holiness. Visiting the church of the Holy Sepulchre, our tour guide spoke quietly as he told us of its history. We also visited a memorial to the victims of the holocaust, a pinpoint of light for every victim. I have tried to find reference to it in the years since we visited to no avail. Into the outskirts of the city to visit The Gardens of Gethsemane and The Mount of Olives.

A long day for everyone, all quiet contemplating everything they seen and heard that day. Was I moved by all I had seen, yes very much so. John not so much by the history of the city, although we knew that an ancestor of his, a crusader was buried in this area, but by the memorial to the victims of the holocaust. Journey back to the ship in the late afternoon, no lecture this evening as the next day would be spent at sea. A special dinner to celebrate our journey being served.

Time to put a jacket on John, girls will be dressed up to the nines and that includes me.

On time for dinner and picked a table near a window (porthole), laid for four people, and waited for our regular dinner partners to arrive. Another couple who had not spoken to us during trip, pulled up seats and sat down to join us. I had the strong impression that the husband (Partner) thought I was a homebody, when his wife (or partner) started flirting with John I was a bit bemused but simply carried on with my dinner. It had been a long day, and I was hungry.

The husband asked me bizarre questions about my life not what I did but where did I live. Was I enjoying the food on board. In other words, not the least bit interested in me, I was observing the flirting going on between the wife and John, when she suddenly started feeding him a strawberry from her dessert, I got the message. I turned to the male at my side and used a voice both of my kids would have recognised as, watch out duck mum's annoyed. Asked him if he was going to deal with this or should I.

He stood and told her to come with him, it's not like the last cruise they were on. They left and I rose to leave as well, John asked Where are you going, scamp. Up on deck to commune with the stars. Do you want some company, only if it's yours, I replied. How he manages to do this, I do not know, but wind me up again he had, exasperated I turned to him as he walked behind me up the stairs, you do not even like strawberries.

Laughing, he said, "No, but I certainly like you."

Commune with the stars we did, always so much fun. Talking to other members of our group next morning as I sunned myself on deck, it transpired that this couple were into wife swapping and how they had witnessed my dismissal of them last evening. Seems I did the right thing. Strawberry's what a wind up.

A full day at sea, I was content sitting, watching the sea and looking for dolphins, John, more like a caged animal, walking around the small deck talking to some of the older group of men. Discovering that some of them had come on this cruise for one purpose, to pass by Gallipoli where an important battle was fought in World War One. They seemed to have plenty to talk about, and the day passed quickly. Lecture that evening about Istanbul and Ephesus, no complaints from John, but I think he was having ancient monuments overflow.

Up early next morning, time to witness entering the black sea via the Bosphorus Strait and seeing the great port famous for centuries. One happy husband, this is what he really enjoys, and I made a mental note for future adventures. Docked early and bus waiting off to Ephesus.

An ancient city in the Aegean region, which reflects the centuries of history from classical Greece to the Roman Empire when it was the main Mediterranean commercial centre. Silt from the river Caister has formed a fertile plain but caused the coastline to move further west. In Roman times, a sea channel was maintained, the original causeway still visible. This is where Anthony and Cleopatra walked on their arrival long ago.

This ancient town filled me with wonder as I thought of all who had gone before. John was enthralled but more interested in the terrain and silting, which had changed the entire region over hundreds of years. Back into the air-conditioned bus, but it was hot. Istanbul, unfortunately the Topkapi Palace was closed, we could only view the outside.

The Blue Mosque, amazing architectural very beautiful, inside sunlight and colourful prayer mats. Shoes in hand we walked and marvelled at the ability of our ancestors. Their knowledge of mathematics, weight distribution and beauty a joy to behold. Later a walk through the streets to our waiting bus, a little late as it happens but nobody seemed to mind.

Nearing the end of our journey, so far one of the most romantic holidays we had enjoyed, happy in one another's company. Perhaps just perhaps retirement could be fun.

Leaving port very early the next morning as we had a full day sailing ahead of us. Back through the straits, heading for the Corinth canal.

This is the part of our journey John had looked into, not the history of its conception, construction of course and the mammoth task undertaken to cut this opening (Canal) between the Gulf of Corinth in the Ionian Sea and the Saronic Gulf Aegean Sea.

This canal has been fraught with difficulties from blocking by landslides. The major problem and is its narrowness 24.6 metres, only passable by small ship's making it commercially unviable. The battle for the only bridge over the canal in the second war world, and the subsequent rebuilding by the Italian Army.

Three years later during their retreat of the German Forces, explosives were used to cause landslides and debris from the original bridge, locomotives etc. dumped into the canal to make it unpassable, this is the area which interested my husband. This is the scene of battles fought during out lifetime. A very sobering thought.

I was interested in the patterns and swirls cut into the rock by the wakes of many ships, looking up at the sheer face and into the sunlight. This had been the dream of man since time immemorial, original construction finally began under Roman Emperor Nero in 67AD. More than two thousand years ago, two different viewpoints, John and I, both based in the ability of mankind.

On leaving the canal we passed by Gallipoli Peninsula, with the Aegean Sea to the west and the Dardanelles to the east. Scene of one of the most terrible battles fought in World War I, the terrain was inhospitable, the Turkish and allied lines were just a few metres apart.

Terrible loss of life on both sides. John left my side at this point and joined the older men who stood at the stern, some weeping for those they had lost. Most grim faced and stoic. John's mother had lost so many of her brothers in this war, I understood his need to stand with those that had travelled so far just to be here. And salute the fallen.

A sad day full of nostalgia, a quiet dinner and finally docking at Itea. Evening lecture about Delphi, our destination next morning, and our last night on the ship. Packing no problem, no need to worry about creases, the washing machine would be busy when we returned home. Last night's sleeping on board but no engine throbbing to send us to sleep.

Next morning found us up on deck watching the sun rise, happy just to be together. Breakfast was noisy as people prepared to leave and say goodbye to the ship's crew, these people helped make this a trip to remember for the rest of our lives.

Off to Delphi, which is between two towering rock formations of Mount Parnassus, a magical place with views beyond imagination. A place written about in the books read by my Uncle Cecil so many years before, the story of it being the meeting point of two eagles released by Zeus, one to the east and one to the west.

Pilgrims came to the site to receive an oracle from Pythia, the goddess of Apollo. A cult and religion influencing the whole of Greece. That withstanding, the buildings, monuments, terraces, temples and treasures forming a strong impression, magical. This area became one of Kohn's favourite memories, the views thrilling, majestic.

Onwards we go to Athens itself, a brief visit to the Acropolis, stood on a hill, this was a fortified site, and the strong walls have surrounded the summit for more than three thousand years. It was a privilege to be able to walk close to the building itself, knowing that this was the birthplace of democracy, philosophy, theatre, freedom of expression and speech.

Did I think of my Uncle Cecil and aunts at this time, I hope so.

Talking to Peter recently, he told me of his visit to the Middle East around the same time, his for work. He and his colleagues made several trips to Saudi Arabia, for Boeing's with 737s, they did hot weather tests in the desert because 737s were sinking into the tarmac up to their wheel axles. Heard the rocks exploding like gunshots. Saudi crew told them there is water in the rock below the surface, and they were disturbing it, that is how sand is made. How parallel our lives are.

Flight home passed swiftly as I slept most of the way, home to the village, itself steeped in history going back to Saxon days. To our normal daily routine, a bit of an anti climax. Allotment to weed, grass to cut and the washing machine to work overtime. Plenty of time to talk about our trip.

Monday morning back to the office for us both, John to an enormous workload, and me to a welcome from the staff and a very subdued office manager. Something was up.

Arriving home, I found the front hall, where my little daughter had loved to sit, covered in a heap of mail. The post office retained our mail for the time we were away, there was a lot. Simply put it to one side, unpacked the groceries and set about cooking the evening meal. Normal routine shower for John and a cup of tea, he took the pile of mail and sorted it. One was for me from the financial institute I had been for an interview with, asking me to contact them on my return from vacation. Oh, dear, I thought maybe not.

Making a call from the office would be a bit tricky but where there is a will there is a way. I had the job, my references had all been received and more than acceptable, the full complement of new staff had not yet been chosen, and employment would commence later in the year, full details would be sent in writing.

John came home that evening, and I went out to greet him, asking what colour car I shall have. He knew exactly what I was talking about. Big bear hug and swung off my feet.

It was late September before I received full details of my new employment, and during that time more members of staff had left the office. To say the manager and office manager were uptight was no exaggeration, the office atmosphere was very unpleasant.

I had not said a word to anyone of my impending job change, something was amiss. My references were the only thing I could think of which had been requested many weeks before. Come September 30th, I received my job offer in writing and immediately handed in my notice.

True to form, the office manager looking after herself, asked me for details of salary offered, holiday entitlement. Offering to increase my salary and extend my holiday quota. The answer was simple, can you add a car and bonus covering sales to that?

The answer was negative, she just stared at me. I must have shown the total contempt I felt.

The manager returned to the office a few days later and simply asked where I would be based and which branches I would be working with, he seemed to know a lot more than the office manager.

Come October 31st, I walked across the road to start the next chapter of my life.

# Chapter Seven
# The Retirement Years, If You Want to Call It That

Moving across the road to my new employment was the beginning of probably the most satisfying stage in my career in finance. I was employed as a mobile financial consultant covering about 10 branches.

The first three weeks, I travelled to each one, introducing myself and explaining my role in relation to their daily activities, this meant no early morning starts as the offices were busy first thing in the morning. This was a very pleasant ease into a new role, which became increasingly busy, over the next few years.

Our annual trip to Spain continued to be very enjoyable and I continued to walk the golf courses with John, with the evenings spent with old friends, over dinner and a few glasses of wine.

John was 60 now and beginning to talk of retirement, after all he had been working since, he was 16 years old, our initial plan to be financially independent, and not a burden to our family was well within our time frame and now we began to discuss how we would like to live our lives in the foreseeable future.

These were not very serious discussions at this stage, as I was only 56 and had just changed jobs, just what we as individuals would like. I admit to having no idea at that point, not a subject I had even considered, but it did make me think of our parents and how bored they all had been when work stopped, and so did they, that was definitely not for me, I wanted something more.

Both of us were soon back to work, with me travelling as well as John, which made him laugh. I was quickly off to an induction course in Nottingham, where I met other members of this new team. Most of them were situated in branches and just a few mobiles like me. It was an interesting start, as we were advised of our forthcoming role. Sales were confined to an insurance company, with very little scope for investment sales.

However, in the coming months, the company would be setting up its own financial products and we would all have to qualify for each product and the Financial Services Act and to retain these qualifications, we would be subject to three monthly exams. This was not a new concept for me, as I had been subject to this standard of supervision for some years.

The role was slow to start as for the staff working in the branches, the concept of a mobile financial consultant was very new, and I spent the months prior to the company setting up its own products, fulfilling the appointments set up for me, by the staff in the branches, these were mainly mortgaging related, so very lowkey advice required. Some mortgages were on an interest-only basis and used endowment policies to accumulate the capital required to pay off the mortgage at the end of the designated term, but a problem was evolving with these policies, as some were not attaining the figure quoted at the point of sale, so they were no longer as popular as they used to be.

Responding to this lack of popularity and after discussion with my assistant, we began to arrange the appointments around the training time for each branch and I undertook training sessions in customer awareness, telephone techniques and the function of each policy being advised to customers. My sales data grew in line with these interactions with the branch staff, and I was reimbursed accordingly.

Following this, the company's new policies came on stream, and they were very good, enabling me to cover all aspects of financial planning with my customers and make a real name for myself as a financial advisor, with a large number of customers.

I really enjoyed these years in this role and my figures reflected this, as did our bank balance and helped me to start thinking about retirement for me and John and what that could look like, including possibly global travel. It was also so good to have achieved this level, considering where I started from, the aunts were always there, believe in yourself.

My company car allowed us both to drive it and John and I took full advantage of this. Long holidays abroad were not contemplated, we simply got into the car that spring of 1995 and headed across the Channel. John had been treated very well when visiting a company in France, taken out and shown the local area, which included Waterloo, scene of the historic battle against the

French. Wellington and Napoleon leading the battle, he remarked at the time how small the area was, and he wanted to take me there. This he planned to do, as well as us visiting one of the Normandy beaches, where some of those young men I had met, all those years ago in Gosport as a child, before the D-Day 1944 landing, died.

We duly set off, like our honeymoon, John organised this trip, leaving me to enjoy the journey. First, we visited Omaha Beach, both shocked at how small it was. A terrible battle had been fought there as the men came off the landing crafts and battled their way up the beach, to attack the enemy, who had the advantage.

Such bravery, as they fought hard for the freedom, that John and I, plus our children, have. We went into the cemetery, which was so peaceful and serene, rows of white head stones clean and well cared for, some with flowers left by relatives, people from all over the free world. We were both deeply moved, and we simply clasped hands, I wept as indeed I am now.

Off to Waterloo, another small area that was fought over, just a green area now. One can picture the lines of soldiers in their distinctive battle dress, guns, explosions, horses and men charging. Again, emotive but not so intense. Travelling south we arrived at Vieuw Beaucoup, more luxurious accommodation in a French holiday complex, around a swimming pool and enjoyed long lazy days, travelling into the Pyrenees or simply walking in the village, visiting local markets. A total rest for me and time to recharge, happy days.

DJ was advancing steadily with his medical training and still based in London, which he seemed to enjoy. He was now thoroughly enjoying rowing with a leading club, sport as ever for him but totally different from John. Tracy had by now finished her university years at Lancaster and now needed to decide what she wanted to do with her life.

Not easy as university life she had enjoyed, she just needed time to consider the way forward. She became frustrated at the time, as she wanted to by a fashion buyer, but the opportunities were limited and she had the wrong degree, she looked at the world of marketing, recruitment and finance, working in the same area as me a possibility but there were no real career opportunities, at the time.

One Sunday morning, I started digging out stuff which had been hidden away over the years, in the cupboard under the stairs. Coming out covered in dust and with a box in my hands, she wanted to know what I was doing, a bit irritated. I handed her the box, saying Do you remember this.

At a very young age, Tracy had lists of girls and boys each having a name, school registers, she used to spend hours giving them lessons, reading them stories and bossing them about and organising a mini school. She smiled at me, of course, education. That September, she began a teacher's training course at Birmingham University, and this was the beginning of a very successful career.

1996 and both of our children now totally independent, DJ a junior doctor and Tracy commencing her teaching career in Slough, living in Bicester, with Richard her partner who she had met at Wendy's daughter Julie's wedding. This was a long daily commute, and at the end of the first year she changed to a school in Leamington Spa and also so she could teach A-level students. They both continued to advance in their careers and lives over the next few years.

John and I continued with our lives, using these busy years to plan to update the house. My irregular hours making this possible, changing the heating from oil to gas, replacing all the windows and doors, we were soon done and just needed to redecorate. The house was much warmer with thick layers of insulation in the loft and cavity foam in the walls.

One weekend early autumn of 1998, we walked out in the fields in the brisk air. Christmas meant a lot to us, and on asking the children if they planned to join us, it became abundantly clear that they might, but leaving the door open should anything else more interesting arise, which it did. This was a bit upsetting for us, but we had enough time to look after ourselves, so we booked our first winter vacation, leaving the UK December 17, off to Canada we went, another adventure but this time further afield.

Travelling overnight, we arrived in Toronto and transferred to our hotel, leaving us a whole day to explore this vibrant city. There was a bitterly cold wind, which had us wrapped up in a jacket and gloves and would take some time to acclimatise to. Our first destination was the CN Tower, which stands on land reclaimed from Lake Ontario, and was the meeting place for many diverse first nations, the Inuit and Metis, for example.

We were taken up 550 metres to the observation platforms, with both of us standing on the platform looking at the view for miles around, what a view, what a privilege. We treated ourselves to lunch in the restaurant, which rotates through 360 degrees in just over an hour, amazing food, much appreciated as we were both very hungry. Did it sway in the wind? Yes, it did.

December and the days are short, this is the first time I saw Christmas lights decorating trees in the parks and along the streets, I remember thinking how very attractive this made everything. We went down to the shopping precinct, which is underground, it was busy, vibrant and very much a winter meeting place, I was a bit disappointed to find a Marks and Spencer outlet, especially as I had one of the jumpers in my bag. We had supper back at the hotel before crashing out. Mid-morning, the next day, we set off to visit Niagara Falls on the Canadian side.

The falls were absolutely awe-inspiring, with the water flowing very fast, despite large ice formations, what a roar the water made. The falls were far bigger than I had imagined, having seen just images. I recommend that anyone visit them if they can. Tourists were well catered for here with many local crafts represented.

We enjoyed looking around the shops, but having not much space for presents in our cases, we had to be a bit discerning. Lunch was in a local diner; the portions were large, which pleased John as he helped demolish half of mine. The specifics of the food I cannot remember, but the coffee I do remember as it was excellent.

The next stage of our journey was by train, from Toronto to Banff and began at 10 am the next morning. This was a train built in the early 1900s and was a classic, which had sleeping arrangements, either reclining seats or suites and observation areas on top of the train and a rear platform. All of which we explored.

The journey was slow, the train went through snowy landscapes, grey rock and dark green spruce. It was just what we needed, rest and relaxation and a great way to travel and see the varied Canadian landscape and travel across the vast country. The train made scheduled stops a few times along our route and we drew into Winnipeg nearly three days later.

John had felt a bit cooped up on the train and felt like a walk during our two-hour layover, stepping out of the carriage, I felt the cold wind burn my skin and got straight back in. John returned shortly after with his scarf around his head and ears, requesting I dig out his bobble hat before we get to Jasper. Jasper is a beautiful place, an alpine town in the Alberta Province and the commercial centre of Jasper National Park.

The sky tram took us to the summit of Whistler's Mountain, both of us in awe of our surroundings. John stood close behind me, saying 'wonderful trip, scamp'; both of us glad we had come. The Yellowhead Museum held our interest for some time before we retired for dinner and sleep. Mountain air is something else for having a good night's sleep. Our journey from this point would be by coach. By the next morning, we were on the Icefields Pathway heading for Banff, another experience. Frozen waterfalls, which were so tall it was difficult to see the top, black dots high up, we realised were people climbing up the ice fall. The coach we were travelling in stopped at a lookout point, enabling those who wanted, to get out for what was to be one of the most exhilarating moments of the trip.

Climbing aboard specially built trucks with large wheels and tyres to enable travel on to the glacier. In these trucks we got as close as we could to the three prongs of the glacier, which looked like a crow's foot, the early settlers had named the mountain crowfoot. We went onward to Banff, another amazing spot and a hotel reminiscent of a log cabin but on a much larger scale.

An incredible town full of young people all out and about. We went to the cinema that evening to see a James Bond Film, dressed in thick jackets and boots, a great thing to do.

The next day saw us at Lake Louise eating lunch at Fairmont Chateau Hotel with an American couple on their way to family for Christmas, having travelled up from Florida before catching the train in Toronto. John so used to travelling the world, was completely at ease and drew these quiet people out, we learnt of their life and reason for moving to Florida, onward bound for British Columbia.

Figure 14—The Mercedes and John and I on retirement.

We took a horse drawn sleigh ride to complete the day, not being very experienced with horses I headed for the seats in the front behind the horses, I was grabbed by my husband and redirected to the rear of the sleigh and I am so glad he did, as steaming manure was collected on a tray behind the horses, right in front of the front seats of the sleigh, somewhat smelly. Trotting round the frozen lake in the snowy landscape was very picturesque, we saw huts set up on the ice, we asked what they were, and the driver explained they were overfishing holes.

Back to our warm and comfortable log cabin hotel, for supper and sleep, before our onward journey to Calgary the next day. This area was a bit disappointing after the last few days, with the remnants of the winter Olympic Games held here 10 years before, looking abandoned. That afternoon was Christmas Eve and after leaving the train we flew across the Rockies mountains to Victoria on Vancouver Island.

We stayed in a very friendly and comfortable hotel, supper and Christmas music around a large log fire, the perfect way to spend Christmas Eve. Upon waking up on Christmas morning, we found a stocking for each of us hanging on the door, which was such a surprise and a lovely touch by the hotel.

We were welcomed into breakfast, which was very lazy and then went out walking, it was so good to stretch our legs, after the days on the train. We went down to the seashore, the beach was covered in huge logs which had broken free from the rivers when Mount Rannier erupted, just a short distance offshore was a large group of sea lions, large and noisy beasts. A Christmas with a difference, we had Christmas lunch in the afternoon at the hotel and then a long sleep.

Onto the last leg of an amazing journey, we took the ferry from Victoria to Vancouver, across the water with views of mountains, small islands with trees down to the water's edge. With the cold wind blowing, we had learnt and wore thick hats and gloves, enabling us to stay on deck for the whole journey across the Strait of Georgia.

Vancouver another vibrant city full of young people. Having a few hours before our overnight flight home, we walked in the park and toured the city. Eating dinner in a local Italian Restaurant, I had the biggest Caesar salad I have ever eaten, John having his favourite beef lasagna, enormous portions. Then we were homeward bound, just the beginning of many such trips.

Arriving back from Canada in time for New Year's Eve, to a warm welcome from the children, and please do not go off on holiday over Christmas again. Seems the parents were missed.

We were still talking about retirement and started searching for the best retirement location for ourselves, thinking another house to stay in for the winter months might be nice, and we began to narrow down our requirements. John immediately talked about cricket and golf, although cricket was not so prevalent, as he could see a lot more of the action in a television broadcast. Just the atmosphere missing, like the university parks in Oxford, as it was still a good place to go and watch this summer pastime.

Having bought two low folding chairs, he seemed to think we would be doing this quite often. I am not sure who was more surprised him or me when he became bored with this entertainment. Participating in a sport is a totally different ballpark to being a spectator. Golf came into its own as this could be played most of the year.

Our winter break in Spain proved that it is not really a good option for winter months, days can be pleasant, but the nights are cold. Having spent a day in the mountains visiting Rhonda and The Alhambra Palace, the day was chilly and windy, making the decision to sell the property much easier.

Reading the paper on his train journey, one spring morning, John located a new house being built on a golf course in Cornwall, the St Mellion Golf and Country Club, he was very enthusiastic as it had a Jack Nicklaus signature course. Come the weekend, we drove down to Cornwall, staying at the golf and country club, to view the property. It was a beautiful house, and we were assured the garden would be landscaped. When we arrived home, he was bursting with delight, asking a question he had not asked in many years. How much money have we got?

I showed him our portfolio and explained that some of it is in bonds which will not mature for some months. Handing him the details, he gave me one of his long penetrating looks and said, "You know your stuff, Scamp."

We could afford the house without needing the bonds and I had one very happy husband. Pity I was busy with work at this time, maybe just maybe I would have done a bit more research. The house was perfect, warm and cosy with a huge gas, imitation log burner, for several months we journeyed to Cornwall as often as we could.

Golf course a challenge but John enjoyed it. I was happy with books and sewing, these were comfortable weekends. Having reached the age of 65 in April, I was not surprised when John decided in August that it was time to retire. This he embraced wholeheartedly and started to relax, but somehow this did not suit him, and he needed to be active. He decided to take on an extra allotment and redesign the garden.

I was still working, thinking in terms of the cost of running two houses, until we decided which one to spend our lives in. Coming home several times to find my husband out playing golf with a group of like-minded men, called The EGGS

(Elderly Gentleman Golf Society). I could see the pattern of life unfolding before my eyes. Well, you know the saying, if you cannot beat them, join them. Sitting down after dinner, I turned to John and said, "I would like to have some golf lessons."

Expecting to meet a young athletic golfer for my first lesson, I arrived at the course after seeing a client, a little nervous but determined, to be greeted by my husband who took me to the driving range and proceeded to give me lessons. Well, if he had not been so good and patient, I would have called him a cheapskate. This seemingly innocuous decision of mine to play golf proved to be one of the most important for our retirement years.

Cornwall during the autumn months did not come up to expectations, course waterlogged, with us having to carry clubs, as there were no trollies or buggies allowed. Living on a golf course, in a beautiful house, was all well and good, but not being able to play golf, well, what was the point? Should have done more research. John was devastated as it was not what he had envisaged, and we made an agreement, one more year to see how it pans out, then the house would be sold.

The New Year of 2000 brought a new era and the beginning of our search for a winter home. Leaving John to think about this, I continued to work until the end of the financial year and then retired to be with him. Retiring was not easy, from a full-on time-consuming career to domestic bliss with golf lessons, that took some adjusting to.

First and foremost, I took a long hard look at myself, I was overweight, unfit, and difficult to live with. All these factors were connected, and it was time to address the situation. I enrolled with Weight Watchers and started speed walking. This activity proved difficult as my lifestyle over the past few years had been poor, eating habits makeshift to fit into my busy schedule, with my body lacking in vitamins and calcium.

Supplements, with diet and exercise, a new approach was required. Come September, I had dropped 26 pounds and life was fun again. John did not complain and just gave me masses of support and encouragement. Retirement was not easy, adjustment, consideration for those around you and learning to relax after so many busy years. Most important of all is learning to like the new you, whoever that may be.

Unknown to me, John had arranged a holiday in October, with DJ opting to join us for a week, one of the things John most enjoyed was looking at travel brochures, and he had located a house for rent in Florida. Flying into Tampa and hiring a car, is how this adventure started, and we travelled south to a place called the Rotonda in Charlotte County.

It was very remote and only a few houses had been built, this was 20 odd years ago, and I am sure this is no longer the case. The three of us drove around, enjoying sitting on Boca Grande beach, watching the grey pelicans diving for food, walking through nature parks and eating out together. The weather was warm so there was no need for sweaters, just shorts and tee shirts.

The men spent time investigating the golf and found the costs prohibitive. We spent time just talking to people to find out as much as possible about the area, and after dropping DJ at the airport we returned to the house and started to discuss possible winters in Florida.

Golf had become important in our lives, I still had a lot of practicing to undertake, but I was getting there, the cost for several months would not be viable, so this needed more consideration. Just a maybe at this point.

It had been a joy to spend time with our son, and hear him talk of his life, as he was now a registrar and enjoying his work, and we discussed him purchasing his first home. Life for him was full, enjoying being a bachelor in London.

Tracy was also progressing in her chosen field, becoming Head of Geography in Bicester, the town where she lived, so no longer long distance commuting every day. Life was busy for both Richard and Tracy, and we saw little of them. My independent daughter, no surprise there. Although John missed her.

Although we were retired, neither of us thought of it as such, with a busy spring and summer, planting, harvesting and preserving, on the allotment and also looking into a possible move from our current home to pastures new. We discovered that we were still looking for adventure, John being a well-seasoned traveller, was still reading holiday destination brochures and he came across a two-week trip to South Africa, so during the spring of 2001 we flew to Johannesburg.

Flying into Johannesburg, amazingly we had no jet lag, which meant we could go straight into the tour. The first part of the tour saw us travelling to Kruger National Park, driving into the park in an open-top jeep. We were so lucky to see animals up close, lions, giraffes, elephants, warthogs and vultures.

Later on, on a night-time safari, we saw water buffalo, and a leopard, that the water buffalo was chained and lying down, and the leopard was used to being the centre of attention, somewhat spoilt the visit. Dinner that night was around a campfire, which was an experience, with the light being very dim as all they had were small oil lamps.

The sun setting was beautiful, dropping down very quickly. Moving on, we visited Soweto, and the apartheid museum, this was very moving, highlighting man's inhumanity to man. We went on and visited the battle areas of the Zulu wars, Rorke's Drift and Isandlwana, where we were introduced to a Zulu chief and witnessed part of the congregation for the local church arrive, a group of mothers and children singing, walking to church barefoot, shoes in hand, which were put on before entering the church.

The tour then moved onto Leopard Creek, which was one of the reasons we travelled to South Africa, this was out of this world. Having seen the golf course on television, John wanted to see it first-hand. Flying south into Cape Town, the plane came in low over the shanty towns, the views were very upsetting.

In Cape Town, we visited a diamond outlet, a pair of earrings took my fancy, a long look from John. *Well, that's a no, no,* I thought. Well, they were expensive. The contrast in wealth in this city was incredible.

Later, the tour included wine tasting at a vineyard not many miles from Cape Town, the wine tasting part was not for me, and John informed me I had not missed much in relation to the wine. The cavernous wine cellars brought back memories of an Anderson shelter, and I was out of there pretty quickly.

The last day was in Cape Town, we were meant to visit Robben Island but the proprietor decided not to run the ferry that day, so we went up Tabletop Mountain instead. We were glad we did, a golfing associate having a property in the area had given us tips on what to look for.

Back to the hotel for our last evening, whilst going down in the lift we were joined by two men both over six feet tall, sportsmen no doubt with bags on their shoulders, one of the men swung round and his bag hit my shoulder and I fell against John.

Luckily, they were very polite, apologising but they were big men. A group of them were in the bar and we were welcomed, asking us to join them for a drink. John was in his element, sportsmen the world over have so much in common. After dinner I left them to it and went to do the packing. Happy days.

Once we were back in the UK, we visited the house in Cornwall, the decision to sell was made, this was not the right place or the right time. A mistake maybe did we learn a lesson perhaps. Would we do more research in future, certainly.

So, the pattern of our lives began to form, summer in England working in the garden and growing produce on the allotment, playing golf three times a week, I had joined Frilford Heath Golf Club with John, but the winters were not really inspiring. Time to rethink and work out what we were really looking for.

One area I had been considering for some time was cars, when I retired my company car was returned and I purchased a BMW. John had not updated his car for around 4 years, the balance was not right, but as ever he did not complain. Mulling things over, or as the kids would say Mum's thinking, watch out, I remembered him describing his first journey in a Mercedes Benz whilst travelling in Sweden, how he thought it handled beautifully, could turn on a sixpence.

So, on the pretext of visiting my sister in Kidlington, I asked him to take me via North Oxford as I wanted to look at something. Into the Mercedes showroom we went. John strolled around and I saw him looking at one car in particular, I knew he would like it, the lines and grace of the car would appeal to his taste. I simply asked what colour would you like?

Surprise, delight and that amazing grin. John ordered his car. This would be ready for collection early May 2002. My husband's pride and joy. A fitting tribute to this incredible man, especially as we were in the position to purchase it outright and brand new. My son in-law owns it now and looks after it with great care, a sign of respect to John and something he would be very happy with.

As with all things in life, sad times come, my mother fell and broke her hip, a matter of days before Wendy's youngest daughter, Susan's wedding. My youngest sister Carol let me know and I was able to go to the hospital on the morning of her operation, sitting with her until it was time to go into theatre.

We talked of the children, how DJ was now an orthopaedic registrar and Tracy head of geography. Then came the surprise, an apology. She was so sorry for what I had to go through, I stopped her short, saying it did not matter, I understood that she had to fight for the survival of her family in the only way she could, she just patted my arm, with tears in her eyes. Onto less emotional matters, we talked of the up-and-coming wedding and the hat I was making for myself.

John and I had arranged to pick up my younger sister, Carol and her daughter, Katie, to take them to the wedding, the following Saturday, being a single mum has many drawbacks, one of which is not being able to enjoy a few drinks, having to always undertake the driving. As they lived in easy striking distance of the hospital, I was able see my mother in hospital complete with hat, which she loved.

Wedding ceremony over and photographs taken, off to the reception, we pulled up outside the Randolph Hotel, in Oxford, where the reception was held, car valet ready and waiting to take the car and park it. Talk about VIP treatment, John laughed and said, "It's not for you, Scamp, it's for the car."

John was driving his Mercedes, of course.

The following Monday, we drove to Snettisham in Norfolk, this area appealed to us as it was near the fens, and a haven for bird watching, an interest we had both enjoyed for many years.

We were very lucky as we saw a bearded tit and a row of baby swallows on a low wire a few feet before us and in a bird hide on Snettisham beach, overlooking a pond, we were looking at oystercatchers squabbling, in an instant they all took off flying overhead, beautiful sight.

I had the most incredible feeling of calmness and happiness, and I knew my mother had just died. Carol called me at the place we were staying, that evening, to tell me of our mother's passing.

Carol and I arranged her funeral and signed all the necessary paperwork. Talking of the music, I remembered my mother singing Jerusalem, the Women's Institute anthem, and Carol remembered my mother teaching all the words as a schoolgirl, then the other piece I remembered but was unsure of the title, in a Persian garden I thought but that was not right, In a Persian Market.

Around this time, I tried to get closer to my youngest sister, but somehow, we had little in common, I suppose we had differing experiences growing up.

It was May 2003 and John and I were off on another adventure, flying from London to Los Angeles.

I had set up a savings plan in 1992, a fixed amount each month for ten years. Maturing after I retired, but the monthly investment amount was not huge, when the cheque arrived, I handed it to John, asking, where we shall go. Big grin and he picked out a brochure from the pile on his desk and said, "I would love to do this trip."

It was New Zealand by rail, road and sea. No small-minded person my husband. What a journey neither of us ever forgot one minute of it.

London to Los Angeles overnight, Los Angeles to Hawaii for an overnight stay. Flying into the island was an experience as we flew along the coast. Ocean colours aquamarine to dark blue, golden sands and lush greenery. The hotel staff greeted us with shell necklaces *Pukas* symbolising protection for sailors and good luck. Beautiful hotel room, wooden but with large windows letting in the sea breeze.

I know we ate, but exactly what I do not remember, just very tired and in need of a shower. Up early to bird song, sunshine and the smell of coffee, guaranteed to get one up and about. Off on a morning flight with our first New Zealand air crew, on our way to the Cook Islands, a hotel complex consisting of cabins directly opening onto the beach. Cool, airy and heavenly. Sitting under the palm trees swishing in the breeze, romantic is not the word. Getting to know the people we were travelling with, in a very small party. Mostly like us of mature years.

Sunday morning, we walked along the road beside the ocean, the road lined with rubber plants creating shade, it was very warm. Joining the local people at church, choirs singing such joy. Amazing. Afternoon dozing on our own private piece of the beach. Sorry to leave as we continued our journeys to Auckland, New Zealand. Hotel suite had a feature we had not encountered before. Washing machine and dryer. Well, a woman's work is never done.

Our journey around the north and south islands, beautiful beyond belief. Bay of Islands, with a trip on the mail boat delivering all manner of things to remote homes. Dogs barking, greeting the boat to advise of its arrival. Traditional greeting *Powhiri* and nose rubbing. Visiting a farm for lunch, what a privilege. Rotorua bubbling mud pools and the 30-metre tall *Pohutu* Geyser. The art and craft centre depicting Māori culture. No guide just dropped off at Frazer Town to catch the train to Wellington.

A great way to see the east coast, rugged areas and sandy beaches. Into Wellington for an overnight stay. John and I were walking the harbour and noting the similarities to parts of the UK. This reminded us of the 1840 immigration scheme. Basically, the diverse regions of New Zealand were matched with areas in Europe, for example, Dunedin terrain is very Scottish and people from Scotland were encouraged to emigrate to this region. Sheep herders from The English Cotswolds. A very progressive method of colonising an area.

Ferry across Cook Strait took us to Picton, a slow journey across enabling us to marvel at the beauty of this rugged region. On to Christchurch, a lively city, and we enjoyed our stay. Eating in the student's quarter one evening. Touring the area around the city and eating dinner at a home in the outskirts. Lovely house all on one floor, garden mainly shrubs but unique. My bad here, I cannot drink alcohol and usually just sip a little wine from a glass, taking all evening.

Unfortunately, I did not notice someone surreptitiously topping up my glass. Soon in a sorry state. John was sympathetic, blaming himself for not keeping an eye on me. Interested in talking to the host, another engineer. Next day was a part of the journey I was looking forward to, the Transalpine rail crossing from Christchurch to Greymouth, but not with a gigantic hangover.

Vaguely remember crossing ravines with water gushing down them in fast raging torrents. Lunch in a box, perhaps not John happily eating both. Will I forgive myself for this stupidity, no, never.

Greymouth lives up to its name and is not inspiring. Staying overnight in a harbour hotel. Warm and cosy evening in the bar and to bed to recover. South along the coastal route looking out to the Tasman Sea, sea lions on the beach. Then inland to the Franz Josef Glacier, taking a helicopter ride out over the glacier, not smooth as I expected but rugged and craggy.

On land again and looking back from tropical heat and plants to the glacier. Onward to The Chateau and a suite of rooms overlooking the garden, which John promptly went out and walked through. The whole trip was full of new experiences and sights, visiting a yellow-eyed penguin colony, out to sea in a very small vessel, with me lodged between John and the funnel binoculars in hand, watching the albatrosses flying overhead, so close you could see the colour of their plumage.

Tiny blue penguin on its way out to sea from Dunedin Harbour. Lunch in a vineyard on our way back to Christchurch, definitely no wine for me. There was also, an art gallery where I saw a picture by a New Zealand artist, an oil painting, trunks of silver birch trees in a snowy landscape. Another regret I should have bought it.

Christchurch again and a homeward bound flight, stopping off in Fiji for two days. Warm again, with tropical rain falls in the afternoon. Cows strolling along the beach. Wading out to the reef and watching the life in the sea below. Halcyon days. Rude awakening in Los Angeles where our luggage was left out in the rain whilst awaiting our onward flight to London. Only an outline of a vacation that spanned four weeks, also a sign of things to come.

The children had worked out that Mum and Dad were happy in retirement and simply got on with their lives. Still looking for the right place to spend winters or even to relocate in the UK. Spending time in Norfolk and West Wales, off we would go, golf clubs in the boot. Off on our adventures, early in 2003, we went to China to see the Yangtze River before it was flooded and to look at the great docks being built in Shanghai.

A country I had not considered visiting, until a discussion one evening over dinner, the damming of the Yangtze River and the building of locks in Shanghai, was of great interest to John. So, the trip was soon booked and off we went. Flying from London to Beijing, the beginning being of most interest to me, the great wall of China, where once again I forgot the heat and suffered heat stroke, bringing my breakfast up and christening the outside of the wall.

John went off with the rest of the group and left me in the air-conditioned bus with bottles of water being handed to me by all and sundry. One lady in particular, took me under her wing and her doctor husband checked on me. Lovely lady. No sight-seeing for me in Beijing, which meant missing the grand forbidden city complex and imperial palace, recovering enough to visit Tiananmen Square, the plaza in the evening. So be it.

On to Wuhan through the rural areas, seeing the farms I had read about many years before, Rice paddies, sesame seed plants, oxen to work the fields and a carp pool. Self-sufficiency. The landscape as I had envisaged was rugged cliffs of golden-hued rocks. John was quiet and not really enjoying this trip so far. The food was not to his liking in any shape or form. Seeing the power stations pumping out black, polluting smoke, not a good sight.

This is an ancient country pulling itself into the 21st century, a long way to go. We left Wuhan and flew to Chongqing, on the River Yangtze. We saw pandas in the zoo, met artists in the gardens and visited the Feng Huang Ghost City, before boarding our boat on our journey to Shanghai. Rickety boat to say the least, as you walked on the decks the twang of flexing metal was distinct.

Down river, we went, through narrow gorges and watching the navigation lights being used as we travelled at night. Witnessing a bloated body floating down the river one morning and the freshly caught fish being brought to the boat, well, I do not like fish anyway. John was still having difficulty with the food, more than happy to queue up for his easy over egg each morning.

Downstream, we were already able to witness the rising level of the water and understanding that we were privileged to see what would be gone, houses, farms, trees and the gorge itself. People would be uprooted, leaving a way of life which had endured for centuries. Into Shanghai itself, witnessing the enormous undertaking of the Three Gorges Dam, men talking of the turbines silted up. John and I looking at the ships being lifted up in huge docks to counteract the different water levels. Biggest constructions we had ever seen. Overnight in a very luxurious hotel, dressing gowns and soft slippers, a very welcome experience after the rustic boat.

During the evening, we strolled around the city taking in the modern buildings under construction, the feeling of energy and vibrancy. Young people stopping us to talk and practice their English, both of us having clear accents, happy to chat, young people the world over are the future. On the flight back, John said you know what I would like when we get back, yes, I replied beef mince. A good trip, an interesting trip, to see a country going through reconstruction as we had post-war. Food a bit of a problem.

On our return, an email from Susan was waiting to tell us Peter had been diagnosed with prostate cancer, this was a bit of a shock, I needed to see him, but to just go for this reason was not enough. Like John and I, they were a close couple, and what affected Peter also affected Susan, to go just to see Peter was not a good feeling. I thought about it for some time, in the end, it was simple, I was 65 in October 2003, and Susan would be that age in May 2004, good reason to visit.

Peter had reached the age of 70, Susan and he had recently found their retirement home in Ocean Shores on the Olympic Peninsula in Washington State. A lovely home very close to the beach. The news that came regarding Peter's health and our decision to visit in May to also celebrate Susan and me reaching the age of 65 was soon organised and we took off for a fleeting visit. Booking a few days in the national park, staying in a log cabin at the top of a beach. Planning to stay with Peter and Susan for a couple of days.

Peter was ill and the effort of entertaining would just be too much. John fully understood this, once again, food being a problem. John was a very active man, and he ate a lot. There is no way Susan could cope with all that this involved and the worry of Peter's health. Our days in the cabin, exploring the beach and venturing into the woodlands.

A warning from the restaurant, *mind the critters*, all good fun. Walking the beach, we both stood in amazement, the rock formations and their unusual colouring, which we had seen in China, were here close to and on the beach. We had witnessed the effect of plate tectonic splitting. The splitting into plates of parts of the earth's crust. Back to the cabin, the evening drawing in and cooling. Before we went to eat, John lit the log burner so the cabin would be warm when we returned. It was warm, alright, had to open doors and windows to cool it down. Out to the beach in the twilight, gulls circling out at sea and whales fishing. Off to Seattle to spend the night with Elizabeth, Peter and Susan's youngest daughter, a family gathering to celebrate the golden girls' birthdays and Labour Day.

9 pm bedtime came as a bit of a surprise, with no curtains at the windows. Crack of dawn, we were both awake and ready for a shower but thought it best to check in case we woke anyone up. Family up and about, teenage son eaten and gone back to bed. Showers for us it was at 5 o'clock in the morning. This is going to be a long day.

Journey back to Ocean Shores would take several hours, John could see Peter was getting tired and suggested he take us to the airport early, allowing him to go home and rest. Prostate cancer is no joke. Spending a few hours in an airport is nothing compared to what Peter was going through. English newspaper for John and a couple of books for me. Soon on our way home.

The children were fine getting on with their lives, Tracy had moved schools becoming Head of Humanities at Banbury School, DJ happy working in the hospitals.

Having visited several places during the winter, over a few years, playing golf in Southern Portugal, and Moliets in Southwest France, we decided in early December to travel to La Manga golf and Country Club in Spain, for a short break, golf clubs were used to flying now, this was just to make sure that Europe was not the place for a winter home.

We had a pleasant time looking around the adjoining area, having hired a car. We looked at a few properties for sale, but it was so quiet nobody was about, and the golf courses deserted. Sitting curled up on the settee when we arrived back, we laughed at one another, we were just having too much fun.

John was an avid newspaper reader and when he found something of interest, he used to tear it out and store in a heap, ready to read at his leisure, rather than keeping the whole paper. After my nagging about the size of the heap, he decided to get rid of some by starting at the bottom, some of it was years old.

A light bulb moment, he found the clipping about a place called the Villages, which was an over 55s community with golf courses in Florida, which he had talked of all those years ago, finding the newspaper advert on the train. What do you think, scamp, shall we get in touch? No grin just a long pleading look. Thus, we found our main winter home, hiding in plain sight.

Thinking in the terms of nothing ventured, nothing gained, we rang the number on his clipping, the office was still open and had a two-week gap in October 2005, which I duly booked. Plenty of time to check passports, visas and car hire in a few months' time.

Travelling for us had become a fine art, one case and two golf bags. We had managed to book a house to rent in the Villages for two weeks during October, no need to pack toiletries etc all can be purchased locally. Flight to Orlando took about nine hours, nothing new there. Car hire, simple as we sorted this out before we left. Just had to find our way north and locate the property during the late evening.

Hilarious written instructions on how to find our destination, no street lighting, had to pull over to try and read them. Succeed we did and soon settled into the rental. Next morning we saw the villages for the first time. Perfect, for our needs, Sumter Landing is a small town situated on the shores of Lake Sumter with a boardwalk along one shore.

Bars, restaurants, shops, all within a short distance. The locals used golf carts for their mode of transport, as they journeyed in from the villages which surrounded the town. Each village had a recreation centre, with tennis and pickle ball courts, a swimming pool, mostly heated. Billiards or pool tables for weekly competitions. Golf courses abound, executive courses with 9 holes and Championship courses with 18 holes. The Championship courses were all set in the Country Clubs. Perfect place for us to spend our winters.

DJ had a discussion with his John, regarding taking a year out to undertake research. John pointing out that this was the year for taking his final consultant exam, but DJ was adamant that this is what he wanted to do. I would like to say all went well, but it was not the case.

The consultant involved insisted that for the first six months, DJ carried out work he wanted done, DJ transferring to a college in London to complete the research first discussed. The bullying he encountered was unbelievable. Completing his research against all the odds, with abusive emails following him back into the hospitals. I was not the least bit surprised when he accepted a fellowship in sports related injuries, leaving for Australia at the end of the year 2006.

At this time, the results of my three yearly routine mammograms came back positive, I potentially had breast cancer. At first, I did not react to this information and having a biopsy was very unpleasant, but positive, it definitely was. The Hospital in Oxford specialised in cancer treatment, so I knew I was in good hands. John was very upset but was right next to me during the whole of my cancer journey. He accompanied me to the meeting with the specialist, listening to the treatment offered and totally supported my decisions, never interfering, just total support.

Wired Lumpectomy operation with radiotherapy treatment for several weeks once the operation site had healed. The operation date was in a few weeks, this is when I finally had a reaction. On the twelfth hole of the green course, having just hit one of the best shots ever, I was crying, tears pouring down my face. A big bear hug, cry it out scamp, cry it out. That slowed up play for the day.

Operation over and onto the ward, so many women having treatment, all suffering different degrees of cancer. Normal routine checks blood pressure, temperature and the drainage of the wound. All good, one would have thought I was pretty fit and slim, but no low blood pressure. I had to drink water, and it was supplied throughout the day. Food of no interest, which was hardly surprising, I was full of water. Offered a sleeping pill that evening, which I accepted.

As it transpired, it was just as well, one young woman at the end of the ward snored loudly all night. Everyone checking to see who it was. Can you imagine the chaos, and I slept through until the early hours when I had to make a dash for the bathroom. Well, I had drunk a lot of water. John came to visit the next day, in the afternoon but could not come onto the ward. No problem, I simply went to talk to him, the grin came as soon as he saw me. You OK, scamp, you, OK? So worried.

That night everyone took a sleeping pill.

There were at least 10 of us on the ward and only one shower. After having the drainage tubes removed, I felt a bit grubby, so I went into one of the bathrooms which had a Douch and cleaned myself up as best I could. Shirt a bit stained but I was on my way home and could shower in comfort.

Wrong, the cupboard was bare, we needed to shop for food. Walking around the supermarket, thinking of dinner, wearing a bloody shirt, and of course you meet people you know. Took John a while but he got the message, I needed to go home. I understood his relief was palpable, but I needed a bit of TLC. Curled up in bed, so glad to be home, and in the best place possible, my husband's arms.

Radiology started six weeks later, no golf during this time. No harm in walking the course though and I soon picked up my strength. At some point, I had to let the children know, and my sister's two aunts had died of this condition, and I felt all should be made aware. Sisters, sisters-in-law and nieces all came back. Simple thank you for letting them know. Children understandably upset, DJ furious and Tracy a bit tearful. My cancer journey with John had been the best way for me, the emotions generated by family more than I could have coped with.

There was to be a big vacation in January 2007, treatment for my breast cancer completed and a few days later we left for Australia. A long flight with a stopover in Singapore, not for long, but a connection with Uncle Bill just the same, bound for Sydney and an early morning connection to Adelaide. Such fun the last part of our trip, breakfast of cornflakes and cold milk, wonderful. Flight attendants and staff were an entertainment in themselves.

Met at the airport by our son's landlady, who promptly told me off for not telling DJ about my cancer. Damned if you do and damned if you don't. Not an auspicious start.

The house, Duncan had rented was a small bungalow just off Henley Beach, a perfect central spot. Oddly, this is when John had a reaction to the months of worry. I knew that I had another 10 days before my energy levels would return, making him coffee, we sat and talked. Not being well enough to help plan this trip was a disadvantage which could soon be rectified. Arranging local trips into the Adelaide hills during the week, saving the more adventurous times for weekends when Duncan could join us, his fellowship being more civilised hours being a private hospital.

We needed to hire a car; Henley Beach is amazing, but this man of mine needed to explore. Car obtained and away we go, exploring the local area, and in particular the beaches. Located in a shopping precinct and more importantly a travel agent. Collecting maps and books about the region, we set about planning our stay. Travelling south along the Ocean Road to Melbourne, seeing the Twelve Apostles, stopping in local hotels on the way there and back.

Ferry across Spencer Gulf from Lucky Bay (near Cowell) on the Eyre Peninsula to Wallaroo on the Yorke Peninsula and south to Port Lincoln and Coffin Bay. Walking in the scrub lands around the bay, male emus with a brood, black snakes and birds. Amazing. One trip north to Port Augusta, then turning south again down the Yorke Peninsula to Marion Bay. Another trip south again to Kangaroo Island and staying in a cottage at the top of the beach called, Flip Flap Flop.

Flying across to Perth, hiring a car and travelling south via Fremantle, Margaret River to Albany. Reading the history of the region and marvelling at the strength of those early settlers. Perhaps the most exhilarating was driving north to the Flinders Ranges, a trip of a lifetime.

429 kilometres north of Adelaide, Wilpena Pound is a place rising from the earth like the cone of an ancient volcano, eye-catching and beautiful. Flying over the area in a tiny plane. Into a 4x4, to really go into the outback. Birds, parrots everywhere. Night-time sitting outside to look at the stars so close, so clear.

A wonderful trip which started badly and ended up remarkable.

The difficult years for our son began, so many things had contributed to his breakdown and a final diagnosis of paranoid schizophrenia was given. He continued living in his apartment, but we were not involved and had little inclination as to what was going on.

Angry, he was so angry at the injustice meted out to him, but mentioning this to his psychiatrist met with disinterest and disbelief. John and I carried on with our life, spending three months of most winters in the Villages, this area, and the lifestyle it offered was just what we had been looking for.

So much so that we decided to buy a property and purchased a plot of land on which to build. The building would commence in spring 2008. Long journey home and almost as we walked into the door, the police came knocking. Aggressive and unpleasant, looking for DJ and adamant that he was here in the house. Our cases and golf clubs were still on the kitchen floor.

John was deep in shock; I was calmer and told them in no uncertain terms that he was not. Take a look around. They left and John broke down, only the second time I had seen him cry and the first and only time I heard him howl. Door locked, kettle on, and time to calm down. I noticed the message button on the phone flashing, that will have to wait, I thought.

Sleep was difficult but sleep we did. This was not the first time our son had gone walkabout, but this one seemed more serious as he had been missing for weeks. No monetary transactions, this information came from his mental health consultant. I was talking on the telephone, so I might as well listen to the messages.

Three of them, Mr Lucas, please ring the Home Office. DJ was in the hospital in Paris, someone would have to go and get him. There seemed to be a bill for around £50,000 involved.

John and I had tackled a few things in our lives, this was a new one. To Paris we go on Eurostar and onto the metro to the hospital on the outskirts of Paris. So glad to see us, hug for his dad, and I simply observed.

DJ was more balanced and happier than I had seen him for a very long time. Three days' medication supplied and off we went back to Paris. Visiting the embassy to pick up a temporary passport for him, eventually on the train and back to the UK.

Dropped him off at the mental hospital, only to be told the medication supplied would not be used, they would re-assess him. All those months of work undone in a moment.

Serious thought time for John and me, we now had no idea what the future held for us. Committing ourselves to purchasing a house in America put on hold. Our life together was important, and we would continue with our lifestyle, summer in the UK and winters away. Keeping an eye on DJ, letting whatever was wrong with him run its course.

Tracy was still as independent as ever, having purchased her first house with Richard in Witney, and progressing in her career to Head of Inclusion at Banbury School. John and I visited them in their new home before our journey to Adelaide in 2007, they seemed very happy.

The next few years were not easy, but the strength of our marriage enabled us to withstand the onslaught of DJ's illness. As gradually he came to stay with us each summer.

Australia was a country that suited John, wide-open spaces and magnificent scenery, and we discussed going back for a few weeks. Duncan was staying with us at the time and decided to join us for two weeks, this related to his medication. Finding accommodation in Western Australia was not an easy matter and we ended up booking two separate houses.

One was a modern house in walking distance of the beach, and the other a beach shack. A holiday with a difference as we took our golf clubs with us. Playing golf among the kangaroos was hilarious, and the locals found it funny that we just stood and looked at these kangaroos that were browsing the grass on the tee instead of driving them away. We travelled north as far as Dongara, stopping in Nambung to view the Pinnacles Desert. Absolutely mesmerising. Ancient limestone spires creating a surreal and breathtaking landscape.

Other than playing golf with kangaroos, which was the highlight of John's vacation.

The local market in Dongara was lively, every stall offering a little shade from the sun, it was incredibly hot. Did I shop well, of course I did, looking at the mouth of the Irwin River and lobsters was all well and good, but a little light relief was needed. Picking up a silk scarf, a mixture of pink and blue, I knew I had to have it. Made in Bali 2500 kilometres away, small world.

Duncan caught his flight home, and we moved to our second rental. Well, it was a beach hut so one should expect a lot of creatures to be present and they were. A few weeks of playing golf and walking the beach for us. John now had an appetite for Australia.

During the summer of 2010, DJ came to stay, our relationship with him was strained, one morning I came down to get breakfast to find DJ had been up all night and drinking coffee. No coffee for breakfast for Mum and Dad, I lost it. He went to the village shop and bought some, then off he went, I shall go away for a few days to allow you to calm down. Left me speechless. Off he went, I assumed back to his apartment.

Well, no, that was not the case. Mental Health Nurse rings up to check on him, not with us, I thought he had gone home. They checked that this was not the case. Police called in, helicopter up checking the area and hovering over the house. The policeman called at the house and asked for a description, he had seen someone looking like that when he drove into the village. Transpired DJ had decamped to the local hotel, walking the river path and hills during the day. John and I looked at one another, life is not boring around here.

Tracy was getting on with her life and had achieved one of her ambitions, Assistant Head Waingels School Reading. The decision not to pressure her life with her brother's illness had been made some years ago, leaving her to get on with her life. Whether or not this was the right decision I am not sure.

It was during this time that John began to talk of retiring to Australia, he really enjoyed the lifestyle, outdoor life and sunshine, what more can a man want?

"Sounds like a rocking chair on the porch," I said. This is not something which appealed to me, but trying to be fair and open-minded, I agreed to research the idea. Pointing out that we had only seen one corner of Australia, perhaps we should revisit, but travel the east coast.

During the summer months of 2013, John was contacted by the secretary of the golf course, A letter had been received for him from Australia, somebody knew he played golf there and had been a member since 1964, an old acquaintance trying to contact him.

Another engineer who had gone to Australia in the 1980s, who had retired from Melbourne to Moreton Island near Brisbane. Australia is huge and to travel the east coast would take a very long time, a guided tour made more sense and John set to work finding one that covered our requirements. Sad news came just before we set off in October that his acquaintance had passed, we no longer needed to make a visit to Moreton Island.

Getting on in years now and a long flight ahead of us, we upgraded our seats and arrived in Sydney for our October guided tour, a little less travel weary this time. Flight next day took us to Cairns, and we began our journey covering almost 3000 kilometres. The Daintree Forest on the northeastern coastline of Queensland, is a very interesting ancient rainforest. Recording the evolution of plant life on earth.

Here, we visited a bird sanctuary and saw beautiful parrots, parakeets, all manner of birds and a Cassowary, so privileged. Boat trip on a crocodile river near Cooktown, where a man had been killed. Sitting on our balcony in the evenings, we witnessed flight after flight of fruit bats flying in roost in the trees.

Our journey south to Sydney began with a trip to the Great Barrier Reef and looking at the reef from a glass bottom boat. Sailing around the Whitsunday Islands, visiting Whitehaven beach, where someone decided to push past me when getting into the dinghy to return to the boat, and I ended up in water up to my chest. I dripped on deck for some time before I dried. Frazer Island was beautiful, and we flew out over the ocean in a tiny 6-seater plane, plenty of sharks down there.

On to Rockhampton and the Tropic of Capricorn, the road taking us through miles of sugar cane plantations, before our journey took us to Brisbane. A young vibrant city which comes alive at dusk, eating out and walking around.

We moved on to Byron Bay, staying in a Japanese style hotel, walking the sidewalks and listening to tree frogs. The area is becoming more built up now, and we took a diversion inland to the inevitable wine tasting. Our first encounter with rural Australia.

We were leaving earlier than most of the group to return to the UK and it was a pleasant surprise when many of them came down to the lounge to say goodbye.

John was heading for his 80th Birthday, and I had to tell him that although I enjoyed visiting Australia, I did not want to retire there. It was not for me, if we had gone all those years before I might have felt differently, but now it's not something I wanted to do. Putting myself first, something I rarely did. That John was willing to go out to Australia, leaving his family, surprised me. As it turned out it was the right decision. I disappointed him, that much I do know.

January, we went to the Villages, Florida, for three months, enjoyable as ever being part of a group playing courses outside of the villages. Visiting restaurants and the theatre.

Contact with DJ was a telephone call, he seemed to be coping, but his speech was a little slurred. Tracy by email, she was climbing high in her career, this was the best way to contact her.

Arriving back in the UK, we decided to surprise DJ with a visit on his birthday. He was not at home when we arrived, we walked into town, a cup of tea would be appreciated, to meet him walking up the hill. John gripped my hand tightly; he was six parts to the wind. Back to the apartment, cup of tea all round. John asked him what he wanted to do. "Come back home with you."

John had understood what would happen, which is why he had given us an option, to move to Australia, leave DJ to get on with it. John told him to put his things together, as we would take him back now, and this option would be discussed. I took a deep breath, grabbed bin bags. Gathered his clothes, found he had no bed linen or pillowcases.

"They did not fit," was all he said.

The bed had broken when he dropped onto it, and he had bought a new one, which was bigger.

*No common sense*, I thought, *sign of things to come.*

Then, to top it all, he had two budgerigars in a cage, he went out and bought a travelling cage, but for only one bird, then proceeded to try and catch them to put in this contraption and of course they flew round the room. Leaving the two men to load up the car, I tried to coax the birds back into their cage.

The little yellow female went in and eventually the other joined her. I think I was steaming by now, my sense of humour missing, took the cage down to the car and put it on DJ's lap, with a firm *Get on with it.*

Discussion around the dining room table as normal, DJ was told he was welcome to come home to live but he had to understand that we would be away for the winter months for as long as we were able. The apartment was to be sold and his furniture put in storage, as we knew that his main worry was the gap between the end from his income policy (60 years old) and the start of his old age pension, this arrangement would enable him to save for this eventuality.

The apartment was in a very poor state and would need thorough cleaning before it could go on the market. This is when I turned to my daughter, the two of us travelled down and set to work, scrubbing and sorting out the rubbish. The estate agent arrived at the apartment, which then went up for sale.

During the summer of 2013, we had applied for a six-month visa to enable us to spend the winter months in Florida. The application was online, and we travelled to London for an interview. Ushered into a large reception hall to sit and wait for our designated number to come up on screen. This took a long time, finally called to a window at a desk, we were asked two questions, do you have a brother residing in the USA and do you spell your maiden name with or without a hyphen. That was it.

Let us not complain that we had our six-month visa.

Six winter months spent in Florida amongst our group of like-minded golfing fanatics, became increasingly important. This was our time, time to talk, time to just be. As ever, walking whenever we could. Not easy in Florida as this is not a recreational American's enjoyment.

Sunny days and warm evenings spent listening to the crickets and frogs. Watching the sun set over the lake, which the house overlooked. Visiting the theatre, into the town to meet our friends and enjoy the live entertainment provided. Invited to jewellery parties, Christmas gatherings, tree lighting ceremonies. Just eating out, talking of the day over our evening meal.

May not sound very much, but compared to the difficulty of living with our son who did not converse, living in his own world, it was very enjoyable. Back at home John used to immediately played rousing music when dinner was ready to be served. Breaking the silence, trying to connect with DJ.

One of John's happiest times had been spent in South Australia, organising our trips. My not wanting to retire to Australia was a disappointment to him, but I was happy to visit. John wanted to visit Australia again, just the two of us. Not an organised tour. On our own renting a house, hiring a car and exploring as we had in 2007.

Being 82 years old, he decided that it was now or never, and would I please help him sort it out. I sorted out accommodation, flights and car, the rest would be up to him. I booked a bungalow in Sellick's Beach on the west coast of the

Fleurier Peninsula, halfway between Adelaide and the mouth of the Murray River.

Absolutely fine, January 2016 we flew into Adelaide, before picking up the hired car and journeying to Sellick's Beach, golf clubs in the boot of course.

A wonderful two months, playing golf and just drinking in the vast differences one finds in this country. Going off the main roads and travelling to the mouth of the River Murray, Goolwa and the Coorong. Privileged once again, seeing a blue fairy wren, so small, when we stopped to see the warning waters at the mouth of the river. Walking over the dunes to see the Southern Ocean crashing into the beach. Our last visit to Australia and one of the best.

This was also the time Tracy achieved her goal of becoming a deputy head at a private school for special needs children in Oxford. I hoped she had a celebration; we toasted her achievement and more than wished her well.

The next two years saw DJ's health improve; he had not had a bad spell for some time. Leaving him on his own for six months proved to be too long, and we started to come back to the UK for 4 weeks over the Christmas period.

Tracy and I started up a new tradition for mother and daughter in 2016. Afternoon tea in the orangery and walking around Blenheim Palace on Christmas Eve, before looking at the light display in the grounds. We thoroughly enjoyed ourselves and it was no surprise when John decided to join us the following year.

In July 2018, we were playing golf on the green course at Frilford Heath, John was having trouble walking, his left foot was swollen, and we had to return home. He also had sore patches appearing on his back.

Appointment with the doctor and diagnosis of gout. Medication helped and movement problems eased. Come back to see the doctor if it recurs. The sore patches did not improve, and the cream bought from the pharmacy, nor the prescription cream from the doctor, cream after cream made no difference. Something was wrong.

I made a list of all his niggling little ailments and took to the internet, not expecting much. An American Clinic had always impressed me with their descriptions of ailment symptoms, it was no surprise that the answer was here. 14 ailments relating to gluten intolerance, John had every single one.

This was Sunday and I was at the supermarket mid-morning. Within days, the discomfort disappeared, movement was a little better, John was much happier. Me, I had to learn to cook gluten-free meals, especially bread.

Florida again in October, taking the golf clubs, the foot problem returned, and walking became very difficult. This was the last time we played golf together, having to use a buggy. It was also the last time we went to Florida together.

Vacations in Florida had come to an end. Still full of adventure, just one more push, scamp, just one more push. What can we do that involves little walking and yet lets one view the world. During our trip to Canada, some years before we met an elderly couple who spent the major part of the year on cruise ships, all their needs accounted for.

John remembered them and said, "Maybe we could do this."

The winter was bleak in the UK, not being a man to give into his frailty, he located a cruise for 42 days. Not a lot of walking involved, and it was something he wanted to do, why not. They also catered for gluten intolerance, maybe I could learn something. Brochures secured and decision made. Sailing from Southampton to Madeira. Not a good start as there was major work being carried out in the engine room, very late leaving port, so no firework display or send off sirens.

Then an overnight stop in Lisbon as someone wanted to get off the ship. Did this set the tone of the trip, yes it did. Afternoon tea at Reid's Palace was a special occasion, and which we both enjoyed. A trip around the island to look at gardens, very different, January is not a good time to visit. Off across the Atlantic Ocean, long days at sea, which we spent on deck as much as possible. Entertainment provided was of a reasonable standard and varied.

One venue for more classical music was a favourite. A young man was giving acupuncture and John decided to have a session, which took thirty minutes. He obviously felt more comfortable after it and booked in for another treatment in two weeks. Arriving in the Caribbean, we visited St Lucia. Coach drives around the island and a visit to a Sandals Resort for drinks. Coffee for me of course.

On now past the coast of Venezuela and into the Panama Canal. I knew of a zip line vacation, golfing friends had enjoyed, that would be different. Perhaps not for me. John was struggling with movement becoming slower, pleased to sit down. Walking around the promenade deck, we both noted the permanent ongoing maintenance being carried out at sea.

Only way to get full 12 months voyaging, but I did wonder. Through the canal and north towards Cabo St Lucas, Mexico. Lovely port, which we enjoyed. This is when an unexpected development occurred, climbing into the tender to get to shore, proved very difficult for John. No matter, we can stay on board when the ship was unable to enter port and stayed at anchor offshore. San Francisco, we were able to go ashore and take a coach south, Monterey and of course Pebble Beach Golf course. More acupuncture for John and he was comfortable again for a further two weeks.

Now, the journey took us to Honolulu and Pearl Harbour, a deeply moving experience. Back on board and a weather warning. A Typhoon raging in the Pacific Ocean, and we would not be able to make our scheduled stops. We spent several days with the ship diverting to avoid the extreme weather. On the promenade decks in chairs watching the sea churning past. Boring to a certain extent, but we were together and had plenty to talk about. Passing French Polynesia, on to Fiji, well, maybe not, the storm raged.

Finally, we reached the east coast of Australia and docked at Newcastle Port, a big cruise ship port of call. Also, a major coal exporting facility. Onward to Sydney Harbour, a place we had visited several times. A busy city, an opera house, a wonder of architectural design. A boat journey around the harbour, well worth the ride as you view the city from the water.

Bondi beach is a joy to visit, but much smaller than one expects. Then the long flight back to the UK. Did I learn anything on this trip? Yes, how to make more interesting gluten-free food, that I was lucky to have visited the South Pacific prior to the cruise. Most importantly, that every second I spent with my husband was precious.

The summer months came, and John was becoming more and more frustrated. Getting down to weed the garden but unable to get back up. He wanted to walk around the village cricket ground, so off we went, he managed it with immense difficulty, and I had to call DJ to come and transport him back home. Walking back on my own, I had time to think.

The worry and concern were clouding the issue. At the time of visiting the doctor about his swollen foot, he was definite, John had not got Parkinson's disease. Wonder what on earth is going on.

Come early autumn, a simple thing changed the situation. I had gone off to the supermarket, DJ was in the study doing his own thing, John decided to walk down the back lane on his own. I arrived back to a heap of muddy jacket, hat, boots and trousers outside the back door.

My son's idea of clearing up. John had fallen and had difficulty getting up, hence mud everywhere. Visit to the doctor's clinic, and a different doctor who referred him to the falls clinic, at the John Radcliffe Hospital.

John had Parkinson's disease and it was advanced.

# Chapter Eight
# Our Final Times Together

John being John did not give in to illness, fighting it the only way he knew—exercise. Walking as far as he could every day, did he need an escort? Of course, he did. Strolling at a leisurely pace, simply enjoying being together, John with the aid of a walking stick.

Christmas Eve, Tracy and I off to Blenheim Palace. Afternoon tea in the orangery, walking around the palace enjoy the decorations. Really well done. Darkness begins early in December, enabling us to walk around the gardens to see the lights, not realising that this would be the last time.

January and February in England, walking during the daylight hours when possible, closer now than we had ever been. John is happy to be at home. With his newspaper and sport on television. Parkinson's disease gradually taking its toll, no longer able to sit or stand in the shower, cleaning his teeth one morning, he toppled backwards in a heap.

Our daily routine started with a wash and a shave; it was funny learning to shave his face. I had washing every day now, John unable to move without help, normal bodily functions needing attention. Body slowing down noticeably. Did I care about any of it? No, just to spend each day with him was enough.

DJ's inability to cope with seeing his father's deterioration, demanding that he go into a home. This is one of the only times I have addressed his situation head-on. Asking where he thought he would be now if John and I had not supported him with his illness. Sometimes, a few home-truths clear the air.

March 2020, the pandemic worsened and vulnerable people were advised to remain at home, shielded. Medication to be collected, through a window at the health centre. To say this was a difficult time would be putting it mildly. Luckily, DJ was driving and able to collect both his and his father's medication. The daily newspaper, centre of John's Day, was a different matter. A young couple living a few houses further on, collected it for him, leaving it on the car boot. Supermarket deliveries came into our lives and life continued as best we could. The close was very quiet with everyone staying inside or in their rear gardens.

Shielding eased in June, immediately John was ready for a stroll. A walk which years ago took about 20 minutes now taking over an hour. No matter precious time together.

When we returned, I helped him off with his jacket, leaving him in the kitchen whilst I went to collect a chair for him to sit on, so I could take his shoes off. Loud thump, he had fallen forwards and injured himself, passed out, I think. Ambulance, hospital, scans, you name it. Alone, no visitors. Luckily nothing broken, a lot of facial bruising. Message came that he was ready to be discharged, please come and collect him.

Tracy and Richard came for me, and we went to fetch him home. John as ever had us all smiling. Deciding to go to the bathroom before he left, he managed to fall. The three of us had to wait whilst he was checked out. All he could say was, I fell on my backside, not my head. So funny.

Unlike most people during the shutdown period, Tracy and Richard were working. Richard was involved in the manufacture of medicines. Tracy had become deputy headmistress of a school for children with special needs, this school remained open during the shutdown to accommodate the normal intake and those of first-line workers. Doctors, nurses, police, etc. Witnessing the stress these two young people had to deal with, knowing that like so many they had begun to question their lifestyle, John and I were worried.

During one of our conversations, Tracy told me of a five-year plan these two had made. To run a guest house in the country, and they were going to save as much as they could to enable this. John and I slept on this, thinking of the saddest thing we had witnessed during the years we had lived in the village. Young people losing parents, the first thing they did was buy a new car.

We had the facilities to help this family of ours and an opportunity few parents are privileged to see. How one's descendants utilise their inheritance. Next morning a decision was made, which we thought was best for Tracy and Richard but turned out to be the best thing for John.

Asking them both to join us for a while the next evening, we questioned where they would like this guest house to be. Cornwall came the answer. Are you sure this is what you want to, affirmative. John answered this one, nothing ventured nothing gained. Over to you two, take your mother with you to look at some properties. Why did I go? Because the decision was far bigger than just the two of them moving, all of us would move. Come September, both houses were on the market.

First guest house had issues, which did not surface immediately, Tracy and Richard had taken more than one trip to Cornwall, and soon found an alternative, offer accepted. This purchase went through very quickly with a completion date set for February 2021.

Christmas was fun, pandemic over we had a happy day together. John just happy to be sat in his chair watching everyone. Enjoying themselves. Happy in the knowledge that at some point in the coming months he would see his beloved daughter every day.

Well, I have been through some difficult times in my life, 2021 was no exception. Our house had sold within days of it going on the market, a completion date before the end of March 2021 requested. Busy time for me, we had lived at this property since 1973, 48 years. We needed a skip. I set about sorting, packing and discarding.

Tracy and Richard had their own house to pack up, notices to hand in. No time to consider the enormous change about to occur in their lives. In at the deep end, they went. Opening the quest house in the spring.

John was in hospital again after another fall, having damaged his ribs more, scans and worry as there was a sign of possible cancer, luckily this proved not to be the case. Still able to pull through this difficult time, the move giving him incentive to overcome the latest setback.

Local services became involved in his care and supplied everything they could think of to improve John's standard of life. A reclining chair arrived and was vetoed, just not comfortable. Advising me he was more comfortable in the chair we had bought so many years before.

Tracy and Richard had adapted to their new lifestyle, how hard that must have been. Richard undertaking to cook the morning breakfasts, together they slowly pulled the guest house to a very high standard. Changing the outside garden area, putting in a large decking area and a garden bar. This was only the first season, John and I looked forward to the next few years, watching them become strong business partners.

Our house was packed up and forlorn waiting for the next occupants. However, our house sale was a mess, not sure who the estate agent was working for, excuse after excuse. Finally, a date was given by the purchasers for one week ahead, ridiculous, every removal firm booked as this was the end of a government easing of stamp duty. Enough was enough and instructed the estate agent to put the property back on the market.

Within two weeks, it had sold again, amazingly to cash buyers. All we had to do was find a house to suit our special requirements. Tracy and Richard had been looking at properties for us all the time they had been in Cornwall, as well as taking on a new role as guest house proprietors.

They found large rooms, doors wide enough to accommodate a wheelchair, one reception room perfect for John, looking out into the garden with a wood burning stove, a bonus, he would be warm in the winter.

This was July, no way am I going to be able to go and view this property, Tracy facetimed me as she walked around the rooms, Richard assured me that it was right for John, first people viewing, put an offer in. Well, I have made some decisions in my life, this was a biggy. Offer accepted.

John's illness was progressing fast and he needed help to carry out his life as normally as possible. Standing behind him and taking his weight as he moved from step to step, heaving him up the stairs, and reversing on the way down. Fine by me, he wanted to be in his own bed next to me. Talking together with me, cuddling him. Sleeping on his back now, unable to curl me into his arms.

Movement very difficult and needing a wheelchair to negotiate the ground floor. I tried to manoeuvre him in the chair out of the door, with DJ's help, DJ went into a panic not able to cope. This move would not come too soon as I was going to need help looking after him.

John's cousin Lynda and her husband John came to visit early in the summer, the house in total chaos as I was packing boxes every day. So be it, they probably did not even notice. The two men had always enjoyed one another's company and a very pleasant time was had by all.

The sale of our house went through very quickly, the main reason being contact between the purchasers and me. Sorting out queries immediately rather than going through third parties. In late August we left the village and journeyed to Cornwall. A logistic nightmare, Tracy and Richard driving up from Cornwall the night before we moved.

DJ packed his belongings and the budgie into his car, Richard driving John's Mercedes, left for Cornwall, leaving Tracy, John and me to remain until the removal firm had completed their loading. Helping John into the car was very difficult, needing help from the neighbours.

Surprisingly, the journey for us three was fun and John was in high spirits, only the night before he said, "Another adventure scamp, wonder where it will lead us this time."

Nothing during the past year had been easy, so it was no surprise to discover that the vendors of the house we were purchasing, dragged the completion date out until we had to threaten, completion by end of October or we will pull out. John Duncan and I moved between the guest house, and David's daughter Jane's home for several weeks. That was an amazing coincidence, the guest house was situated in the same village as Jane, we had no idea.

Finally, the house was ours, and we moved in. A lot of things needed Attention but they were insignificant. Wood burner lit and John was quickly asleep in his chair. Stair lift was input during the first week, with John having to sleep on the old settee in the meantime, not that he worried.

Another wheelchair was purchased, more comfortable with soft padding, now we had one upstairs and one down. The house needed new furniture, curtains, etc. Tracy and I went shopping, not a problem, as daily visits had John smiling with joy each time she walked in through the door.

Sad time for me, David had died in 2020, we were unable to attend his funeral because of the pandemic, Trevor died two weeks after we moved in. This was one funeral I did attend, Tracy stayed to look after John, Jane accompanying me. Moving service, and I was able to read out a tribute from Peter and the rest of us.

Christmas was fun, the house decorated to the nines, my husband a happy man. That is all I cared about.

Tracy and Richard had been partners for many years, for them to marry was a very special day, just four of us at a no-frills wedding, one very happy husband. His little girl was married, so important to him. They celebrated that evening we needed to wish them well. What did I do, I heard no mention of a wedding cake and proceeded to make one.

Worst wedding cake I have ever seen, but it did the trick together with a glass of bubbly, DJ had decided to stay at home rather than attend the ceremony and was able to wish them well, very important to him.

The garden view from the snug was bare and I set about filling John's view with Azaleas, spring flowers and potted shrubs.

Months and weeks, spending as much time with him as possible. Ramps supplied by the local authority enabling me to manoeuvre him and his wheelchair out into the garden. Under the umbrella as it danced in the breeze. Glorious sunny days surrounded by bees, birds and flowers.

Lynda and John drove down from Reading, staying at the guest house, spending time with us. It was good to see them, although the time together was short, John not able to cope.

Still able to walk for a short distance with me providing a steady base to work with, I came into the snug to find him standing at the table holding the back of a chair, I knew instinctively what he wanted. Slipped between him and the chair and snuggled close for our final bear hug.

The illness was progressing, affecting his ability to speak. Needing help to feed himself. Not a word of complaint just a smile.

DJ was not handling this situation, unable or unwilling to help me look after his father. Having taken control of his own illness, I was unable to talk to his mental health team as I had in the past. Eventually, we had to seek help, getting him back on track. I am sure he cannot remember all that he did or said.

Christmas was a very quiet time, Tracy finding John the perfect present, being very thin now his shirts gaped at the neck, making him chilly, she bought him some neckkerchiefs; old-fashioned but perfect.

The winter brought a chest infection, antibiotics were in very short supply, only for children and vulnerable patients. John was prescribed medication which helped for a short time, but the infection persisted. Doctor finally called to see him and prescribed antibiotics. Staying in bed not something John liked. Deciding he had enough he tried to get out of bed and of course he fell, those legs of his no longer able to take his weight.

Off we two go to A&E, for x-rays. Equipment linked up and his heartbeat looked strong, breathing was very difficult. Monitors clipped to his finger. Consultant came down to check on him before taking x-rays, removed his monitor to enable moving the bed, and John stopped breathing. I was upset to say the least, pulled him into my arms, told him.

What a privilege it had been to know and love him, his face tranquil and relaxed. The poor consultant in shock, we thought he had died.

The nurse took one look and said, "He is breathing."

How lucky was I to have those special moments in which to tell him how I felt. Tracy and I had another special moment when John had been given a pain killer drip, unable to speak now, he pursed his lips, which in any language means give us a kiss. No problem, duly given with much laughter, and he turned to his little girl, same thing. What a man was able to show how much he cared in any possible way. Tracy left the ward in tears. We just held hands.

Visiting every day for a very short while, it came as no surprise when Tracy and I were ushered into an office and told that John needed palliative care. Simple answer, he comes home. I went back to John, slipped my hand into his, and asked him, if he wanted to come home. Just a squeeze in reply. Enough for me.

Wheels were set in motion, we emptied the small sitting room in the front of the house, a bed was delivered. John arrived by ambulance mid-afternoon, that wonderful smile as he reached out his hand to me. I smiled and said, "Ready for a cuppa."

During the next few days, his health deteriorated, but he still found the energy to mouth the most important words I shall ever need. I love you.

John died with both of his children spending time with him during the night. I came down in the morning and knew he was no longer with me, walked through to the snug, as with my mother, a bird flying across the garden and swooping away. Off you go, my love, I will feel you in the wind, and I finally wept.

Paperwork…loads of it; luckily, I had Tracy to help; how anyone manages to undertake this on their own, whilst arranging for a loved one's funeral, is beyond me. Emotional at this time, not really, I seemed to be frozen inside; funeral service, not really; celebrating a life well lived, definitely. Just four of us saying goodbye to him with a video link to Peter, Susan, Lynda and John.

A moving tribute for this incredible man.

But grief is a painful business, finding it difficult to remove the memory of his illness from my mind, I decided to go where we had been, so happy just the two of us, the difficulty of dealing with our son's illness left behind. Our winter home in Florida.

Booking flights no problem, something for me to work towards as I negotiated the dark nights. Daytime I kept busy, understanding that I was not the only one suffering. The whole family missed him, he had such a presence.

Summertime, now I turned to the garden, filling it with flowers. This I could do for John as he had made gardens for me. Having brought rose cuttings with me from our previous home, I planted them in pots. Is this the best way for me to communicate with him, yes.

The paperwork involved with our affairs was almost complete, just the inland revenue left, which is no surprise, and John's credit card he used with his business. This was with the bank I had worked for when I first started work, I called into the local office to close it. I had come full circle, reception desk manned by a female not just any female, the manager. Women had forged ahead in banking and maybe just maybe I played a part in that.

November, Tracy, Richard and I flew from London to Florida. Did I take my golf clubs, oh yes. Walked into the house and knew immediately that I had done the right thing. Relaxed and at peace, we three explored the area together.

Feeling bold, I suggested we fly up to Seattle to see Peter and Susan, which Tracy immediately set about organising. Just a short trip for a few days. It was good to see them both, Kat and her husband Sean calling in to see us. Lunch at the local pub, an Irish pub in a remote part of Washington State—who would have believed.

Tracy and Richard went off walking, well, reminiscing golden oldies can be a bit much. Peter is an artist, and I was amazed to see his painting of birds, red eyes he called them, sand cranes I called them. John and I used to stand and watch them flying into Florida, in huge V formations and soon learnt to avoid them on the golf courses.

How parallel Peter and my life have run. Noting that both Peter and Susan had mobile phones, I started texting them both most days. This became important, communicating on a regular basis, we drew close again after so many years. Gradually more family members are joining in the daily round of texts.

4 July 2024 and big celebrations on the beach in Ocean Shores, here in the United Kingdom a celebration of a different kind. The appointment of the first female chancellor of the exchequer—I can hear my aunts cheering.